Parish and Place

PARISH AND PLACE

Making Room for Diversity in the American Catholic Church

Tricia Colleen Bruce

OXFORD
UNIVERSITY PRESS

UNIVERSITY PRESS

Oxford University Press is a department of the University of Oxford. It furthers
the University's objective of excellence in research, scholarship, and education
by publishing worldwide. Oxford is a registered trade mark of Oxford University
Press in the UK and certain other countries.

Published in the United States of America by Oxford University Press
198 Madison Avenue, New York, NY 10016, United States of America.

© Oxford University Press 2017

CIP data is on file at the Library of Congress

ISBN 978-0-19-027032-2 (pbk.); 978-0-19-027031-5 (hbk.)

9 8 7 6 5 4 3 2
Paperback printed in Canada by Webcom, Inc.
Hardback printed by Bridgeport National Bindery, Inc., United States of America

CONTENTS

Acknowledgments   *vii*

Introduction   *1*

1. Parish   *12*

2. Boundaries   *45*

3. Decisions   *70*

4. Difference   *108*

5. Fragmentation   *137*

6. Community   *170*

Conclusion   *194*

Appendix A: The Study   *207*
Appendix B: National Survey of Personal Parishes   *215*
Notes   *219*
Bibliography   *229*
Index   *243*

ACKNOWLEDGMENTS

Community and place arise as central themes in the forthcoming pages. My journey through the conceptualization, research, and writing of this book is indebted to multiple communities, in a variety of places.

Perhaps it won't come as a surprise that one of those places is social media. Back in 2009, then pregnant with my first child, I received a Facebook message from my former graduate school colleague, Bob Ngo. After a visit to Texas (his home state; mine, as well), Bob sent me a thought-provoking message about how Vietnamese Catholics in his hometown had raised money, acquired property, and started their own churches. "These churches are huge," he wrote. "People oftentimes travel long distances to attend, rather than go to one that is close to their house." Bob then relayed a conversation he had with his mom about it, who shared that "the Vietnamese people were not very satisfied with the way that most parishes handled the Vietnamese congregation. They were only offered one Mass per Sunday, when it was clear that more than one was needed." One of the new churches he described was mere blocks away from where his family attended as a child. "And seriously," Bob wrote, "it dwarfs the old parish."

I was intrigued. A cradle Catholic, I knew how the territorial parish system worked. Sure, I (like many American Catholics) visited a few parishes whenever I relocated, seeking the best fit for my singing, guitar-playing self. But I'd never heard of new parishes with a stated purpose to serve a particular community—parishes that didn't subscribe to the territorial rule. Personal parishes. As a sociologist, I knew this novelty was worth exploring.

My acceptance soon thereafter as a fellow in the Engaged Scholars Studying Congregations program provided an invaluable context in which to articulate and work through these questions (infant in tow!). Conversations with R. Stephen Warner, Nancy Ammerman, Omar McRoberts, John Bartkowski, Orit Avishai, Lynne Gerber, Christine Sheikh,

Christopher Brittain, Margarita Mooney, Helen Rose Ebaugh, Barbara Wheeler, Lawrence Mamiya, James Nieman, and Gerardo Marti—and the stunning backdrop of Cape Cod—shaped the direction of my research. I am grateful for this Lilly Endowment-funded opportunity.

Two additional sources of funding made it possible to scale my research nationally using mixed methods: a grant from the Sociology Program of the National Science Foundation, and a Project Grant for Researchers from the Louisville Institute. Feedback from anonymous reviewers of my NSF proposal was formative. Support from the Louisville Institute brought the added benefit of a fruitful cross-disciplinary Winter Seminar, where I received meaningful input from Jim Lewis, Terry Muck, Don Richter, Penny Edgell, Ryon Cobb, and Melissa Guzman, among others.

Conducting this research pulled me into national conversations about the organizational and ministry needs of diverse Catholic populations. Invited to lead a study of Asian and Pacific Islander American Catholics by the US Conference of Catholic Bishops' Committee for Cultural Diversity (joined by collaborators Jerry Park and Stephen Cherry), I found myself privy to the insights of diocesan leaders deciphering practical organizational strategies to meet pressing needs. In this, I came to appreciate more than ever that the questions I posed were not merely theoretical.

I also gratefully acknowledge transformative conversations that have occurred through *The American Parish Project*, co-initiated with Gary Adler and Brian Starks. Gary and Brian have advanced my thinking about parishes considerably: thank you. So, too, did all who participated in our 2015 seminar on the sociology of the parish (and preceding discussions): Brett Hoover, Kathleen Garces-Foley, Jerome Baggett, Kristy Nabhan-Warren, Mary Jo Bane, Maureen Day, Kristin Geraty Bonacci, Mark Gray, Courtney Irby, Aprilfaye Manalang, Tia Pratt, Nancy Ammerman, John Coleman, and Mary Ellen Konieczny. I hope that this book furthers these parish-centered conversations, along with the spirited network of scholars voicing them.

I am thankful, too, for invited presentations that sharpened this analysis: to Jim Martin and all at Fordham University's "Vatican II at Fifty" conference; to Mary Ellen Konieczny, Charlie Camosy, and Notre Dame's Polarization conference (especially Hosffman Ospino, Susan Crawford Sullivan, and Nichole Flores); and to interlocutors at the Society for the Scientific Study of Religion, the Association for the Sociology of Religion, and the Religion Section of the American Sociological Association.

During data collection, I found willing and capable collaborators at the Center for Applied Research in the Apostolate (CARA) at Georgetown University, especially Melissa Cidade and Mary Gautier. Several people previewed my national survey with helpful feedback, including Deacon Sean

Smith of the Diocese of Knoxville, Bill Clark, Bob Miller, and several sociologist colleagues. Maryville College students aided me at key moments in this research: among them, Jordan Tarwater and Stacey Padilla (who endured a more than ten-hour snowy drive to one case study diocese!), Marcus Azevedo, Caroline Anglim, Tri Ninh, Doan Ninh, and Allison Bradley.

Further thanks go to Maryville College and Dean Barbara Wells for supporting a one-semester sabbatical. I extend a special shout-out to the Social Science Division and my weekly writing companion, Frances Henderson. I'm also indebted to my online community of writers in the Academic Writing Club (insert emojis here!). Several colleagues beyond the college read and reacted to drafts at pivotal stages (among them R. Stephen Warner, Kathleen Graces-Foley, David Yamane, and Damon Maryl): I thank you for the time and dedication that this kind of intellectual labor requires. My (second-time!) editor Theo Calderara and publisher Oxford University Press believed in the imperative of telling this story; for this, I am grateful.

With special gratitude to my study's participants: I sincerely appreciate your willingness and candor, made transparent in the voices I attempt to capture in the forthcoming pages. Hundreds of diocesan and pastoral leaders filled out my survey or sat down with me in person to share their expertise, experience, and opinion. You remain anonymous here, but I know and *thank you* with a full heart. This book is forever indebted to your willingness to engage these complex and difficult questions.

My aforementioned little one, in utero at this project's conception, is now seven-years-old; her brother, five. As I have read, inquired, and written along this journey, they, too, have adopted the art of reading, inquiring, and writing. My desire to educate in truth and justice is born equally of my training as a sociologist and my parental urgency to bequeath a better world. Sonoma Colleen and Carson Kimball—for your unceasing encouragement while Mom was writing her "really long book!"—I thank you. I love you. Finally, to Brandon. Between the two of us, we have (thus far) brought into the world two amazing humans, multiple books, a successful company, a home, and a love strong enough to withstand all the challenges en route. Boom.

Introduction

Blouses and Shirts: Neckline within two inches of the top of the sternum; Loose-fitting not form-fitting; Sleeves should be at least to half (between shoulder and elbow); Opaque not see-through. Skirts and Pants: Skirt length should cover the knee when seated, no slit above the knee; Loose-fitting not form-fitting; Opaque not see-through. Men should wear neat and clean pants; no shorts. Veiling is welcomed and appreciated.

—Posted Notice, Traditional Latin Mass Personal Parish

My attire is minimally compliant on this hot Texas day—my blouse a bit low, my skirt a bit high. I am grateful for the small woven basket in the foyer lending veils and bobby pins to cover my thick blond hair. Already a few minutes past nine o'clock, I sit down discreetly in an overflow-area pew and abide by the proximate posted notice: "SILENCE PLEASE."

The building is nothing aesthetically special. I'd almost missed it entirely, detoured by the Waffle House and seeing no exterior sign marking the former Methodist church as now Catholic. To be fair, the Honda bumper sticker reading "You can't be both Catholic and pro-abortion" offered a reasonable clue. Inside, drop-ceilings, a center aisle flanked by pews, and a rendering of Michelangelo's Pietà atop a tripod easel substitute for ambiance during renovations. Large Catholic families fill the pews; an oversized stroller blocks one aisle. A hefty man pinned "usher" unfolds extra chairs one-by-one, accommodating pregnant and young mothers first. A bound paper worship guide—one in English, one in Spanish—aids newcomers unfamiliar with the Traditional Latin Mass. An elderly woman drops a broken rosary into a basket for repair.

"In nomine Patris, et Filii, et Spiritus Sancti." Cue the kneeling. I reach for a foam rectangle to ease my discomfort, though none around me seem fazed. "Dominus Vobiscum." Moms breastfeed. A dad rushes through glass exterior doors with his young son, who promptly throws up on the lawn. "Laus tibi, Christe." The sound system pops, clicks, and adds recurrent silence between discernable words of an English-spoken homily. Urgency translates, nonetheless: all are charged with baptizing a child in case of impending death, freeing him or her from original sin. Instructions are quite specific. "Oremus." The temperature rises. The usher drips. None protest.

Adorned in an elaborate tapestry, the Eucharist in its ornate golden monstrance receives heightened reverence. The young priest covers his hands so as to not touch it directly. Quiet prevails amidst the shuffle of a packed space; the faithful await communion. An a cappella choir breaks the silence to unify voices throughout. "Tantum ergo, Sacramentum Veneremur cernui." I sing along. All remain until the conclusion of the two-hour service. "Ite, Missa est." The 300 or so in attendance genuflect and amble out, quietly. An adjoined hall welcomes friendly post-Mass banter over coffee, in sharp contrast to the earlier reverence.

Parishioners feel at home, in their parish, in their place. They take pride in their church's formal status in the diocese. Theirs is a *personal parish* in the US Catholic Church, devoted exclusively to the Traditional Latin Mass. Community—and distinction—is palpable.

* * *

EL FESTIVAL HISPANO

Mr Chiquitito	Music by DJ
Miss Chiquitita	"Hispanic Food"
4:00–5:00 p.m.	Tacos, Quesadillas, Empanadas,
Caritas Pintada	Tostadas, Chicharrones, Elotes,
Brincolin, Bailables, Cantantes	Frituras, Flautas, Tamales, Beer
	—Flyer, Hispanic Personal Parish

* * *

I see the advertisement for the upcoming festival hanging from a road bridge on my drive to the church, in a town just north of a large Midwestern city. The mix of English words translates to the town's overwhelmingly non-Hispanic residents. The Virgin Mary (Nuestra Señora de Guadalupe) occupies the upper left hand corner of the vibrant green and red poster.

Arriving at the parish around 12:30 Saturday afternoon means overlapping with shoppers at a rummage sale on the back side of the church. I find a parking spot up front, close to the parish school. Our Lady of Guadalupe greets me on a large street-facing brick wall. She appears again, near the concrete stairway entrance, and again, inside the church—her image sewn into a hanging blue tapestry, and wrapped around a four-foot column in subdued golden hues. A blue shoebox sitting atop Our Lady's column-wrapped image invites donations.

The main worship space—white walls, pendant lights, modest stained glass windows—is full of sound and life, but not from Mass. The pastor (a middle-aged white non-Hispanic, Spanish-speaking priest) has agreed to meet with me for an interview. He is just finishing a baptism. The celebrating Latino family has everyone in tow—the newly baptized infant adorned in white, her siblings, parents, grandparents, godparents all well-dressed to mark the occasion. They congregate joyfully and talkatively around the altar. Older siblings take turns jumping off the priest's chair and dipping hands into the baptismal font. Neither activity seems to faze the pastor. He takes his time.

Once the space empties and quiets, I introduce myself. The priest switches to English. An echo in the main church, we instead step into the sacristy behind the alter. It's filled with vestments, candles, linens, and papers . . . but no chairs. We stand. He signs a consent form; I turn on the recorder. The parish is home for Hispanic Catholics, he tells me: they don't always feel welcome elsewhere. His parishioners want to pray in Spanish. Our Lady of Guadalupe means home. Theirs is a *personal parish* in the US Catholic Church, established by the archdiocese some eight years prior, canonically decreed in ministry to Hispanic Catholics. Will it be needed years from now, the pastor wonders aloud, his feet shuffling as he stands. Maybe, maybe not; but today, it is.

* * *

This book is about *personal parishes* as an organizational response to grassroots transformations in American Catholicism. Unlike their territorial parish counterparts, personal parishes are decreed not primarily by geography, but by purpose. Whether in terms of ethnicity, liturgy, mission, or "some other reason," per Catholic Canon Law no. 518, personal parishes carve out sanctioned spaces for expressing Catholicism in ways that distinctively cater to Catholics' identities, preferences, and needs. Local bishops establish personal parishes with explicit purpose, apart from territory. Catholics throughout the United States have consequently found in personal parishes places of welcome, immersion, and home among other Catholics like them: a parish, a purpose, and a place.

Just under half of US dioceses have established personal parishes in the last thirty years, for a total of 192 new personal parishes since 1983. Combined with older "national" parishes that remain open, there are some 1,317 personal parishes in America today. This constitutes a small but meaningful fraction—8 percent—among all Catholic parishes. Nearly every diocese (96 percent) has at least one personal parish. Even as the total number of parishes is decreasing, the proportion of dioceses with personal parishes grows each year.

Many of today's personal parishes serve ethnic Catholics, now overwhelmingly non-European. But unlike national parishes formed to serve earlier Catholic immigrants (today subsumed under the "personal parish" label), new personal parishes also serve myriad other purposes: among them, devotion to the Traditional Latin Mass, to social justice, charismatic Catholicism, Anglican Use, tourism, and more. In catering to niche populations, personal parishes illuminate an institutional response to diversification. They depict a strategy deployed by leaders of the largest American religious group: an answer to demographic change and heterogeneous lay preference along fundamental lines of difference. *Parish and Place* tells this story.

CONTINUITY AND CHANGE IN THE ORGANIZATIONAL STRUCTURE OF AMERICAN CATHOLICISM

Catholicism in America has been shaped by two fundamental principles of organization: place and purpose. The former was codified in church law some 450 years ago. *Parish* came to mean a bounded territory, with a pastor appointed to serve all those living inside its geographic limits. An individual Catholic's domicile determined his or her parish. Not unlike polling places or public school districts, all are assigned. All belong. "Parish" means place. Still today, every geographic inch of the United States is allocated to a territorial parish—each a part of a larger diocese. Parish boundaries assert the authoritative, administrative control of the institutional Church over local, organized religion lived out by individual Catholics.

But a purely territorial model of parish proved an awkward fit for American religion. Catholicism's principle of parish-as-place clashed with a driving force of religion in America: congregationalism via voluntary association. Absent government-established religion—and amidst a plethora of options—Americans have long embraced the freedom to choose their religious communities. Consequently, religious assemblies—Catholic parishes among them—came to exhibit participants' preferences. Paired with the vast immigrant roots of US Catholicism, Catholic parishes acquire personas superseding (even undermining) territoriality. Lived, lay behavior spawned the need for an alternative organizational form.[1]

Thus, a second fundamental principle—purpose—simultaneously undergirds the organizational structure of Catholicism in the United States. Millions of earlier European immigrant Catholics—othered within a predominantly Protestant American milieu—built separatist Catholic worlds in schools, hospitals, charities ... and national parishes. The urgency of Catholics' divergent language and cultural needs meant that they weren't always willing or able to congregate together. As Catholic historian Jay Dolan writes in *The American Catholic Experience*, "The national parish was a pragmatic response to this problem, and it became the principal institution the immigrants established in their attempt to preserve the religious life of the old country." National parishes offered an organizational strategy whereby the US Catholic Church could reconcile the twin forces of purpose and place. It compromised Catholic leaders' interest in retaining adherents, and lay Catholics' desire to keep their cultural heritage.[2]

Sociologically, observers of this latter trend—following the influential work of R. Stephen Warner—contend that American Catholicism is another iteration of "de facto congregationalism." Voluntary association set a trajectory for local religion derivative of individual choice and relative autonomy from centralized denominational authorities. Catholics, following this line of theorizing, pick and choose parishes with little regard to church hierarchy or formal regulation. Local religious organizations, accordingly, emerge from grassroots agency. And, indeed—American Catholics carry a reputation for following their own conscience above hierarchical pronouncements. Churches exhibit these preferences—whether for language, liturgical orthodoxy, short sermons, guitar-based hymns, and so on and so forth. The parish has been well-theorized as a cultural product born of religious agency and the reappropriation of a shared tradition. But does this mean that parishes are fully congregational? Are they (or *all* local religious organizations in America) mostly the product of agency, cultural work, and lay appropriation of shared traditions? What might this look like from the top?[3]

SEEING LOCAL RELIGION FROM THE TOP

Viewed through Catholicism's own organizational history, the structure of local religion also reflects institutional strategy. National parishes flourished in nineteenth-century America. But in time, US bishops' pivoted away from national parishes, re-emphasizing territorial boundaries (a dynamic explored more fully in subsequent chapters). Later immigrants encountered a very different Catholic context of reception than that which had greeted earlier arrivals. The organizational strategy of the Church had changed: its leaders urged the laity to join territorial parishes, rather than to create new national ones. Parish petitions from newly-arrived Latino and Asian immigrants were typically denied. Further still, the Second Vatican Council (1962–1965) encouraged territorial parishes themselves to embed distinctive cultures. In short, an older model of parish organization appeared to meet extinction within an increasingly heterogeneous, pluralist, and integrationist American Catholic Church.[4]

But organizational strategies in the US Catholic Church have pivoted . . . again. The most recent Code of Canon Law (issued in 1983) granted bishops greater discretion and control over when and for whom to establish personal parishes. Its application also widened to include not only language and ethnicity but also "for some other reason," a phrase with enough ambiguity to be leveraged in creative ways.

Today's American Catholic population exceeds 81.6 million. One in five American adults self-identify as Catholic. Racial and political diversification is reshaping Catholicism from above and below. Non-Hispanic whites now constitute just over half of the Church; growing numbers of Latino and Asian Catholics set Catholicism at the forefront of linguistic and cultural diversity in America. A plurality of political and ideological views further diversifies the US Catholic Church. Accompanying these changes on the ground are declines in priestly ordinations, the enduring ramifications of clergy abuse, rampant diocesan restructuring, resource contraction, and contested leadership.[5]

Nowhere are these challenges put more into focus than in the parish, which continues to operate as the locus of church-going Catholics' religious lives. Much of American Catholic practice takes place at or in association with the parish, given its monopoly on the celebration of most sacraments. While the overall Catholic population is growing, the total number of parishes nationwide is shrinking. Parish establishment dates average nearly a century old. Fewer parishes and fewer priests serve a historically large average number of parishioners, relying increasingly on pastor-sharing or lay (non-ordained) ministers. Multiracial congregations are more common in the Catholic Church than in any other Christian denomination.[6]

In the language of organizations, territorial parishes act as *generalist* organizations aiming to serve all in a heterogeneous market. They target the middle, accessing the highest number of "customers" (parishioners). Parishes offer an average of four Sunday/Saturday vigil Masses a week, and many Catholics describe an "important difference" between services at the same parish. A third of parishes offer Mass in languages other than English at least once a month. Theologian Brett Hoover uses the term "shared parish" to describe the ways in which single church spaces serve multiple cultural groups—often Latinos and whites—who maintain distinctive languages, customs, and activities therein.[7]

Territorial parishes that don't celebrate Mass in languages other than English or Latin (two-thirds of all parishes) are overwhelmingly white. Other racial groups rarely attain a parish presence exceeding 5 percent. Latino Catholics—who comprise nearly a third of the total US Catholic population—are most likely to attend predominantly Latino parishes. Spanish-fluent Latino Catholics are even more likely to attend such parishes. While only a quarter of African American Catholics attend predominantly Black Catholic parishes (which are far fewer in number), among those who do, Mass frequency and parish satisfaction are higher. Asian Catholics are particularly likely to attend services at multiple locations, typically their territorial parish as well as another offering culturally specific activities.[8]

In a territorial parish marketplace, Catholics are choosing parishes. Within single parishes, Catholics are choosing Mass times. The panacea of integrated, diverse, generalist territorial churches—drawn together by residential proximity—is often contradicted by American Catholics' lived behavior. The more heterogeneous a population, the more difficult it is to appeal to all through a generalist organization. Even so, territorial parishes remain canonically bound to place despite lay behavior to the contrary. As the late Cardinal George put it, "objective relations do not depend on subjective ratification."[9]

Today's personal parishes emerge as an organizational alternative: an institutional response to diversification and purpose-driven parish selection among American Catholics. They are not generalist but *specialist* organizations, catering to a narrower, intentionally homogeneous sector. While less common than territorial parishes, and not at the level of prominence that national parishes once had, new personal parishes appear each year, meeting an array of ethnic and non-ethnic purposes. Personal parishes respond to the needs of a particular market, audience, or niche. They encapsulate a world of their own, wholly focused on the people and purpose that canonically defines their existence.[10]

What explains the (re)emergence of the personal parish as a contemporary organizational form in American Catholicism? Such as in the diocese of Omaha, where Catholics devoted to the Traditional Latin Mass gained a personal parish in 2007. Or San Jose's Vietnamese Catholics, who in 1999 secured approval for a personal parish, resolving decades of intense petitioning. Or, in the Archdiocese of St. Louis, where nine new personal parishes for various purposes were established in 2005 alone. Grassroots change begets new organizational forms.

Some kinds of institutional change can be linked to dramatic, historic events, such as that introduced by progressive bishops at Vatican II. But personal parishes' contemporary emergence is more prolonged. Theories of congregationalism help to explain lay behavior, but fall short in explaining that of institutional elites. Patterns of personal parish formation embody decisions made by the American Catholic hierarchy. New personal parishes reflect a judiciously applied, institutional, organizational strategy for accommodating difference. Their formal, canonical status distinguishes them from those whose elective purpose is born of attendees, neighborhoods, leaders, and histories rather than through authoritative decree. Personal parishes are not de facto; they are de jure.[11]

I wrote in my first book, *Faithful Revolution: How Voice of the Faithful Is Changing the Church*, about lay Catholics who built a grassroots movement to change the Church in the wake of abuse.[12] Theirs was what I called an intra-institutional social movement. Voice of the Faithful's form, identity, and tactics were heavily influenced by their desire to remain within the Church (banned by some bishops, even). Ultimately, this led them down a path that replicated some of the very institutional dynamics they set out to change. Knowing this, I found it curious when I began my study of personal parishes that the literature on local religious organizations skewed so much in the opposite direction, underplaying the impact of institutional authorities on lay organization. This kind of theorizing does little to explain formal parish establishment, which ultimately resides in the hands of local bishops. Personal parish designation matters especially because it does not reside in the hands of laypeople.

Accordingly, I turn here to the logic of organizations to rethink religious collectives from the top: as institutional strategy, rather than primarily the product of autonomous believers' behavior. Doing so expands current thinking about local religion and institutional change, interweaving insights from congregational studies, organizations, authority, geography, race, and power. Local religion is a structural, organizational reality as much as it is a socially constructed, cultural one. Organizational change is contingent upon institutions; outcomes are influenced by institutional authorities even as they are born of participants' own agency.

THE CHAPTERS AHEAD

This book builds an understanding of institutionally managed organizational change from the top. It is one that privileges *interdependence*: parish decisions are connected through higher-order processes and wider conceptions of space (here, via dioceses). Local religion belongs to an interlocking structure. Seeing beyond congregationalism means accounting for what connects local religious organizations to each other. This broader view, moreover, better accounts for mobility across space and place, along with the territorial and social boundaries that guide such movement.

The forthcoming chapters trace the implications of this perspective through a variety of angles:

- Chapter 1 (Parish) unpacks the meaning of "parish" and the significance of formal parish status. It asserts the weight of institutional authority in defining local religious organizations. This chapter also profiles the characteristics of personal parishes in the United States today.
- Chapter 2 (Boundaries) shows how personal parishes resolve an institutional tension: Catholicism's tradition of territoriality and boundaries, on the one hand, and the realities of American Catholics' mobility, preference, and agency, on the other. It shows how institutions adapt organizational forms to accommodate new realities on the ground.
- Chapter 3 (Decisions) offers an insider look at how bishops make decisions to establish personal parishes . . . or not. While sources from the top and the grassroots play a role in the origins of new personal parishes, diocesan leaders nonetheless adjudicate personal parish outcomes.
- Chapter 4 (Difference) describes the institutional rationale for accommodating difference through non-assimilative, named, specialist organizations. Personal parishes show that multiracial congregations are not the only strategy used to accommodate racial diversity in local religion. Heterogeneous populations and uneven integration in territorial parishes introduces the need for organizational forms that cater to specific purposes.
- Chapter 5 (Fragmentation) discusses fragmentation as an inherent consequence of specialist adaptations to organizational structures. Personal parishes represent Catholicism's accommodation of religious agency from the top: a way for institutional leaders (as opposed to individual Catholics doing culture work on the ground) to make room for choice and difference, organizationally.
- Chapter 6 (Community) looks at the implications of personal parishes for building community across difference. It advances an approach to local religion that is necessarily interdependent, viewed across wider

conceptions of space, and framed by both territorial and social boundaries. For the Catholic Church, this means that leaders see community across the diocese rather than isolated within individual parishes.

- The Conclusion summarizes how personal parishes—defined not by territory but by purpose—enable the Catholic Church to respond institutionally to grassroots change and diversification in American Catholicism. A structural view of organizational change reveals multiple organizational forms to meet divergent needs, facilitate unity, and maintain institutional control. This carries lessons for understanding local religion, the future of personal parishes, and the place of purpose in a heterogeneous (Catholic) America.

All told, this is a story of organizational change amid internal diversification. American Catholics are changing, and American parishes are changing . . . always intertwined within broader structures of authority. Personal parishes enable the US Catholic Church to reconcile voluntary association with authoritative hierarchy . . . and Americans' penchant for preference with formally constituted, institutionally sanctioned church homes.

A NOTE ON METHODOLOGY

This book's focus is especially on personal parishes established after the promulgation of the 1983 Code of Canon Law, and those with earlier founding dates that remain open today. The change, ascendency, and innovative application of personal parishes in the past thirty years is a story that, until now, went untold.[13]

The research upon which this book is based includes an original, national study of personal parishes fielded to all US dioceses (the "National Survey of Personal Parishes," hereinafter NSPP). After first conducting a pilot study in a single diocese, I sent the NSPP in Fall 2012 to all 178 US (arch)dioceses inquiring about the presence, origins, and rationale for personal parishes. Eighty percent of (arch)dioceses responded. This produced a comprehensive national portrait and list of personal parishes in the United States. Where possible, I supplemented data from non-responding dioceses using diocesan websites and the 2012 Official Catholic Directory.

With this big-picture data in hand, I next selected twelve (arch)dioceses across eleven states for in-person field visits and interviews (see Appendix A for selection rationale and further methodological detail). I conducted visits between April and October 2013, attending Mass at every personal parish in the diocese and interviewing personal parish pastors. I also interviewed diocesan representatives including bishops, multicultural staff, pastoral planners, and canon lawyers. A total of 68 in-person parish visits and 62 interviews (with 67 individuals) comprise the core ethnographic data informing this study.

This book does not approximate the experience of all Catholic parishes, nor that of all Catholics. The study intentionally examines a parish form that remains in the minority today, privileging an exception to the (territorial) rule. Personal parishes grant a window into how the Catholic Church changes amidst a changing Catholic population. The Church is a phenomenal absorbent of difference; that difference now expands farther than ever.

CHAPTER 1

Parish

I pick up two of my Vietnamese international students in the Maryville College parking lot at 7:15 a.m., the sun not yet out on a chilly fall morning. They had agreed to accompany me to a daily Mass of the newly established Vietnamese mission in Knoxville, Tennessee. My car is stuffed with kiddo paraphernalia; the students are gracious to climb aboard and around the mess of toys and crayons.

We head north toward Knoxville, to the church housing the Vietnamese mission ... or so we thought. The diocesan website promised that daily Mass for the Divine Mercy mission would be at Immaculate Conception, Tuesday, 8:00 a.m. But upon arriving to the stone church downtown, the only signs of life are from a small construction crew doing maintenance on one side of the building. There are no cars. Although this seems odd, we guess that Mass attendants may have arrived on foot, or found parking elsewhere. But, upon walking a short distance up to the front of the church, we find the doors locked.

Large bells gong at exactly 8:00 a.m. There are no people; there is no Mass.

Standing for a while longer and walking around, confusion on our faces, one of the construction crew asks if we need assistance. We inquire about the Catholic community that we expected to see here this morning. "Oh, the Vietnamese group? They meet at All Saints now." All Saints is another parish in a different part of Knoxville, some 13 miles away. The man says he thinks they started meeting there two or three weeks ago. He calls someone to confirm; we wait. We listen as he apologizes for the early call, talking about "a woman here for the Vietnamese service." Our eavesdropping infers confirmation that, yes; they are now meeting at All Saints.

So, back in the car we go, suburbia-bound. All Saints is a much larger church, proximate to the city's only Catholic High School. We arrive just before 8:30 to a parking lot full from activity at the high school. Announcements and bells ring in the background. Peering inside the main liturgy area, we see a lone, elderly white woman praying. No Mass. No gathering of Vietnamese Catholics.

We direct our renewed confusion to a smiling woman organizing handouts in the narthex area. She says yes; the Vietnamese community does meet here now. But they are already done. The priest just left. Their weekday services are now Tuesdays and Thursdays at 7:30 a.m. in the church, she tells us, and Sunday mornings in the high school. She speaks kindly of their priest (a "nice man"), and points toward a small chapel where they worship, a space set apart from the larger, main area. It's empty at that moment, of course. My students and I depart for campus, our coffee en route being the only tangible outcome of the morning's goose chase.

Our experience is telling of an itinerant Catholic community without formal, canonical "parish" status. Knoxville's Vietnamese Catholic group had no physical space to call their own, no predictability or stability in their Mass offerings, and no publicity to newcomers advising any change. They were a Catholic community without a home: neither a territorial parish nor a personal parish. Mission status afforded them a priest, but not the permanence of a pastor. Absent a church, they borrowed available space without meaningful symbols, saints, or imagery to embody distinctive Vietnamese expressions of Catholicism. Divine Mercy was not (yet) a parish.

* * *

In a climate of religious freedom, it is tempting to presume that a group of Catholics can gather, claim a suitable space, identify a leader, and hang a shingle to indicate that they are "open for business," so to say. With its separation of church and state, the United States lays fertile ground for novel religious organization, entrepreneurialism, new religious movements, and thriving communities of the faithful.

But while this spirit of religious agency bears truth in practice, it most certainly does not (fully) describe Catholic parishes. Catholics' religious enterprises are circumscribed by top-down polity. Parishes subsist at the intersection of authority, territory, and community. *Authority*—namely, a local bishop—prescribes when and for whom parishes are created, and when or why they merge or close. *Territory*—or the boundaries in physical space that define a territorial "parish"—stipulates belonging, unless a special population is identified otherwise. And *community*—both ascribed and achieved—transforms a parish from abstraction into a viable and lived, shared experience of religious and social meaning. A parish is not just a building. Starting a discussion about *personal parishes* requires a preliminary framing of Catholic parishes overall, situated over time and across space. From here, we can better understand the scope and meaning of personal parishes as an emergent organizational form in the US Catholic Church today.[1]

THOSE LIVING NEAR OR BESIDE

"Parishes" identified Christian communities as long ago as the second century. The Greek source of the term—*paroikia*—translated to "those living near or beside." A "paroikos" was a neighbor. Perhaps paradoxically, the word was also used to describe those living as foreigners in a land, with no right to citizenship. As such, the original connotation was as much theological as it was organizational: early Christians saw themselves as outsiders to the world, but insiders together.[2]

In time, paired with the Latin translation "paroecia" and (for a while) used interchangeably with the Roman administrative term "diocesis," parish took an increasingly territorial meaning. A parish identified the jurisdiction of a local bishop. "The idea of sojourn in exile was lost when the parish received fixed boundaries, and the idea of a community of people was replaced by that of the governing authority of the bishop."[3] Terminology grew more uniform in the sixth century, as "parish" came to refer to a local congregation served by a priest, grouped together within the larger territory of a bishop; the latter labeled a diocese. Although an exhaustive history of the ecclesiology of "parish" in the Catholic tradition is beyond the scope of this book, acknowledging its origins as linked to dwelling together in community—and to unifying marginalized populations of the faithful—sets the tone for its contemporary use.

Territoriality, moreover, plays a pivotal role in the story of Catholicism as an emergent global religion. A territorial-religious union was particularly evident in Europe, where churches became "territorial realities," "manifested at every level of society."[4] Cities emanated from a church building at the town center; parish was the primary administrative unit. "The idea of the parish," writes geographer Patrick J. Duffy, "in contrast to its buildings and possessions, was virtually indestructible: its burial grounds, sites and boundaries were indelible in landscape and embedded in local memory."[5]

Even so, parish boundaries were not strictly determined prior to the Council of Trent in 1545. Pastors served all who came to them, domicile notwithstanding. The Council of Trent levied a partial indictment of this territorial agnosticism, replacing it with a strict conformity to boundaries and their delineation. A pastor needed to know whom (and whom not) to serve. The desire for pastoral jurisdiction trumped the original connotation of parish as a unified community. Parish came to mean isolated, individual geographies of people, with fixed boundaries, under the rule of a local bishop. [6]

The first official compendium of rules and regulations governing the Catholic Church did not come until much later, with the 1917 Code of Canon Law. Although this first official "rulebook" of the global Roman Catholic Church did not explicitly define "parish," it did identify a parish's legal components. These included "(1) a territorial section of the diocese; (2) with a portion of the Catholic population assigned to it; and (3) having a proper pastor who looked after the care of souls." A parish was, in effect, a territory of Catholics led by a pastor. Notably, the focus of the parish was on the pastor, not the people. Parishes were the ideal administrative, pastoral, organizational structure to be followed universally.[7]

Pastors could be either territorial, national, or personal.[8] A parish priest was most commonly assigned to Catholics on the basis of domicile. This necessitated clear boundaries. "Since parishes are in the [1917] Code of Canon Law principally indicated according to territorial lines, it is necessary that they have well defined boundaries, because it is within these limits that parishioners belonging to a particular parish will be found. Their affiliation with a definite church and a particular pastor will depend upon their place of residence."[9] Territory implied individual Catholics' parish affiliation.

But territory was not the only constitutive characteristic of parishes, even in the 1917 Code. A second, non-territorial form of parish constitution also existed—one that resonated more so with earlier etymologies, unifying outsiders marginalized within an otherwise homogeneous community. Joseph Ciesluk's 1947 commentary on the 1917 Code describes this alternative variation as such:

> It appears from canon 216 *4, that there is another principle by which parishes are determined, besides the principle of territoriality. It is true that the most convenient basis of partition is that which is taken from the division of territory, because it is commonly accepted in human society that races and people be organized into political subdivisions by proper and distinct boundaries. Under circumstances in which the population was homogenous, the faithful who lived within the limits of a certain country could, with comparatively little difficulty, be subdivided into distinct communities with definite territorial limits, constituted under the authority of a proper pastor. But for various reasons it becomes

evident that another principle must be taken into consideration ... whereby parishes are distinguished not according to the territory which they embrace, but by reason of certain people or families that happen to belong to them. Authors give them the generic term of personal or family parishes, as distinguished from local or territorial parishes.[10]

This alternative form is the personal parish, existing apart from—or in combination with—territory. Personal parishes define membership by the people who belong to them. Given the emphasis on persons rather than (primarily) on territory, they carry the moniker of *person*-al parishes. A "personal pastor," ergo, "is one who is appointed for a certain number of persons or for some family."[11]

The national parish was a subcategory of personal parishes, designed to serve Catholics whose language or customs set them apart from other Catholics. A "national pastor" would "receive their people by reason of nationality without regard to the boundaries of other parishes ... [these parishes] do not observe the territorial limits of all other parishes but include territory also belonging to other parishes which are territorial."[12]

Personal parishes, thus, find their roots in early iterations of church law. Canon law carries the legacy of both Germanic and Roman conceptions of jurisdiction: the former linked to territory; the latter to person. Territory and person cannot be fully divorced, of course, as Ciesluk notes: "the people who belong to these [personal] parishes are not scattered throughout the whole world, but are presumed to live, and actually do reside, in a more or less determined locality."[13] But it is personal title that determines affiliation for personal parishes, not domicile.

"PARISH" IN THE UNITED STATES OF AMERICA

Jurisdiction by person rather than by territory has always been an exception to the rule. But this is not to say that such exceptions did not exist: in the United States, they abounded. By many measures, America presented an exceptional case for the global Catholic Church. Its vast territory remained a missionary dependent of Europe well into its development as a nation. This meant that local Catholic organizations emerged in the United States with limited oversight from European bishops an ocean apart.

Further complicating things, many early American Catholic organizations were legally incorporated under the names of lay board members, rather than priests or dioceses. The nation's civil laws—modeled after more autonomous, Protestant systems of governance—fueled this unplanned congregationalism. A "trustee system" in the Catholic Church empowered lay Catholics at the helm of local organizations, pitting them against a hierarchical Catholic polity. "The evils of trusteeism," Catholic historian Fergus Macdonald writes, manifested in countless debates over property ownership and (especially) pastoral appointment, some even violent. He details:

> The precise point around which trouble usually developed was the limit of the trustees' power. . . . Such intrusions were made by some congregations, enthusiastic for democratic ideas but ignorant of the divine constitution of the Church, who thought they had the right to engage any pastor they wished, to keep him as long as they pleased, and to get rid of him when it appeared advisable for them to do so. Since the trustees held the purse strings, they clearly had power in this regard. If they chose to back some recalcitrant cleric, the bishop was hard put to remove such a person under this system. The results were bound to be serious.[14]

Trusteeism (i.e., congregationalism) threatened the institutional authority of the Church.

American Catholicism's laissez-faire emergence required greater lay input. But, especially once met with the appointment of the first US Bishop, John Carroll (consecrated in 1790), this lay empowerment in local religious organization butted heads with the top-down authority delineating "parish" in Catholicism globally since the Council of Trent.

There is, perhaps, no greater illustration of this clash between organic, bottom-up "parish" development (quotations intentional) and authoritative, top-down parish development than the historic rise and subsequent proliferation of national parishes in the US Catholic Church. The trend began with German American Catholics in Philadelphia, who successfully petitioned Bishop Reverend John Carroll to erect a church of their own. He reluctantly agreed, "for the preservation of charity, and in the hope of its being hereafter conductive to the interests of religion."[15] Holy Trinity opened in 1789 as the first exclusively national church in the United States. It was a personal parish. The request came from lay Catholics; the realization of Holy Trinity as a parish came at the behest of the only US bishop.

National parishes offered American Catholics the promise of cultural preservation in an otherwise hostile country. The exception to the territorial parish rule was birthed of American Catholics' extraordinarily diverse immigrant character. Millions of immigrant Catholics with myriad cultural needs, a proportionately small number of priests, a vast US territory, and widely dispersed churches made it difficult for territorial parishes in the United States to comply with standards born of entirely different circumstances. "As a result there was not always a strict adherence to the ideal methods as prescribed by the common law of the Church for strict parochial organization."[16] The US Catholic Church was exceptional. American parishes married purpose to place.

National parishes grew by leaps and bounds between 1820 and 1920, fueled especially by Catholic emigration from Ireland, Germany, and France. Entrepreneurial efforts by lay and ordained Catholics emphasized the imperative of specialized, non-territorial parishes. Although US bishops made efforts to comply with the Council of Trent's emphasis on territorial boundaries, the 1866 Plenary Council of Baltimore "adverted to the fact that the existence of parishes along strict territorial lines in this country was not yet possible."[17] Even territorial parishes were predominately Irish, or a mix of Irish and German.[18]

Canonically, national parishes occupied by Catholics in a burgeoning US Catholic Church sat on a shaky foundation. Haphazard institutional compliance likely hastened restrictions brought by the 1917 Code of Canon Law, which instilled a near moratorium on national (personal) parishes for decades henceforth. Existing communities of American Catholics gained their status ipso facto, ushered in as canonical parishes despite their less-than-compliant and less-than-territorial origins. A 1922 statement by the prefect of the Commission for the Authentic Interpretation of the Code of Canon Law settled the matter officially with ex-post-facto forgiveness, stating that no special decree would be required for churches already erected in the United States. This regulatory action reasserted the institutional hierarchy's authority to define parishes, following this period of heightened lay agency and instability.[19]

America's national parishes remained an awkward exception to territoriality under the reign of the 1917 Code of Canon Law. They had a pastor, they had a church, but what about territorial boundaries? Were they even parishes? While some theologians at the time contended that this left their status in limbo, others (ironically) argued that they did have a territory— be it an entire city or entire county—but a territory, nonetheless. "To say, then, that national parishes have no territory would not be absolutely correct, because besides the primary characteristic that they exist as personal parishes for a definite language group, their secondary characteristic is that the latter group is composed of a particular people in a certain locality within reasonable distance of the church that is erected for them, and that the parish is therefore also territorial."[20] By this logic, canon lawyer and priest Joseph Ciesluk argued in 1947, "there seems to be no element lacking to prevent national parishes from enjoying the status of parishes."[21] But clearly, some saw discrepancy.

Adding enforcement to the 1917 Code of Canon Law, the discretion to establish new national parishes did not reside with the local ordinary (the bishop). It required Vatican approval. Per the 1917 Code:

> Parishes based on diversity of the language or nationality of the faithful found in the same city or territory cannot be constituted *without special apostolic indult*, nor can familial or personal parishes; as to those already constituted, nothing is to be modified *without consulting the Apostolic See*.[22]

So, while national parishes already established in the United States could stay (without modification, unless approved), new national parishes would require an official thumbs-up from the Vatican. American exceptionalism and the influence of congregationalism had spawned hundreds upon hundreds of national parishes. But the 1917 Code reigned in this spirit for compulsory Vatican oversight.

These regulations severely dampened personal parish establishment for much of the twentieth century. Lay people had to petition their bishop; bishops had to petition the Holy See. Centralized Church authority ceded congregationalism to clericalism, surmises historian Jay Dolan.[23] The institutional Church had reaffirmed place as the constitutive element of a parish.

Soon after the Code's 1917 release, Chicago's Cardinal George Mundelein and New York's Cardinal Francis Spellman led the way in discouraging new national parishes. Mundelein "declared full-scale war on the national parish system in favor of 'territorial parishes,'" writes Catholic historian Charles Morris.[24] National identity and separatism yielded to shared, integrated, territorial American parishes (structurally, if not in reality). An "Americanization paradigm" privileging integration triumphed in the organizational strategy of the Catholic Church after 1920.[25]

The 1917 Code and its chilling effect on personal parishes remained in place as immigration to America ebbed after 1920, all the way through the abolition of federal immigration quotas in 1965. A third of national parishes active in 1940 no longer existed by 1980, by then suppressed or restructured as territorial parishes.[26] "Ironically," writes historian Timothy Matovina, "in their efforts to accelerate the process of Americanization the bishops sought to abolish an institution that had facilitated the gradual integration of numerous Catholic immigrants into U.S. church and society."[27]

This institutional change to organizing religion locally meant that American Catholics worshiped together in territorial parishes ... or, under the illusion of togetherness, at least. Contemporary Latino theologian Hosffman Ospino assesses this historical development as such:

> As the United States emerged from the Great Depression, however, the policy of proliferating national parishes came under question, particularly in large cities that attracted successive waves of newcomers. Accordingly, a different model for the Hispanic parish emerged. Sunday sermons and pastoral care were delivered to Spanish speaking Catholics within existing parishes, often in the basement church. Even when physically, pastorally, and linguistically separated, this model united the parish in one building. Many Catholic parishes operating this way had dual choirs, separate pious societies (Holy Name and the Legión de María), and different catechetical programs. Hispanic communities by and large did not become clones of their Anglo counterparts but developed alongside these. In many places Hispanic communities eventually became more numerous and the source of vitality for entire parishes.[28]

In effect, Latino Catholics created their own national (personal) parishes in the basements—both figuratively and literally—of predominantly white territorial parishes during this period of retrenchment.

One sociologist's 1948 assessment of national parishes based upon the Catholic Directory reported that there were then some 1,535 national parishes in the United States, most established pre-1917.[29] This equates to roughly 10 percent of all parishes at the time. The largest percentage served Polish Catholics, followed by Italians and Germans. I recreate this tabulation of national parishes in table 1.1, with an additional column indicating the percentage of each group's parishes among all national parishes.

Personal parishes numbers do not mirror proportions of ethnic Catholics at that time. Immigrant groups' years of arrival, bishops' corresponding attitudes toward personal parishes, and rural versus urban settlement patterns all impacted whether particular ethnic groups started (or received) national parish designations. Special needs and experiences of discrimination also predicted different outcomes. Italian Catholics, for example, outnumbered Polish Catholics eleven to one at the time, but Polish Catholics were far more likely to seek and gain national parish status. Even in an era of general disapproval, national parishes were instrumental in carrying ethnic culture and mitigating against discrimination.

Table 1.1 ETHNIC COMPOSITION OF NATIONAL PARISHES
IN THE UNITED STATES, 1948

Ethnicity	Number of National Parishes	Percentage of National Parish Total
Polish	466	30.4
Italian	314	20.5
German	206	13.4
Slovak	152	9.9
French	114	7.4
Lithuanian	103	6.7
Mexican	44	2.9
Hungarian	36	2.3
Bohemian	33	2.1
Portuguese	23	1.5
Spanish	11	< 1
Romanian	10	< 1
Maltese	7	< 1
Hollandish	5	< 1
Belgian	5	< 1
Chinese	3	< 1
Filipino	1	< 1
Cape Verdian	1	< 1
Tyrolese	1	< 1

Source: Adapted from Harte (1951): 162–163.

VATICAN II AND THE PARISH

The meaning of "parish" met renewal in the global Catholic Second Vatican Council (1962–1965). Vatican II elevated the idea that local dioceses had distinctive needs and diverse cultural expressions, and that local bishops were best suited to discern how to serve Catholics therein. Catholic scholar John Vandenakker writes that "Vatican II still endorses this concept of the essential universality of the church, but it also seeks to make more explicit how the bishops in their local settings share in their own way in the apostolicity, catholicity, and communion of the one church."[30] The Council, in other words, acknowledged and empowered bishops to more autonomously adjudicate the particular needs of local Catholics.

Vatican II, moreover, "helped to restore a more communal and collegial sense to what it means to belong to and participate in a parochial assembly of the local church."[31] Pastors were urged to cultivate community locally.

Laity, too, as an "ecclesial family," were invited to build ministry emphasizing community and purpose.[32]

Even while drawing attention to the local, the Second Vatican Council simultaneously affirmed the decision-making power of the bishop, the "high priest of his flock," in whom it was entrusted the discretion to start parishes.[33] Bishops occupy the helm of a "particular church"—a phrase denoting divisions of the universal Church: typically, dioceses. Dioceses function not as appendages but as local embodiments of the entire, unified Church.[34] That said, since "it is impossible for the bishop always and everywhere to preside over the whole flock in his Church," this requires also the use of parishes ("lesser groupings of the faithful"), under an appointed pastor.[35] Parishes are part of a particular church (a diocese). The phrase "particular church" or "Church" should not be misinterpreted to mean an individual parish. Parishes operate within an interconnected diocesan whole.

Vatican II did not overhaul territoriality in the organizational structure of the Roman Catholic Church. Parish still meant place. A parish was still the basic administrative unit, led by a pastor, under the jurisdiction of a local bishop. But the Council did shift the relationship of bishops (and pastors, and laity) to the parish—previously attending primarily to administrative organization, but now to localism and community. "What was revolutionized was the manner of lay and clerical participation in the life, liturgy, and mission of the parish. What was not foreseen was the way in which these latter, more fundamental changes, coupled with the effects of rapid socio-cultural changes, would lead in a very short time to new experiments in structuring parish life."[36]

A newly revised Code of Canon Law was not delivered until 1983, nearly two decades after the conclusion of the Second Vatican Council. It was described by Pope John Paul II as "the last Conciliar document" and "the first to integrate the whole of the Council into the whole of life."[37] This meant that core ideas expressed in Vatican II documents finally received juridical authority through the promulgation of a new rule book for the universal Roman Catholic Church. With it came a conceptual innovation (or historical recovery) that would reenergize the organizational option of the personal parish.

Canon 515 in the new (1983) Code of Canon Law defines a parish as follows:

Can. 515 §1. A parish is a certain community of the Christian faithful stably constituted in a particular church, whose pastoral care is entrusted to a pastor (*parochus*) as its proper pastor (*pastor*) under the authority of the diocesan bishop.[38]

The word "community" appears as constitutive in the meaning of parish, in addition to the pastor ... and without specific reference to territory. Territory appears elsewhere; here, parish gets added emphasis on people, community, and purpose.[39]

The new Code of Canon Law clarifies the enduring importance of territoriality in Canon 518. But with it comes the pertinent mention of personal parishes as a justifiable exception to the rule:

> Can. 518. As a general rule a parish is to be territorial, that is, one which includes all the Christian faithful of a certain territory. When it is expedient, however, personal parishes are to be established determined by reason of the rite, language, or nationality of the Christian faithful of some territory, or even for some other reason.[40]

The 1983 Code ratifies personal parishes' use as a coexistent option for building communities of Catholics. Place or purpose could justify a new parish.

The new code codifies a local bishop's discretion to respond to the particular situation of his local church. Says Vandenakker, "the significance of allowing other kinds of parishes is that it frees the bishop to respond creatively to the pastoral needs of diverse groups within the diocese."[41] Territory is not the sole adjudicating factor; "pastoral need is sometimes best served by forming parishes along other lines as well."[42] Potential factors, moreover, include the highly flexible "some other reason" ... a novel innovation.

The contemporary personal parish option for organizing local Catholics presents bishops with a social basis to facilitate pastoral care. Parish membership is implied through "belonging to the group for which the parish was established."[43] Commentary on canon law states in this regard:

> In a sense, each parish is both territorial and personal, but its designation as one or the other indicates which of these two characteristics is dominant. If a parish is considered *territorial*, all the persons in the territory belong to it (whether they have "enrolled" or "registered" in the parish, or not). If the parish is considered *personal*, it still has some territorial limits (at the utmost, the territorial limits of the particular church).[44]

The two prevailing rationales—social and territorial bases for parish establishment—are not mutually exclusive. Personal parishes may even overlap with territorial ones: for example, a territorial parish could be simultaneously erected as a personal parish for university students, or for all Hispanics of a diocese.

Far from purging the "national parish" once and for all, the current Code of Canon Law effectively encourages it as an organizational option. It empowers bishops to consider whether to instill geographic parish boundaries at all, or to instead prioritize social boundaries. Franciscan priest-theologian Kenneth Davis states that "the fact that the 1983 Code makes it easier to erect personal parishes implies encouragement of them." He opines further:

> In fact, if we seriously consider everything required by canon law, it is obvious that much is best served by a parish without boundaries, especially if that parish serves a people who, due to their language or nationality, have a longing for belonging.[45]

The Catholic parish—and the *American* Catholic parish in particular—can be purpose-based or place-based. The personal parish option means that this can be achieved through the formal structure of the Church, sanctioned (and overseen) by institutional leaders.

In sum, the history of "paroikia" from its origins, to the promulgation and reign of the 1917 Code of Canon Law, through the Second Vatican Council (1962–1965), until its replacement with the 1983 Code of Canon Law showcases stubbornness in the American context. On the one hand, the notion of territoriality steadfastly endures as the rule for local religious organization. Communities of purpose are the exception (and for years, an unwelcome one). Territorial regulations reigned in excessive lay control.

On the other hand, this history demonstrates that the Catholic Church responded to lived behavior among (American) lay Catholics by adapting its organizational options. Law and tradition stipulate parish as territory. America's diverse immigrant Catholicism stipulates parish-as-person and parish-as-purpose. Rather than the latter undoing the former, changes to canon law now accommodate both through a dual organizational structure: territorial parishes to serve all on the basis of domicile and proximity, and personal parishes to serve specialized local need. Both forms reaffirm the power of parish-building as ultimately residing in the hands of the hierarchy—not lay Catholics.

PARISH STATUS MATTERS

A core contention of this book is that official parish status matters. A de facto community of Catholics is not equivalent to a canonical parish in Church law or in sociological assessments of power, function, and substance. Specialized groupings of choice do not a personal parish make. To be counted as a parish canonically, a Catholic community requires a juridical (i.e., legal) status that cannot be generated through community alone. Although parishes may (and frequently do) originate as non-parish communities desiring formal status, it takes a bishop's decree to formally constitute the community as a parish.[46]

This important technicality runs counter to definitions of "congregation" that prevail in the sociology of religion. If congregations are, per leading congregational scholar Nancy Ammerman's 2009 definition:

> Locally situated, multi-generational, voluntary organizations of people who identify themselves as a distinct religious group and engage in a broad range of religious activities together [47]

... then, surely Catholics who gather together voluntarily, with an identity, in religious activity, constitute a parish. They look and act an awful lot like a parish—with the trappings of a priest, rented space, and stable community of faithful attendees. But herein lies a major point of distinction: *Parish* is an official, canonical status. Personal parishes are bound by both "parish" and "personal parish" definitions in canon law. Their existence is contingent upon the institutional Church; they are dependent upon and tied to the polity of its structural regulations. In this, authority offsets congregationalism. It is insufficient to conclude that a Catholic organization is real in its consequences because the formality of Church law does not make it so.

Parish status (whether personal or territorial) matters in material and symbolic ways. The privilege of parish status is signaled by Catholic pronouncements that a given community's status has been elevated to that of a parish. Personal parishes share behavior with other non-parish organizational entities, but there is an implicit and explicit hierarchy of statuses. "There's plenty of Masses around, don't get me wrong," said one pastor of a Traditional Latin Mass personal parish in our interview, "but for us to have that full formative aspect of it, to really become biblical, you really need the parish." Being a parish affords a host of tangible and intangible goods. Status shapes interactions with the diocese, the priest, and parishioners, and impacts the legitimacy and continuity of a given community.

The distinction is metaphorically similar to citizenship. To draw the parallel: while one may "feel" like an American citizen and act as such, there are certain rights and privileges not afforded to non-citizens (namely, the right to vote, to run for public office, and to hold a passport). The status is not merely symbolic. Non-citizen status, moreover, carries greater instability and risk: legal residency may be revoked, one's opinion may not be heard in policy matters, and the right to speak imperiled. So, too, with parishes in the Catholic Church: status carries more than semantic and symbolic value.

While the substantive meaning of parish status plays out over the forthcoming chapters, here I review three of the more transparent canonical privileges: (1) presumed permanence/stability; (2) an assigned, suitable pastor; and (3) a physical church home.[48]

A Stable Community of the Diocese

Arguably the most important dimension of canonical parish status is stability. As James Coriden frames it, parishes have a distinctive right to "existence": they are erected with continuity and permanence. Parishes privilege stability and permanence in ways that other local Catholic organizational entities do not. "Canon law gives a strong presumption in favor of its endurance in being."[49] This means that—once established—a parish is and should be difficult to suppress (close). Other Catholic groups, by contrast, come and go more readily, based on need (or politics). Parishes are intended to be long-term entities with staying power.[50]

A decision to establish a parish is a serious decision, treated as they are in Church law as "juridic persons," subject to rights and obligations like individual Catholics.[51] One diocesan planner in a western diocese summarizes this notion with his assessment in our interview that "once you canonically establish a parish, it's very hard to destroy it." Restructuring (i.e., redrawing parish lines) is often messy and contested. Parish establishment may follow a prolonged period of gathering within other, less canonically stable forms of community. "It's quite a step when they're actually made a parish of a diocese," shares a personal parish pastor. "It's harder for [the bishop] to take it back," adds another. Gaining parish status—and the accompanying assurance of stability—is a big deal.

For personal parishes, in particular, this stability extends materially and symbolically to the assurance of service to particular populations and purposes. A territorial parish's internal mission may vary over time, with leadership and neighborhood change. But a personal parish's origins commit explicitly—through decree and canonical status—to serving a named people and purpose. "The position of the Latin Mass, the permanency of the Latin Mass is assured here," one Traditional Latin Mass personal parish pastor shares with confidence. Parish status creates not just a stable structure for any proximate Catholics to worship and build community: it assures a stable structure for a specific community of Catholics. So long as the people remain, the parish and its purpose endure.[52]

Unlike other Catholic organizational entities, parishes are not seen as a temporary or precarious step toward something else (e.g., full integration into the territorial parish to which they are linked, parish status on their own right, or disappearance altogether). A parish is embedded in the fabric of the diocese rather than dependent upon another parish's pastor and finances. This is an attractive position, as one personal parish pastor describes:

> People like the parish. They don't want to be a mission, if they can have the power to support themselves. When you're a mission, the money you take in goes to—not to you, but it goes to whomever you're a mission for. . . . Being a parish is just great. You can have your own societies. You can have your own religious education, and you have full control over how it's run. You don't have to have somebody come in and tell you, "You have to do it this way," or "You have to do it that way."

As this pastor alludes, parish status affords control (monetary and otherwise). Unlike a mission that borrows space from a "parent" parish (with an option to "drop us if we were a drain on their finances," says this pastor), parishes manage their own finances through a pastor and canonically mandated financial council. This means greater autonomy in resource allocation.

This same pastor (of a Traditional Latin Mass personal parish) goes on to say that parish status is especially important for personal parishes with atypical liturgical styles:

> You have some parishes that may not like this or that, and then – you're not being able to do what you feel is necessary for your culture. Particularly if the culture is different . . . the culture ought to be allowed to have its own parish.

The countercultures of personal parishes may make their acceptance in the diocese more precarious. Personal parish status brings greater stability for uncommon or marginalized forms of Catholic practice.

Many describe a discernable difference between parish stability and non-parish instability. One pastor speaks of the confusion this can carry:

> It was not a clear status. The pastor of the parish had almost nothing to do with the community, so they paid their own chaplain. The position of the chaplain was also not clear, because the canonical status was not clear. Baptismal, marriage, and all the other accommodations would be written in the parish.

The durability of parish status—and accompanying parish name—can reassure interested Catholics that they can join and belong as long-term parishioners. Two pastors explain how this happened with their personal parishes, solidifying a community that was previously far more precarious:

> That's when more people came in, because they felt: this is permanent. It's not something that's going to go away tomorrow. When you're a mission, the church you're a mission to could say "Well, we don't want to sponsor you anymore." . . . Therefore, what are you going to do? You're out on your own! You have to look for somebody to sponsor you.

* * *

> There's certainly a level of increasing freedom. From the point of view of the people, there is increased security in this situation. People feel secure, because a parish is a canonical reality. It's canonically erected. We told the people here and we made sure that they knew that in order for the bishop to suppress this parish, he had to apply for permission. He couldn't just get upset one day and, with the stroke of a pen. . . . They feel more secure that the priest is not going away, the parish is not going away, the community is not going away, it's here to stay. It's stability.

Another pastor of an African American parish celebrated the security that canonical parish status brought for his long-standing community:

> In the process of the merger, we made it clear that we needed to safeguard the parish as a personal parish for African Americans. We felt that that was an important thing to have happen, because we don't really have any other black priests coming up, and you could easily get someone in here who just has a whole different view of things, and wouldn't necessarily respect that. So it's a canonically established reality and so, therefore, needs to be respected, in that sense. If it wasn't, you'd get somebody else come in here and just . . . whatever.

Parish status prioritizes continuity.

A personal parish decree can also imply stronger (or at least more explicit) support from a local bishop for the specified community. Bishops commit in writing to maintain a stable community, with a pastor, for the given purpose. Not every Catholic group is granted parish status. Those that do find unique legitimacy within the diocese. One pastor is quite open about how his bishop's support through parish status has been the life-blood of their community:

> There's something special about being a pastor of a personal parish. You have support of the archdiocese that's more explicit, in some ways, than it is for

geographic parishes. If we had to maintain it ourselves, we would have been closed a long time ago!

Another pastor acknowledges, similarly, how parish status communicates bishop approval to a wider audience:

> It sure makes a difference to a parish, knowing that they have the blessing of the authority—the bishop—to recognize the ministry that they do, as far as the reason they're a personal parish. Their boundaries are, in a sense, open. I think it helps us to stay focused, and it helps us to know that what we're doing is being recognized by the bishop.

The external validation embedded in official parish status can matter even more when a new bishop is appointed. Barring continued support, parish status protects a community's existence above other organizational forms. That is "when it matters," as an African American personal parish pastor puts it:

> When it matters is if you get a new bishop, or you get a new pastor who wants to change some things. Or doesn't understand some things. I mean, the most likely thing that's going to happen here is we're probably going to get a Hispanic speaking priest. Because, I mean, they've got more of them than they've got Black. If you get a Hispanic speaking priest in here, of course his emphasis is going to be on the Hispanic community. There's a lot that he'll be able to do, but at a certain point, there's a limit. And that limit has to do with, well, this is a parish designated for African American people! There are certain things you can't do, or you're threatening that. There are certain things that you *should* be doing, if you're not doing them. So, that's why it was important to me that [personal parish status] be done.

A personal parish decree stabilized and ensured service to black Catholics, outlasting transitions in pastoral or diocesan leadership.

Entrusted to a Pastor

The stability proffered by parish status comes also with (and through) the promise of an appointed pastor. Per the canonical definition of a parish, "pastoral care is entrusted to a pastor."[53] In the United States, a pastoral appointment is made for a renewable six-year term.[54] For a personal parish, an appointed pastor must necessarily be trained and able to meet the decreed need or purpose of the personal parish constituency. This commits the diocese to identifying, appointing, and supplying a suitable pastor.

An appointed pastor—and the promise of future pastors with a similar skillset—offers Catholic communities an essential resource internally, and point of leverage externally.[55] A Traditional Latin Mass pastor shares how this protects his community beyond his own tenure there:

> They're guaranteed that when I leave, the Mass continues. With a different priest, of course, but the Mass is the same. That is so important. Some [priests] are more apt than others are, but in the end, people aren't totally shaken up by changing pastors. The pastor is supposed to be stable. . . . That is one of the envisioning strengths of [parish status].

By contrast, Catholic communities with a capable priest who is not their assigned pastor lack this protection. One lay leader recalled how "There was a monthly Mass at a [territorial] parish, but that priest was reassigned, and that was the end of that monthly Mass." Parish status avoids this kind of uncertainty.

Pastors, themselves, appreciate the stability and clarity that parish status provides them in ways that other organizations do not. One contrasts his current appointment with his previous role as a priest to a non-parish community, saying that "When we were a chapel, we were under the auspices of [another parish]. I had to go and get permission from the priest there, 'cause he was technically the pastor here." This is a common theme: priests trying to manage Catholic communities without parish status—and therefore without pastor status—who constantly had to ask permission of a relatively absentee pastor in the conjoined parish.

A personal parish pastor, by contrast, has "all the authority you need; you have the rights of the pastor. . . . You don't have to ask a local pastor permission to do things." The pastor has autonomy and control not available to priests (or laity) leading other forms of Catholic organization. One pastor from a university personal parish acknowledges this freedom, saying that, "I hardly ever have to ask anybody's permission to do much of anything that I want to do." Absent personal parish status, "the pastor within which we were located would be able to overrule me." Having a dedicated pastor empowered with decision-making and administrative control—as opposed to a priest without pastor status (however dedicated he may be)—separates Catholic communities with parish status from those without.

A Parish in a Place

A third category of status privilege has to do with the physical structure housing a community. While not explicitly mentioned in the canonical definition of "parish," it is typically coterminous.[56] A parish needs a place. Property acquisition (subject to diocesan oversight and approval) is among the distinctive rights of a parish, as compared to lesser forms of Catholic community. As a "juridic person," parishes are "capable of acquiring, retaining, administering, and alienating temporal goods according to the norm of law," per Canon Law 1255. Temporal goods include a church building.

Personal parishes necessarily find a physical home in a dedicated space (confusingly, often referred to as "parish"). A community may gain parish status before acquiring their own space, remaining itinerant as they work toward the financial goal of church ownership. Typically they rent space in another parish, but without any administrative ties to it. One pastor of a Traditional Latin Mass personal parish tells of how his community is fundraising to acquire their own space:

> I do fully realize the need to have our own parish building. The parish life is associated with it . . . having a situation that allows the type of parish life and full liturgies associated with, "This is our parish," and the identities that go with that. . . . Once we achieve that (and I'm very hopeful that we will), that will bring forward additional benefits, I'm sure, to how we grow, and the metrics that are associated with our parish.

Another describes how "having our parish live in a temporary location is problematic and difficult" and that "the establishment of a more permanent residency, with our own building, is certainly an ultimate goal . . . and one that we're all working towards."

Paired with the material acquisition of a physical church home (such as the new space shown in figure 1.1), parish status gives personal parishes traction to attract and retain parishioners. One pastor describes this enthusiasm:

> When people see the plans—the artist rendering and all, it's like, "Yeah, I want to be a part of that!" And so they did. Parish status, it's not . . . that's intangible; you can't see it; it's not like seeing a building. But still, it gives you that sense of pride [that] equates to enrollment or registration, and then with the increase in the revenue.

A church building begets parishioners . . . and parishioner contributions.

FIGURE 1.1 Acquiring a place is a key criteria for parish establishment. This personal parish raised funds to construct a new worship space.

Some personal parishes benefit from the suppression of older parishes that leave behind empty—often quite beautiful—buildings. One pastor shares how his community repurposed an old cathedral in their diocese:

> They put [the personal parish] in this parish because, as a diocesan official later told me, it had a high altar and low attendance. There were no permanent modifications for Mass facing the people, and they did not remove their altar rail. And it was rather underutilized church that had been very active. It was large. It had a central location.

The space fit Traditional Latin Mass needs perfectly. This reflects a best-case-scenario for a diocese: entrusting an older building to the care of a vibrant new community whose purpose resonates with the architecture. This also pairs the expense of an old building with the finances of a thriving community.

Matching new personal parishes to old buildings, of course, can lead to some curious combinations, such as a Korean personal parish in a church with Irish shamrocks, or buildings many miles away from parishioners' homes. Personal parishes also repurpose non-church buildings, such as one Vietnamese parish that renovated a gas station, or another that remodeled a space formerly occupied by Seventh Day Adventists. But again, a parish is not just a building. And a building is not a parish. Infrastructure—and its related polity—matters: canon law mandates diocesan oversight, even while day-to-day administration is handled by the parish and its pastor.

Parish Limits

Parish status offers stability, a pastor, and a physical home. It links a community of Catholics in formal, material, and symbolic ways to each other, and to the diocese in which it sits. Together, these characteristics set parishes apart from other types of Catholic (and non-Catholic) collectives. A "certain community of the Christian faithful" is not sufficient to constitute a parish in of Church law; the community must be "stably constituted in a particular church" and "entrusted to a pastor as its proper pastor" which falls "under the authority of the diocesan bishop."[57] Granted approval, parishes occupy an organizational form in the US Catholic Church that is the most visible, legitimate, and stable of all.

Institutionally, bishops are well aware of the ways in which parish status—unlike other organizational forms—brings communities of Catholics into the fold of the diocese and its formal administrative oversight. This is both a right and an obligation: a parish must necessarily comply with "everything," says one bishop. "That's a prerequisite for becoming a personal parish. They have to follow all the guidelines and the norms established as policies of the archdiocese." This can improve otherwise ad hoc or unknown diocesan activities. One bishop explains:

> Without being a parish, we have very little control over that. They are like groups
> of people functioning independently. So, it's better to give them the status of
> being a parish. The pastor of those communities was only like a chaplain to
> them; but now they get a pastor. And he becomes much more integrated in the

life of the local church. They become part of the deanery system, they take part in all the clergy kinds of programs that we have. They work together, and get great support from the diocese. As well as lay people—they enter into our training programs. And they could never do that on their own.

He expands upon how this facilitates diocesan (and bishop) oversight:

> To take full benefit of the life of the church, the local church, there are a number of procedures that [parishes] must follow in terms of financing, permission to build, and things of that nature. They've learned it's much easier if they are officially recognized as a parish—a personal parish. Because that gives them entrée to follow the same procedure and process that every other parish follows. They have to submit their books, and their finances, and things to the scrutiny of the diocese. And make sure that everything is always above board, and properly done. And the money that they are collecting from people under the aegis of being a Catholic community: that money is being properly spent, properly accounted for.

Parish status, in other words, reaffirms a local bishop's authority over finances and other matters.

Of course, the obligation and oversight that accompanies parish rights makes some Catholic communities weary to seek it. One pastor in a Midwestern diocese suggests that becoming a parish is not always preferable:

> The other side of it is this: that if they become a parish, they come under regulations of the diocese that they wouldn't be under otherwise. And if the regulations are going to be things that don't fit in too well with what they're doing, then they would prefer not to be a parish.

Becoming a parish means losing some flexibility, even as it means gaining privileges. One pastor describes the paradox that this introduces:

> They have to take up the annual collections of the diocese, if they're a parish, you know. And there are certain other regulations like that, that every parish does. . . . If they're Traditional Rite, they're independent for that—but they're not independent for their other functioning things. So, they may or may not want to be a parish. But it certainly improves their status if they're made a parish.

This pastor's reticence circles back to finances: specifically, the cathedraticum, a "tax" levied on every diocesan parish. Parish status is "a better connection," he says, "and at the same time—for us—it's a more heavy burden."

Personal parishes bear official, canonical, parish status. They serve diverse and specialized Catholic populations. Like their historical counterparts, today's personal parishes form cultural sanctuaries, but now accommodate many arenas of difference.

The National Survey of Personal Parishes (hereinafter "NSPP") shows that:

- There are currently 1,317 personal parishes in the United States.
- Personal parishes constitute some 8 percent of Catholic parishes overall.
- Most American dioceses (61 percent) have at least one personal parish.
- 192 "new" personal parishes have been established in the United States since the release of the 1983 Code of Canon Law.[58]
- New personal parishes constitute 15 percent, or not quite one in seven, of all personal parishes currently open. This equates to just over 1 percent, or about one in one hundred—of all US parishes.
- Most personal parishes—old and new—serve ethno-racial/national groups. The rest serve myriad purposes, the Traditional Latin Mass foremost among them.
- Among new ethnic personal parishes, the highest proportion serve Asian American Catholics—most commonly, Vietnamese and Korean Catholics.

Personal parishes constituted approximately 10 percent of all parishes in 1951, 11 percent in the 1980s, and 8 percent today. Even so, more American dioceses each year since 1983 are adding new personal parishes, just as they close old ones.[59]

(Arch)dioceses in the Northeast are more likely than any other region to currently have a personal parish in operation. Their higher numbers are not surprising, given the greater concentration of national parishes begun by immigrants years ago. While nine in ten dioceses in the Northeast report having at least one personal parish (most of which were established pre-1983), just half of Midwestern dioceses report as such. Southern and western dioceses lie in-between—boasting more parish growth overall in recent decades (60 and 57 percent have at least one personal parish, respectively). The more urban a diocese, the more likely it is to have established a new ethnic personal parish. Dioceses that already had personal parishes pre-1983 are more likely to have established new ones.[60]

There are two major categories of personal parishes in the US Catholic Church today. The first category includes those established before 1983—most at the turn of the twentieth century, under the rubric of the national parish—usually in service to European Catholic populations. Many of these personal parishes are now more than a century old. A substantial proportion has been suppressed. Others remain open in service to Catholic populations vastly different from that for which they were founded. The average founding date of personal parishes established before 1983 and still open today is 1912. Among those established after 1983, the average founding date is 1998.

These older personal parishes are often the first on the chopping block during diocesan restructuring. Even the very first national parish—Holy Trinity in Philadelphia—lost its parish status (though it still stands as a church, offering irregular Masses). The NSPP asked whether dioceses had recently closed, suppressed, or merged parishes originally erected to serve a specific population of Catholics (e.g., as a national parish); 43 percent of dioceses responded affirmatively. Dioceses closed an average of eight such parishes during restructuring in the past decade alone. Another 10 percent of dioceses reported that the canonical status of at least one parish had changed from "personal" to "territorial" since 2002. This status transition impacted an average of two former national parishes among dioceses nationwide.

One Philadelphia diocesan leader describes in an interview how, in his diocese, "We just closed 14 parishes, and last year there were about 15 that closed. And many of those are national parishes, or they were national parishes that have now become territorial parishes because of the mergers." Generations of European Catholics have long since assimilated and departed their national parishes, leaving behind younger Catholics with different sociocultural needs. Another pastor tells how this is happening for the Hungarian population in his Midwestern diocese:

> The Mass at 11:00 is for the Hungarians. They're getting older and older. We don't have any children with us; it's mainly grandparents. Their children and their grandchildren are all absorbed into parishes around—they're not so anxious to be in a Hungarian Church, and all that. It's mainly the grandparents, and they're getting older and dying, and so the number is going down.

Other parishes still attract Catholics who share the ethnicity of the original parish decree, but many lack knowledge in its language or traditions. One priest serving an old Italian parish says, "The [Italian] language is pretty much dissipated. I don't hear Italian." Funerals are a common request, as one priest put it: "Well, it's a changing role. The parish is still the personal parish, but it doesn't really serve that community . . . except when people die."

Closing older national parishes matches the narrative that (white European) Catholics' ethnicity has met its "twilight."[61] Less anticipated are those parishes whose survival (and current vitality) rests almost entirely upon an ethno-racial group . . . just not the one the parish was originally founded to serve. Saint Joseph parish in the diocese of Omaha, Nebraska, for example, was established in 1886 to serve German Catholics. Today, its parishioner population of more than 1,500 is 98 percent Hispanic.

This kind of demographic shift has saved many older personal parishes from closure. New generations of Catholics—especially Hispanic and Asian Catholics—cluster and worship in national parishes not originally meant for "them." Occasionally during diocesan restructuring, an old parish will receive a new decree, thereby establishing it officially for the ethnic/national group now actually there. Otherwise, the parish retains its original decree as a home for the occasional Mass or street festival honoring the designated heritage, absent a critical parishioner base of co-ethnics.

Occasionally, keeping an older personal parish is a political or financial move to appease (wealthy) co-ethnics. One priest hints at this:

TCB: *So, in the case of the older—especially the Italian personal parish, and the Portuguese one—why retain that status, if they serve so few members of that original group?*
Out of deference to the older people.

Further still, old national parishes may occupy churches in urban cores of metropolitan areas, such as the once-heavily Catholic immigrant neighborhood depicted in figure 1.2. Newer immigrant Catholics whose socioeconomics parallel those of immigrant Catholics a century ago now fill the pews.

Not surprisingly, America's old personal parishes have—by and large—aged, closed, dwindled, and/or found new functions. While parish status can protect a purpose, it cannot produce the people. Among white European national parishes that have survived, their average establishment date is 1909. This spins a truthful but incomplete story that national parishes are

FIGURE 1.2 Economic and demographic changes to historically Catholic neighborhoods can leave behind empty churches.

a thing of the past. This can be heard in remarks from one older national parish pastor:

> There's always going to be a loss of culture, and a loss of language. Ethnic parishes, as they were known years ago, don't really exist anymore . . . except nominally, or older people that are holding on. You'll find there's a new kind of ethnic parish, with a new kind of ethnic immigrant. You know, Hispanics. And Asians.

White American Catholics no longer exercise their ethnic "options"[62] as readily as before, their specialized parishes rendered unnecessary through "successful" generational assimilation. This grants the illusion that personal parishes "don't really exist anymore," to echo this pastor's words. But they do . . . for that "new kind of ethnic immigrant," and more.

Post-1983 Personal Parishes

The second category of personal parishes—those established in or after 1983—comprises the main story of this book. They are new(er). They arose in different institutional and cultural contexts. They satisfy new institutional needs. Of all personal parishes open today, 192 were established by American dioceses in the thirty years following the implementation of the new Code of Canon Law (1983–2012).[63]

Forty-four percent of US dioceses established at least one personal parish during this period. The number of dioceses with new personal parishes grew modestly but steadily throughout the thirty-year period following 1983. Collectively, the increase in dioceses with new personal parishes portrays an image of an American Church turning cautiously but increasingly to creative, non-territorial options for local Catholic organization.

Three-quarters (77 percent) of new personal parishes serve specific ethnic groups. Dioceses in the South are twice as likely to have established ethnic personal parishes in recent years. This differs from the historic association of personal (national) parishes with the Northeast, but mirrors southern dioceses' overall higher likelihood to start new parishes. Expanding, younger, and increasingly non-white Catholic populations fuel growth in southern and western dioceses.

Post-1983 personal parishes are markedly distinct from their older counterparts in that they also serve myriad non-ethnic purposes. Nearly a quarter of new personal parishes do so. This includes personal parishes devoted to offering the Traditional Latin Mass exclusively, to college ministry, to social justice, to Anglican Use, to the elderly, to tourism, and other areas tailored to local diocesan populations.

Table 1.2 breaks down today's personal parishes into eight categories: five ethno-racial categories (Asian, Hispanic, European, African/African American, and Native American), and three non-ethno-racial categories (university, Traditional Latin Mass, and other purposes). This parish count includes only those personal parishes established in or after 1983. It does not include parishes that remain open today whose establishment date precedes 1983.

Table 1.2 CATEGORIES OF PERSONAL PARISHES ESTABLISHED, 1983–2012

Category of Purpose	Number of Parishes	Percentage of Personal Parish Total
Asian	82	43
Hispanic/Latino	34	18
Traditional Latin Mass	24	13
European	22	11
Other (non-ethnic) purpose	14	7
University	7	4
African/African American	6	3
Native American	3	2

Note: Includes only those parishes open as of 2012.

Parish establishment dates imply the date of canonical parish decree. This is typically not coterminous with the date a community first gathered or acquired a church building. It also cannot be conflated with the founding date of the parish community previously housed in the church. A new personal parish may postdate a church building (or prior communities therein) by decades. Sometimes a creative new name honors this complicated legacy (e.g., "Santo Nino at St. James").

Newly decreed European personal parishes (11 percent of the new personal parish total) usually signal that an older national parish was granted personal parish status anew during diocesan restructuring. Diocesan restructuring is common: more than six in ten dioceses (62 percent) suppressed or merged parishes in the decade between 2002 and 2012. Personal parish establishment is more common during diocesan restructuring. Dioceses with recent parish closures are more likely to report new personal parish establishment. An overall decrease in the number of diocesan parishes, moreover, increases the likelihood that a diocese will start a new personal parish. Destabilizing the parish "market" spawns innovation in the form of personal parishes.

As observed historically, today's ethnic personal parishes do not mirror each ethnicity's proportionate population size among Catholics at large. This is especially notable for Hispanic and Latino Catholics. Hispanics make up a full 38 percent of adult Catholics,[64] but only 18 percent of new personal parishes. To explain this, it is helpful to pair personal parish numbers with another question on the NSPP about the use of personal parishes relative to other, alternative ministry options for specific groups.

Table 1.3 (ARCH)DIOCESAN USE OF PERSONAL PARISHES AND OTHER
APPROACHES TO ETHNIC OR LANGUAGE MINISTRY

	Percentage of dioceses that use personal parishes	Percentage of dioceses using non-personal parish ministries
Vietnamese	20	46
Koreans	20	27
Polish	19	23
Hispanic/Latinos (combined)	17	76
Italians	16	9
African Americans/Blacks	11	44
Mexicans	6	35
French	6	8
Native Americans	5	25
Filipinos	3	29
Deaf/hearing-impaired	2	51
Chinese	2	13
Puerto Ricans	2	10
Africans	1	32
Brazilians	1	16
Haitians	1	15
Dominicans (Dominican Republic)	1	11
Cubans	1	8
Salvadorans	1	8

Note: Dioceses could select more than one option. The table conflates non-personal parish options into a single "non-personal parish ministries" category. For many groups listed, dioceses did not report *any* specialized ministry form.

Dioceses clearly prioritize specialized ministry to groups of Catholics based upon ethnicity, language, nationality, and liturgical preferences. Purpose has a place. But most often, dioceses opt to form non-personal parish structures to deliver this ministry. Not having parish status for a given community of Catholics is far more common than having parish status. Dioceses report that other approaches—namely, dedicated parishes without personal parish status, missions, apostolates, and integrated parishes offering special Masses or ministries—are more common. Personal parishes remain an emergent organizational form among dioceses, not (as of yet) achieving the level of prevalence that national parishes once did. Table 1.3 shows the percentage of dioceses selecting each option for the language, ethnic, or national groups listed.

While upward of three-quarters of dioceses offer other ministry options for Hispanics and Latinos, for example, only about one in six use personal

parishes. A number of factors help to explain this. Hispanics are comparatively more numerous and dispersed territorially. Territorial parish priests
are more commonly trained to speak Spanish. Spanish is the most common
non-English Mass offering. A pan-Hispanic personal parish risks erasing
ethnic specificity. Hispanic diocesan ministers are more inclined to promote integrated organizational spaces.[65] New personal parishes do exist
for Hispanic Catholics, though, and are typically pan-Hispanic—merging
multiple ethno-national backgrounds (leading at times to inter-ethnic
tensions).

By contrast, Asian Catholics are the most common racial group served
by personal parishes. Although Asian Catholics do not constitute the largest minority in the Church (far outnumbered by Hispanic Catholics), they
are more likely to be first generation Americans. Asians' rate of migration
to the United States now surpasses that of Latinos, and America's pro-
Catholic pull brings a disproportionately Catholic population as compared
to native Asian countries.[66] Personal parishes serving Asian Catholics have
much newer establishment dates: 1992 on average, as compared to 1924
for personal parishes overall. There are no pan-ethnic personal parishes for
Asian Catholics, due foremost to substantial linguistic diversity therein.

Dioceses also elect different routes to meet the needs of specialized
non-ethnic groups: for example, those desiring the Traditional Latin
Mass (TLM). A large percentage of dioceses (eight in ten) report celebrating the extraordinary form of the Roman Rite at territorial arch/diocesan
parish(es). Far fewer have established TLM personal parishes.[67] This data
confirms that territorial parishes still handle the bulk of specialized ministry. Questions about when, how, and for whom personal parishes find
livelihood shape the chapters to come.

CONCLUSION: CHANGES PARISHES IN CHANGING ENVIRONMENTS

American Catholics experience Catholicism together in communion, in the
collective. The shared experience of Catholicism, through the parish, lies at
the core of the faith tradition. And parishes are more than the sum of the
individuals therein. They constitute "the basic social unit" of the church
and "the point at which the institutional, hierarchical church and the people encounter one another."[68] Parishes merge symbolic and material realities to define local community and house Catholic culture.

While the meaning of parish does not stop at its canonical definition, it
necessarily starts there. Parish status matters materially and symbolically,

in both its presence and its absence. Individual Catholics may neither know nor appreciate (nor care, nor need to) about parish status. But ignorance or apathy does not nullify the significance of institutional status and power. In the words of one aforementioned personal parish pastor, "it doesn't matter until it matters." Rights inaccessible or revoked are surely more noticeable. Parish status is the most clear regulatory marker of the institutional Church, and the most transparent measure of an emergent organizational form. It is only with these formal parameters established—that authority and polity in the Church matter when it comes to "parish" (and, here, to "personal parish")—that one can understand and appreciate symbolic and sociological meanings beyond the canonical designation.

Parish status has even become more consequential over time. Increased oversight centralized in the 1917 Code of Canon Law reigned in the grassroots, laissez-faire parish development epitomized by America's early national parishes. Personal parish establishment lay dormant for decades. The new (1983) Code generated an opportunity to reclaim the earlier organizational form, and with it, an assurance of diocesan oversight. Contemporary personal parishes—through formal decree and endowment of promises—generate purpose-driven organizations.

All new organizational forms combine and permutate their historical counterparts; they are historically path-dependent.[69] Institutional changes in 1983 (the afterbirth of Vatican II) fostered innovation using an older organizational form. The national parish for ethnic Catholics underwent a genesis to become the modern personal parish, serving not only ethnic Catholics but also myriad non-ethnic purposes. Personal parishes are necessarily read as a structural response by Catholic hierarchy to changing institutional environments.

Circling back to this chapter's opening vignette: some two years after my students and I embarked upon our goose chase to attend Mass with Vietnamese Catholics in Knoxville, the Divine Mercy community fundraised and gained permission to acquire a physical church home. Outgrowing the high school chapel, they moved to the high school gym. Outgrowing the high school gym, the local bishop identified a church where they could celebrate Mass, teach the Vietnamese language, and convey Vietnamese culture. "It's one of my great joys at the moment. They're just great folks," the bishop shared. "You know, we bought the church, I think we closed like on a Tuesday or a Wednesday, and by the following Tuesday it was all painted! People just showed up . . . thirty people with paintbrushes . . . !"

Their new home is a former Protestant church on ten acres with seating capacity for 300, classrooms, and a house. Parishioners set up the sanctuary with Vietnamese statues and a baptismal fountain. They brought their own chairs while awaiting new pews. But when I interviewed the local bishop, they were still not a parish, canonically. I asked him about this.

> TCB: *So do you think that that community—which still has mission status at this point—will be moving towards parish status soon?*
>
> My guess is within a year. Because they're really a firmly established entity, and they have a priest, and they have a location now. So, it's one of the conversations I'll probably have with them before the end of the year.
>
> TCB: *Okay. And you've identified most of the things that would take it to that point: the number of people, the resources (by way of finances), they have a building, they have a priest . . . is there anything else that you would add to that?*
>
> They have the enthusiasm.
>
> TCB: *The enthusiasm, yeah.*
>
> They're all—I think it has all the right conditions.

Sure enough, in 2014, "The Church of Divine Mercy became the Diocese of Knoxville's 49th parish on November 23 when Bishop Richard F. Stika elevated the church's status during a special Mass."[70] The Vietnamese Catholic community became the diocese's first personal parish.

CHAPTER 2
Boundaries

A behemoth architectural relic in an otherwise downtrodden New Jersey neighborhood, St. Joseph's Polish Catholic Parish embodies more than a century of change. Its 1892 founding came in the wake of large-scale Polish emigration and expanded US industrialization. Jobs at Campbell Soup, RCA Victor, and the New York shipyard made Camden a viable immigrant destination. St. Joseph's arose as one of several hundred Polish national parishes serving some two million Polish immigrants. Before gaining their own church, many of Camden's Catholic Poles ferried across the Delaware River, walking three miles to a Polish parish in Philadelphia. St. Joseph brought Catholic Poland to Camden. The founding pastor's entrepreneurial establishment of a savings and loan association enabled parishioners to build and purchase homes in the church's immediate vicinity. Discounted and discriminated against, Catholic Poles came to form a tight-knit community known as "Polishtown." Activity abounded through Polish Masses, a parish school, a convent, citizenship classes, and cultural events.[1]

Attend Sunday Mass at St. Joseph's today and one encounters a neighborhood changed. Surrounding blocks contain boarded-up and graffitied row houses; "R.I.P." tags one home across the street. A stained-glass church window depicting a Polish saint is interrupted by a bullet hole. With a poverty rate among the highest in the country, the City of Camden has felt keenly postindustrial urban decay. Economic decline and white flight in the late twentieth century led most Polish Catholics to relocate. Today, whites comprise less than 2 percent of the neighborhood, now overwhelmingly African American, renter-occupied, and minimally Catholic. The parochial grade school and convent have long been demolished; the once high school now houses a thrift shop.

Inside for Sunday's Mass kneel a handful of Polish Catholics, their presence dwarfed by the soaring Baroque nave. Lights and oscillating stand fans flip on a few minutes before 9:00. A visiting priest celebrates Mass in Polish. Communion offered at the chair rail takes just moments, elongated only by the recipients' protracted journey up the long center aisle. Polish organ hymns fill the emptiness. Pope John Paul II paraphernalia marks the space as Polish, as do the Polish and American flags flanking the alter. Friendly Polish banter follows the forty-minute Mass into the parking lot, to a soundtrack of nearby hip-hop. Attendees' cars are clearly not from the neighborhood. The finely dressed, white, and generally older Polish crowd has driven in from a considerable distance. Parish and neighborhood no longer align.

* * *

Personal parishes override boundary lines to serve certain Catholics. While physically, temporally, and socially rooted, personal parishes arise in and apart from place. They need not mirror their neighborhoods, finding livelihood in the absence of parish boundaries. But how does this mesh with the Catholic Church's long-standing tradition of territoriality? Understanding personal parishes entails understanding the functions (and contradictions) of parish boundaries.

This chapter traces the evolving role of parish boundaries alongside American Catholics' heightened mobility. Personal parishes' contemporary emergence can be explained, in part, as an institutional response to the shifting character of boundaries. We see this exemplified through parish choice, diocesan boundary-drawing, parochial school reform, and renewed understandings of a parish "home."

BOUNDED TERRITORIES

In the Catholic Church, territorial parish boundaries exist as a way to manage things, administratively. Like public school boundaries or political districts, they specify which Catholics go to which parish church, and which parish church (and pastor) is responsible for which Catholics. "For the faithful, territoriality means that the Church is not a membership organization in which you pick and choose your place or degree of affiliation," writes Francis Cardinal George.[2]

Organizationally, boundaries enable institutional recordkeeping and reporting. As one pastor shares, "A lot of times the reason for parish boundaries is just more organization, you know. Who has responsibility for reporting this wedding or this baptism." Boundaries—and the accompanying allocation of American Catholics—provide a sense of order for the local church. Another pastor describes the value of having "every square inch of a particular archdiocese" within some parish as providing "a certain order." Abolishing boundaries in the Catholic Church, says another pastor, would make things "very messy":

> I think it might be a little bit of a disaster administratively, if you would just do away with [boundaries]. Because there's a really nice system of how parishes run themselves and how they keep sacramental records and that type of thing. The way it works now in the church is: the church that you're baptized in becomes your sacramental church. And so, when you receive subsequent sacraments, you always have to get a copy of your original baptismal certificate, and you go back to your sacramental church. I don't see the Church ever doing away with that. It's just ... there's too many canon laws, and it would do away with a lot of privileges of the parish that would make the administrative aspect of it ... that would make this very messy.

Parish boundaries help the Catholic Church to function locally.

Record-keeping begins with baptism in one's "sacramental church." As Catholicism urges infant baptism, this means that administrative documentation in the Church typically begins shortly after birth. The parish where one is baptized becomes one's "church-of-record." A baptismal certificate remains physically at the baptismal parish. Any new parish will request a copy of the baptismal certificate preceding future sacraments (e.g., confirmation, marriage). A notification of subsequent sacraments also goes back to the church-of-record, documented alongside the baptismal certificate.

Parish boundaries outline the scope and limit of pastoral responsibility. Territorial parishes encompass a given geography; pastors are charged with caring for all Catholics in the parish.[3] Quoting Francis Cardinal George again, "For the parish priest, territoriality means that he is responsible for every Catholic residing within his parish boundaries, regardless of whether they are registered, use envelopes, go to Church, or make their presence known."[4] This binds even those (substantial numbers of) non-Mass attending Catholics to the parish. "Somebody has to have a certain amount of responsibility for people in a given area," shares one bishop in an interview.

Boundaries safeguard the care of all local Catholics. One diocesan blog clarifies that it is not just a matter of "organizational policy," but that "canon law says that priests are responsible for the spiritual well-being (ensuring the sacraments, etc.) of the people within his 'domicile.'" A diocesan planner adds in our interview that this obligates a priest to the people (and their needs): "Having boundaries in canon law is really probably necessary to put the onus on the priest to serve the people." Absent territorial parish boundaries, one pastor concludes, "people would fall through the cracks . . . there is no one that would be looking for them." Parish boundaries (theoretically) guarantee that the needs of all Catholics therein—regardless of background or circumstance—get addressed.

By this rationale, boundaries are as much about the pastor as they are about the people. They serve a needed institutional function. One Midwestern diocesan planner describes how the bishop manages this allocation of pastoral responsibility across the diocese:

> [The bishop's] view of boundaries was that boundaries existed to put the onus on pastors not to ignore people that they should be serving, not to corral the lay people. And so, he let the pastors have a gentlemen's agreement, so to speak, to work it out. In other words, if you want to come to my parish and you don't live in my boundaries, all I have to do is exchange a note with your pastor saying, "Tricia is now in Our Lady of Good Counsel," and it's just: "Okay." It bypassed the bishop. And, "If anybody wanted to ask me," he said, "I never refused it."

Similarly, a multicultural director in a large northeastern archdiocese summarizes his bishop's approach:

> The archbishop's vision here is that a pastor is responsible for the people that live within his parish. And so—it doesn't matter what language or culture they come with, the priest is responsible; the pastor is responsible for them. So that is the goal. I don't think we're always as good at it as I'd like to see, but our goal is just that. So, if you find in your parish you have Spanish speakers, people from different countries in Latin America, then you need to be asking yourself, "What am I going to do? How does our parish need to adapt and change according to the people that live here?"

Parish boundaries compel pastors to do their job. Or the opposite, one Texas pastor speculates: "Priests can sort of sit back and be lazy, and say, 'I've got my people. They have to come here.' As a result, I think that you don't even have to try terribly hard. Because those people would have to come anyway."

By default, an American Catholic's home parish is the parish within which he or she physically resides (parish meaning territory). Territory denotes membership. Parish registration (or "joining" a parish, for that matter) is technically unnecessary. The very idea is a largely modern, North

American phenomenon; registration does not exist in canon law. Territorial ascription eliminates the need for it. Unlike in many Protestant denominations, there is no "membership transfer" in Catholicism. If St. Mark's parish boundaries include your block, you are a member of St. Mark's canonically, even if not in practice. It is your home parish.[5]

Historically, "place was fate for Catholic parish choice."[6] The 1917 Code of Canon Law offered clear instructions to fulfill one's "Easter obligation" in the proper parish.[7] Sacraments sought outside one's home parish (notably, marriage, baptisms, and funerals) were difficult to attain, and subject to nullification if not approved by the home pastor. "When boundaries were enforced, they were enforced," recalls one pastor.

Territorial ascription of a parish home was once fairly straightforward: your parish was the only parish. Rural living meant that parish boundaries didn't require strong oversight. When St. Joseph's and Polishtown arose, concrete roadways were not yet commonplace. Groceries, schools, and churches stood within walking or carriage distance. Uneven roads and unsavory conditions challenged otherwise mundane journeys. Distance discouraged Mass attendance.[8]

Birthed in this historical context, American Catholic parishes necessarily found their place near population centers, or were reasonably spaced geographically to accommodate dispersed attendees. Early boundaries lacked careful demarcation, as parishes fairly obviously served nearby Catholics. One diocesan pastoral planner relays this history:

> Boundaries came about when the parishes were formed. And many of our rural parishes came about, say, in the 1880s. . . . And I mean, you had a rural community and then you had nothing for 15 miles. So the whole concept of a strict boundary between here and there: Why would you even need that? So, when they were forced to write something down, perhaps in the [19]20s, it was basically, "You go down to the big rock in the road . . ."

Not unlike the once-dominant model of a one-room schoolhouse, parishes acted as the single, one-stop shop for Catholic organizational life.

Accordingly, the quintessential neighborhood parish helped build community around shared, localized experience.[9] The parish was an extension of the home, the family, the community, and the weekly routine. Parishes were immovable; American Catholics generally stayed put, too. One canon lawyer affirms that "territoriality is part of our legal tradition and it has served the church—and I'm talking specifically in this country—pretty well for quite a number of decades, because we had a situation where people didn't really travel, they didn't move."

Suburbanization began to change all this. Prosperity and economic growth following World War II welcomed large numbers of Catholics into the middle class. Upward mobility combined with assimilation into mainstream religion to increase Catholics' self-efficacy. Business, shopping, and church sprawled ever farther from city centers. The iconic one-room schoolhouse met near extinction. Highways ushered in a new era of mobility and access for millions of cars then occupying American roads, thanks to Henry Ford's revolutionary auto production. The 1956 Federal-Aid Highway Act, the largest public works project to date, introduced 41,000 miles of interstate highways. Provisions enabled the government to purchase land to establish rights-of-way for interstate construction, demolishing some churches in their wake.[10]

Parishes stayed immobile, but people were moving. Catholics did stay longer in their neighborhoods, grounded by parishes.[11] But many neighborhoods met substantial change or demolition ... among them, idyllic manifestations of the walkable, neighborhood parish home. Construction of the Mark Twain Expressway to St. Charles County on the perimeter of St. Louis, for example, spelled the demise of several downtown churches despite lay protest. Among those that remained was St. Mary of Victories, a former hub for German and Hungarian immigrants. Today the church sits in an urban ghost town. "Pray that our historic and beautiful church, now standing in the shadow of highways and warehouses poised on the brink of a revival, will continue to be Holy Ground for metro St. Louisans for the next century and beyond," its description appeals.[12] Parish boundaries root churches within defined territories, but cannot always root Catholics therein.

A PARISH MARKETPLACE

Increased mobility and suburbanization meant that American Catholicism met a new era in the twentieth century: an itinerant faithful. The default neighborhood parish gave way to a broader, open marketplace of parishes, now accessible by car. Adding to this, the Second Vatican Council (1962–1965) advanced the idea of a parish home built upon community and local culture. This begins to change how Catholics identify their parish home, using a rationale less wedded to place. It also plants the seeds for personal parishes' reemergence, prioritizing purpose over place.

Vatican II replaced the formerly universal use of Latin in all Masses with the vernacular—the language of the people. It also introduced new stylistic options: innovative musical instrumentation, seating arrangements, and liturgical ornamentation among them. Post-Vatican II churches could incorporate architectural styles facilitating greater lay participation, where altar rails no longer separated priest from parishioners. Priests could celebrate Mass with the laity as participants rather than spectators. Parishes became communal spaces for "the People of God."[13]

In terms of parish boundaries, this diversification meant that a boundary line was no longer the most meaningful line of difference between one parish and the next. Territorial parishes could look and act distinct from one another. Catholics saw beyond their designated territorial parish home to consider a marketplace of options. The freedom that characterized American religion overall paired with de jure elements of Vatican II to fuel Catholics' sovereignty in parish affiliation.[14]

Two personal parish pastors summarize this formative, post-Vatican II phenomenon as such:

> Especially since the time of the Second Vatican Council, people have rethought the way geography works in the parish. Mostly, it's a more Protestant mindset, where: "We like this other church, and we will go there." There's no sense of me belonging to this geography anymore.

* * *

> People basically are going where they're finding what they need. There are people who drive through three or four parishes to go to the parish that they count as their own. I've come across people who should belong to [ ] parish and never set foot in there, for whatever reason—either they grew up in some other parish, or they didn't like that style.

Parish diversification destabilized territorial parish belonging. American Catholics started choosing.

Evidence of this appears in the years following Vatican II, parish "shopping" on the rise. The 1980s Notre Dame Study of Parish Life noted that some 15 percent of American Catholics at that time crossed boundaries to attend elsewhere, attracted by "the quality of pastoral care, friendliness of the people, style of worship and quality of preaching." Researchers reassured that, nonetheless, "the concept of parish as the neighborhood church community remains dominant among American Catholics."[15]

The proportion of parish shoppers has since more than doubled. A 2012 study found that nearly a third of Catholics live closer to another parish than the one they attend. The tendency to choose is even stronger among younger Catholics, minority Catholics, and Catholics living in populated urban centers with a higher parish density (i.e., more options).[16]

This broods the chief irony of parish boundaries in the modern American Church: American Catholics are less and less likely to abide by them. Catholics "go where they go to receive what they want to and need to," shares one personal parish pastor. Fueled by an American ethos of individualism, Catholics frequently decide for themselves which church community constitutes home. From below, the penchant for choice and cosmopolitanism overrides territorial compliance.[17] From above, these behaviors beg pressing institutional questions about the organizational structure of parishes.

Dioceses feel the effects of parish choice acutely in their efforts to track and manage local populations. One diocesan researcher shares how it plays out in his diocese:

> One of the things that I have been doing for the last eight years is taking all the addresses of all the Catholic households in the diocese, and geocoding them. And doing maps of parishes to show where people live vis-à-vis their parish boundaries. What we have found over the last eight years I've been doing this: each year, there's a higher percentage of people worshipping in parishes outside of their boundaries. Eight years ago, archdiocesan-wide, 68 percent of Catholics worshipped in the parish in which they lived. That has dropped about a half a % per year. Last year, it was 64 percent.

He estimates that the percentage of Catholics attending their home parish would have been closer to 90 percent forty years ago.

Other diocesan researchers report that their parishes have as few as 57 percent of parishioners coming from within assigned boundaries. A more typical range falls between 67 and 77 percent, consistent with national findings that 31 percent of Catholics drive by a closer church to attend another that they prefer.[18] "People are now choosing consciously where they wish to worship," shares one pastor, affirmed by another: "Nowadays, with people traveling around, they're more inclined to go to the parish they want to go to." A canon lawyer and a lay leader in a personal parish articulate their own observations of this shift:

> We live in a very, very mobile society. People are moving all around, and just to say this: the [Church] law has not caught up with the reality. The purpose of the law—the mind of the church—is that parishes be real communities of people. And territoriality has served them well, because when people are living together in the same neighborhood, generally speaking, they're facing the same issues, the same challenges, the same problems that their neighbors are facing. And, again, that tends to build community and immunity. But that dynamic is shifting.

* * *

> Our places of worship also tended to be the places where we spent the majority of our lives. Unlike previous centuries, we don't spend our whole lives within

a mile of our home! But I think a lot of that—the modern definition of our understanding of faith really comes into that. Our relationship isn't with the community immediately around us anymore. We're so mobile, so involved in a very technological world. The idea of being able to go elsewhere to find faith is so relatively new. And even within the Catholic Church, to be able to go to different churches . . . ?!

Both comments acknowledge the tension between canon law defining local religion, and Catholics' lived behavior.

The advent of territorial parish selection "canonically, poses all kinds of problems," says one canon lawyer. A bishop tells me, for example, that boundary-crossing complicates the Church's ability to minister:

Well, it creates a lot of practical problems and questions. I'll give you an example. Geographically, I'm located in this particular parish. But I don't like the pastor. Or I don't like the liturgy. Or there's something about the parish I don't like. Its architectural style is not what I like. I like big pillars and things. And I have certain personal tastes that are not really to the core of our religious tradition. So, I like to go to my old parish that I used to grow up in, I like it very much. Although I *presume* I'm there. What happens is, they get caught, sometimes. Because the pastor of the parish is constantly looking at the people in the parish who are registered, and trying to register people so he knows who's in the parish: who he's ministering to, and how many parishioners he's got. And that helps him budget, and decide what kind of programs. Then, that person who hasn't been going to their own geographic parish for a long, long time dies or something. Has a death in the family. The problem is—they come back to the pastor, or the office. And they say, "Well, are you a member of this parish? This community? There's no record of it." "Well, I live here." Well, yeah, but you don't go to this parish. You go somewhere else. And they get caught in that bind.

Catholics' lackluster adherence to boundaries, in other words, challenges diocesan authority over a lay flock.

The disconnect between administrative authority and lay compliance can be problematic for Church leaders. Boundary-crossing undermines the order and administrative function of the territorial parish. Close adherence to canon law (and its stipulation of territorial parish boundaries) allows a bishop to referee parish membership. One pastoral planner shares how immensely boundaries mattered to the bishop who led his diocese:

I'm laughing, because I don't think you're going to find a more stringent diocese in the United States. Our bishop was a canonist; his understanding of the whole concept of boundaries was, for him, the lynchpin of all of our parishes and holding everything together. And it's like . . . where do I start? He was really insistent on following parish boundaries. To the point that, when he came in, he let the priests know that if a parishioner from outside the boundaries wanted to sign up—and he's speaking to the *priests*—wants to sign up, and be a member of your parish—you cannot do that.

Few requests to cross parish boundaries were approved.

How do dioceses reconcile the phenomenon of mobile, unbound Catholics (in behavior, if not canonically)? A local bishop sets the tone. One pastor shares that in two of his appointments, the dioceses were "much, much more clear about parish boundaries," but in his current diocese he "[doesn't] really hear much talk about parish boundaries." One multicultural director guesses that his own diocese "is an anomaly, in the sense that I think they're probably one of the only dioceses in the whole world that still adheres to territorial parishes."

Dioceses must adhere to territoriality, administratively. "Pastors still adhere to that, even though people don't," says one multicultural director. The politics of territory has financial implications, for one. Diocesan staffers recall arguments over which parish a major benefactor belongs to. Pastors lobby for the financial contributions of Catholics living in their catchment area but attending elsewhere. Registration lacks the canonical teeth to prevent donors' envelopes from going back to their ascribed parish. As one pastoral planner explains, "There's people strong on both sides: One saying, 'This is the boundaries, we need to do that' and the other saying 'That's ridiculous; we need a pastoral approach!' to which the first one says, 'Okay, people can go wherever they want, but their Sunday collection *must* return to the boundary parish.'"

Some dioceses try to reduce Catholics' noncompliance. One diocesan website, for example, communicates that "parishioners are required to register at the parish within whose boundaries they live" and that "decisions about any exceptions relating to church registration are made per the pastor's discretion and done on a case-by-case basis." Webpages typically provide maps or searchable fields to "find your parish" or verify "where is your home." Shaded blocks on parish maps indicate where the territory of a given church ends. Clickable parish names pop up with a bounded catchment area. Other diocesan websites deemphasize parish ascription, instead inviting Catholics to enter a mileage range up to 100 to "find a parish" . . . a subtle indication, perhaps, that parish selection is bound more by fuel budget than explicit sanction.

Strict adherence to canon law can be a difficult message to convey to Americans accustomed to religious agency. One diocesan respondent shares his own experience at the nexus of this paradox:

> It's tough to tell the people. My heart is really reaching out, and is breaking for all of the people who are on the edges of the church—either on the outside looking in, or about to leave—and see the church as impersonal. And it can be. And then, I'm the one that has to tell them! Now, you try to soften it. You say, "Well, you can go to Mass there all the time. You can affiliate. But you can't join." And basically, what it's like is, "You can't really be a family member. You can always be the guest on the outside looking in, but you really can't be a family member."

Another pastoral planner shares her alternative approach to questions she receives from newcomers looking to find a parish:

> When somebody calls me and says, "I'm moving here, what parish do I belong to?" I will say, "Canonically, you belong to Our Lady of Sorrows, you belong there. But you are actually geographically closer to Star of the Sea, which has a school. And since you have children, you may want to attach yourself there." Or, "You're older, you want to do a lot of volunteer work, you might want to go to St. Matthew's—because they have a very strong senior ministry that's had a lot of outreach in the community."

Her response communicates informal flexibility in defining the parish home. It's one that many pastors also embrace, such as the pastor who says he'd never tell Catholics not to come to his parish "because there's something that's speaking to them; they're probably much more energized, and probably much more socially conscious and much more active Catholics by coming here than if they were in their own parish."

Some dioceses strike a balance between personal attachment and canonical compliance. One diocesan document on boundaries states, for example:

> Recognizing that parishioners have emotional and spiritual attachments to their parishes, and not wanting to place undue burdens on these people, registered parishioners will be "grand-fathered" in their current parishes. That is, validly registered Catholics will be allowed to remain registered in their parishes. After a date to be determined, however, Catholics moving into a new area will be allowed to register only in the parish within whose boundaries they reside.

This delivers an institutional hardline in a softened tone, aware of incompatibility with lay behavior. This document adds that "Exceptions are made, of course, for national and personal parishes." Personal parishes are where an allowance for those "emotional and spiritual attachments" resides, canonically.

REDRAWING BOUNDARIES

Restructuring the overall number and distribution of parishes serving a diocese will invariably raise questions about boundaries. Diocesan restructuring has been rampant of late, driven by priest and financial shortages nationwide. Some 62 percent of US dioceses have closed, suppressed, or merged parishes since 2002. More parishes closed than opened in the same decade. Periods of diocesan restructuring present a primary prompt for personal parish establishment because they instigate boundary conversations at the institutional level. Navigating the growing paradox of territorial ascription and individual Catholics' parish selection, dioceses may look to personal parishes as a compromise. Personal parishes present an institutionally sanctioned means to preserve boundaries while also enabling lay choice.[19]

Technically, a Catholic parish does not close. Rather, the territory formerly assigned to one parish is reallocated to another.[20] The boundaries change. Catholics living in the affected area are rezoned to another parish. This means that the Catholic Church's response to neighborhood change differs from that of other religious groups. Sociologist Nancy Ammerman writes in *Congregation and Community*, for example, that "When it becomes apparent that the neighborhood in which the church is located no longer matches the profile of that church, some congregations solve the problem by establishing a new place for themselves."[21] By contrast, lay Catholics cannot relocate their parishes. Catholic bishops redraw parish boundaries.

Determining parish boundaries, of course, is not a neutral enterprise. Canonical compliance and Catholics' lived behavior may act in opposition. While a searchable diocesan map conveys a relatively straightforward cartography of parish assignment, it was likely generated through a convoluted and politicized process of boundary-drawing by institutional elites. A close inspection of parish boundaries may reveal that they are in "bad shape," as one diocesan pastoral planner put it. One Midwestern diocesan report revising parish boundaries and the principles behind them began with the statement that: "Most parishes in the diocese have boundaries that are either ambiguous, or in conflict with neighboring parish boundaries."

Parish boundaries encapsulate communities in a particular time, geographic space, and demographic moment. Grassroots transformations can, in time, render boundaries conflicting, or incongruent with contemporary realities. Diocesan staffers tasked with codifying, "fixing," or reassigning parish boundaries know this well. Modern technologies including geographic information system (GIS) software assist diocesan researchers in revealing and reforming outdated boundaries.

Three pastoral planners from different dioceses around the country share their discoveries and frustrations during this process:

[Pointing to the map] If you live in one of these—it's like a six-square block area—you are within the physical boundaries, the official boundaries, of five parishes! Because they were all overlapping! What happened, over time, is that the boundaries of one parish would change. And nobody would realize that the hipbone is connected to the knee bone. And that was the reason for saying you can't do boundaries. Well, then [the bishop] gave my assistant and I the task of redoing boundaries. So, we worked on this for about five years, going back and forth. Because they were a real mess.

**

I go on mapping software in order to map out our boundaries. It was phenomenally difficult, because many of the boundaries were made when it was wagon trails. So it would say, "The wagon trail between these two properties" you know. "Farmer Jones and . . ." like that. Or, "Due North from the dam, the regional dam." Well, that dam has been gone for 100 years! So you have, as I'm doing this, as I'm trying to lay this out on the grids . . . it was just, it got unbelievably difficult! And you ended up with a lot of conflicting boundaries. And no one had ever realized that there were conflicts, or paid any attention.

**

One of the problems we have, especially in some of our more suburban and some of our higher growth [counties]—the boundaries out there are kind of crazy. Because they were drawn 100 years ago, when everything was farmland. Well, now you have these subdivisions, and in many cases the subdivisions are so much nearer a different parish than the one whose boundaries they're actually in. So they've all decided to go to the parish that's closest to them.

Territorial parish boundaries are often found to be ambiguous and outdated, thus confusing and difficult to enforce.

When redrawing or establishing new parish boundaries, diocesan planners prioritize clarity. "If parish boundaries are going to be useful, especially to the laity, they must be logical and easy to understand." Follow easily recognizable geographic features, for example. Highways, rivers, county and state lines make for better boundaries than creeks, subdivisions, or imaginary lines. "Vague references not rooted in geography" are discouraged. One diocesan planner shared that her message was typically, "If you're going to set boundaries, please use civil boundaries as much as you can. Keep within the same county. Keep within the same school district if you can, because otherwise, the pastor is dealing with four different school calendars."

Although the process for boundary establishment varies across dioceses, it typically involves an exchange between diocesan planners who propose boundaries, pastors who approve or contest them (in conversation or conflict with bordering parishes), and final approval by the bishop. The latter step is affirmed in canon law, which states that "it is only for the diocesan bishop to erect, suppress, or alter parishes."[22] Again, it is the boundary, meaning the geographic space and not the physical building or lay community, that forms the canonical, territorial parish. As such, decisions about boundaries suddenly become decisions about jurisdiction, power, and authority. As one pastor puts it: "When we talk about authority in the Church, it's usually associated with geography."

Ironically, (re)drawing parish boundaries can retrofit formal canon law on parish belonging, encoding Catholics' grassroots parish selection. To illustrate: diocesan planners share that their mapping process typically involves first geocoding the home addresses of all registered parishioners by parish. This reveals exactly where a given parish's attendees live and how dispersed they are across the diocese. Diocesan staff then use this data to propose new parish boundaries, best approximating actual behavior. A pastoral planner describes this process:

> I went through and geocoded all of them by parish boundaries. I found out where those boundaries were—the official descriptions—and geocoded them. I found out that there were some cases where we had conflicts between two adjacent boundaries, so I thought maybe we should go and change some boundaries. And I saw some places where it was obvious the boundaries needed to be redrawn, because most of the people in this particular community want to go to this church rather than this one. So, we redrew them.

In other words, Catholic officials encode lay behavior by altering parish boundaries. The tail wags the dog.

Even those Catholics residing within the territorial bounds of their parish may have moved into the neighborhood because of the parish. Historian John McGreevy describes how real estate ads once advertised homes by parish assignment.[23] Catholics were encouraged to purchase within parish boundaries to stabilize the neighborhood. Today's Catholics, whose commutes expand ever further, may still make real estate decisions based upon desired parish. One pastor shares, "If anyone in the neighborhood is wanting to sell their house, they'll usually contact that parish and say 'Is anyone in the parish interested?'" Another pastor says similarly that newcomers to the area will say "Okay, well, what parish do we want to be involved in? . . . then, they'll simply congregate around the church." This kind of parish selection precedes (and predicts) parish ascription. While territoriality officially contrasts congregationalism (meaning parish choice), the fact that people choose a neighborhood based upon parish preference complicates this. Choice begets territory; territory begets ascription.

American Catholics' parish choices act back upon the formal, institutional definition of parish. Preferences build boundaries. This has the latent effect of enabling territorial boundaries to exacerbate social ones. Parish lines bind demographically similar neighborhoods that Catholics already self-selected into (or out of). This is not to say that boundary-drawing intentionally privileges homogeneity. But by drawing boundaries based on extant behavior, when at least a third of Catholics attend parishes that are not closest to them, it is a predictable consequence. Boundaries codify choice.

REBINDING UNBOUND CATHOLICS WITH UNBOUND PARISHES

Personal parishes are frequently an outgrowth of diocesan attempts to map and (re)define parish boundaries. Through the procedures described above, some parishes turn out to attract Catholics from all over the diocese. One diocesan pastoral planner shares how difficult it is to draw boundaries for these kinds of parishes:

> People were coming from all over. And when Bishop said, "Okay, give them boundaries," boy did we work hard! We did the dots, and we said, "If we were to draw boundaries based on the dots—we would have to expand the boundaries so much that it would start taking away, big time, from the neighboring parishes." So, I said, "There's absolutely no way this could be a territorial parish." Well, they struggled with that. One of these parishes was originally formed to serve the Germans, so it was just continued. What do you do about a parish that's a charismatic parish, and so there's no population? So, they ended up saying—I mean, this is [laughing] . . . I mean, only a canonist can find all the little loopholes!

The institutional "loophole" is a personal parish designation. Personal parishes canonically establish a parish without territorial boundaries.

Canonically, a personal parish sits geographically inside another (territorial) parish. Personal parishes may gain non-territorial status because no boundary lines sufficiently encompass their parishioner population. Stymied by unachievable boundary lines, diocesan staff may propose to the bishop that territorial parishes be restructured as personal parishes through new decrees. One diocesan pastoral planner states plainly that:

> Some of these parishes were formalized as personal parishes only because the boundary structure would not fit. Because, if you did not do that, and you insisted on the boundaries—You might as well close it down.

The personal parish offers a structural, organizational solution to the complex institutional problem of parishes with dispersed or overlapping attendant populations. As they draw Catholics from distant places, formal boundary-drawing rubber-stamps a parish's purposeful and placeless status ... because territorial boundaries don't fit. Social boundaries rewrite territorial ones.

Personal parishes are an attractive option also because redrawing boundaries and reallocating territory—colloquially, "closing churches"—is an incredibly painful, not to mention heavily contested, process. Parishes are communities of Catholics. Parish closure represents "a reality provoking the most profound grief for those whose religious identity and history was anchored to it," writes Michael Weldon.[24] One pastoral planner recalls this difficulty in his own diocese:

> We came to the conclusion we needed a lot fewer parishes, and a lot fewer schools. So, after a couple of years of work, and parish meetings, and meeting with parish leadership, and going through the pain ... and that was painful! It was one of the most painful experiences that I have ever been involved in. So, it was a very difficult situation.

He continues, explaining, "In the final analysis, people are so committed to their communities, that unless you really have to close them—why just make everybody mad?" "But," he says, "then we've got the problem of declining priest resources."

Bishops go to great lengths (and boundary innovation) to avoid parish closure. One strategy involves "merging," or consolidating multiple churches into a single, unified parish. Merging parishes raises its own set of boundary questions. Dioceses describe it in varied ways, among them "consolidation," "collaboration," or "clustering." Generally, the affected churches will have their former selves canonically suppressed, then reconstituted as a single, combined, new parish—under the leadership of one pastor. Merging, a concept that does not even exist in canon law, is another institutional compromise to territorial parish suppression.[25]

Merging can create innovative territorial parish set-ups, stretched across multiple church sites. Interviewees describe how such consolidations honor separate communities, within the constraints of a priest shortage. Far from being a straightforward process, mergers, too, uncover a complex mix of territorial and social boundaries. If territory were the sole factor in determining which parishes would merge, those most contiguous would combine. But more often, this is not what happens. Determining which parishes merge involves a dance between territory and people/purpose. A merger may bring two parishes together that are less geographically proximate, but more compatible culturally. To put it another way, some neighboring parishes won't merge because they are too different (often, racially). Social boundaries act against territorial ones.

Even upon merging, parishes may be reticent to renounce their former, autonomous selves. Some merged parishes operate as virtually separate churches, using multiple buildings on different properties and virtually non-overlapping communities. One diocesan planner explains:

> Where we have tried to merge parishes, the parishes will not give up their identities, their personal culture. So, we're not asking that at all. We're having collaboratives: they will share a pastor and priest personnel, but they will have separate other things, like that.

Two distinct communities; two physical spaces; one territorial parish.

In another scenario, a territorial parish grew to such a large size that it spawned several "satellite" churches nearby. This staved off a canonical division of the geographic parish into separately bound territories (which parishioners did not want). In church law, it remains a single parish. But its attendees worship and commune in multiple, physically separate spaces. The canonical and lived complexity of "parish" upends the typical sociological definition of "congregation."

Personal parishes offer an alternative way to satisfy the social and territorial impulses that bind modern Catholics' religious lives. Personal parishes openly acknowledge what separates local Catholics. One diocese, for example, decreed a personal parish home across two churches, acknowledging two distinct parish identities: one nearly all black; the other nearly entirely Hispanic/Latino. The pastor describes:

> This thing of, "We're one parish, we should be doing everything together, we should be doing everything in the same place." ... In the beginning, nobody wants to do that. Nobody wants to do that! We want our stuff here; you keep your stuff over there. And I'm like, "Well, cool." I'm not even going to battle that. I'm not even going to argue about that. Since we do have two churches, cool. Alright, I'm not gonna argue. But you know, there's a different basis for us to be community, a different basis for us to be one parish. It's not based on that we all worship together in the same space, at least not immediately. So, we're kind of working our way.

Their multisite personal parish does some things together, for example, the Easter Tridiuum and confirmation (the former, canonically required). But having two separate buildings means that the two communities can exist as two churches, each defined by purpose, and neither by territory.

This model of organizing parishes differs from one that serves all in an ascribed catchment area. Separate spaces alleviate the tension of blending diverse Catholics. The same pastor shares:

> It's definitely a challenge, and it's a new way of thinking for a lot of people. And some people don't necessarily buy into it. But, see, the other thing is: to fight a fight of forcing people to come together that don't want to be together ... ? I didn't feel like I had to do it, thank God, because I had two churches. Now, if I had one church, that might be a whole different ballgame. But we had two churches. So I was like, "Well, look, I'm not going to force people to come together. I'm not. If they don't want to come here, or they don't want to go there – cool."

Symbolic boundaries separate two uniracial, non-overlapping churches ... here, contained in a single, canonical personal parish.

Resource shortages (especially priest shortages) make compliance with territorial boundaries all the more challenging. The fluidity and at times contradictory application of boundaries elevates institutional tensions commanding alternative organizational forms.

PARISH AND SCHOOL

One additional layer to the story of parish boundaries' institutional function and contemporary challenge is the parochial school. By definition, "parochial" means "of or relating to a Church parish."[26] Parishes and parish schools form an interlocking history in the United States. "The parish, of course, *is* the school," explains one bishop I interviewed. Parochial schools acted historically as sites of socialization, community, and retention for American Catholics, in the minority religiously. They also underscore parish boundaries.

A common charge as Catholicism took hold in America was to build the parish school first, holding Masses there until funds could support the construction of a separate worship facility.[27] Many national parishes began exactly this way. Nearly every Catholic parish established before Vatican II had its own school. In the Northeast and Midwest, where parishes are older on average, parish boundaries were often coterminous with those of parochial schools. The proliferation of parochial schools, many served by communities of religious sisters, met the needs of growing Catholic populations. Younger parishes (including those in southern and western states) are less likely to have been founded with schools, inferring a parish boundary function less wedded to school enrollment.[28]

Parish boundaries increase in salience when dovetailed with parochial schools. With the benefit of admission and subsidized tuition extended first (or only) to parishioners, parish boundaries determine which students can enroll. The classic parochial school model thus prioritizes—necessitates, even—living within parish boundaries. "Clear boundaries help make orderly Catholic school enrollment possible" states one diocesan document. Reflecting on his own childhood, one bishop recalls how "If you did not live within the parish boundaries, you would not be going to our school . . . because the schools were all jammed."

Today, many Catholic schools still give priority to those living within parish boundaries or registered in the parish. Pastoral planners explain how school preference can drive parish preference, because parents join parishes with parochial schools. If diocesan policy disallows registration anywhere other than one's territorial home parish, then residence and parish registration are synonymous. But accepting parish registration in lieu of residency means that diocesan, parish, and school leaders balance ascription with achievement to identify which Catholics belong. Donation envelopes may validate membership.[29]

Since 1975, the number of students enrolled in Catholic elementary schools has decreased by more than a million. Catholic school closures and consolidations now outpace school openings.[30] Like parishes, Catholic schools close, merge, and consolidate. Consequently, multiple territorial parishes now feed into single, shared Catholic schools serving ever-larger territories. A canon lawyer and a pastoral planner describe this change:

> What has exacerbated this [boundary issue] is a phenomenon that we've seen the last 15 years or so, with parish schools closing and merging. People go where the children are. So, if I'm in St. Joseph's parish—and my school has closed, and my children are going over to St. Ann's—well, they want to be with their friends. There are things going on at the parish that are related to school. So, I'm going to start going over there. I'm not gonna blame them; I'm just saying it causes . . . it's a challenge that the [canon] law really doesn't address.

* * *

> You belonged to St. Patrick's parish, or you belonged to Sacred Heart parish and you went to this certain school. But, one of the things that's happened here, as has happened in other places: they combined some of the schools. So, Sacred Heart and St. Patrick Schools merged into Providence School. At that point, forget the boundaries between Sacred Heart and St. Patrick's! I mean—some people went and moved over to Sacred Heart, other people came over to St. Patrick's, irrespective of where they lived.

If not every parish has a school, and if parishes share schools, then it is not surprising that Catholics will drive past their assigned parish to attend another one. This complicates otherwise intransigent territorial boundaries permitting (or denying) parochial school attendance.

The contemporary restructuring of parochial schools further muddies the bounded nature of territorial parishes, the institutional oversight of lay Catholics, and diocesan attempts to organize local religion. When Catholic schools reconstitute—or wholly neglect—parish boundaries, it has a spillover effect for parishes. Parents of school-age children cross boundaries to worship where their children attend school. Neighborhood Catholics see boundaries as porous and nonbinding, feeding into consolidated spaces and determined by family need. Boundaries stretch and congeal. Ironically, parochial schools (perhaps now less-aptly named) concretized but later undermined the institutional stability of parish boundaries.

A PARISH HOME

The only official, canonical route to boundary flexibility requires a personal parish. Established without boundaries (apart from those of the diocese), personal parishes embolden a pastor's responsibility beyond the neighborhood. One personal parish pastor says:

Since my jurisdiction geographically ends at the curb, it doesn't matter from where I draw. In this broader sense, everyone in the archdiocese who is of Hispanic descent and who wishes to be part of this . . . that person is my parishioner. I think that's the main difference. [My parish] can draw from farther away, on a more official level.

Pastoral responsibility does not stop at a specified line; it extends to all who share a particular need or desire.

Personal parishes embody—structurally—the transformative power of mobility on Catholicism in America. "I don't know too many people who feel like they're stuck going to the church where they are," says one multicultural director from the Northeast. A southern pastor echoes:

> I don't think the idea of "territorial parish" is as important as it once was, because as we know, people are . . . with this ability to travel, and that sort of thing . . . this mobile society where we live, parish boundaries are kind of meaningless now.

Increased movement fundamentally transforms individual Catholics' relationship to their parish. Grassroots transformations generate new ways of belonging based not just on proximity or canonical regulation, but on taste. In this, dioceses meet both occasion and urgency for a new way of organizing: personal parishes.

Bishops must come to terms with the discord between the canonical reality of territorial boundaries and Catholics' search for a preferred parish home. One admits that "with geographic parishes, the normal procedure, you get certain canonical procedures that come into place regarding boundaries, and some people get anxious about that." Another shares how his pastoral advice is to "take anybody." But when Catholics break the rules of territoriality, it "becomes a really uncomfortable thing." "That's not a good way to do pastoral ministry," he adds. "That's why I'm not in favor of people running around everywhere and doing their own thing."

Another bishop rationalizes the discord through his broader desire for area Catholics to find a church—whichever church—to call home:

> Well, as a bishop, my territory is the diocese. So, I'm pastor of all parishes. So I want people to feel at home. And again, I'm speaking just for this diocese. You might be in the territory of one parish but actually closer to another parish, it depends on where you live. And a lot of our parishes, territory-wise, are spread out. So if a person finds a home, I'm happy. We have [several] schools, so we're not driven by overcrowding in our schools, like there might be in other places.

His conception of territory and home is wider. It stretches across the diocese: the thick boundary line, so to speak, rather than any single parish's catchment area. Porous parish boundaries and personal parishes are a retention effort.

What does this mean for the idea of a parish home? Territory and fixity battle choice and movement. Parish evokes propinquity, but behavior prompts translocalism. Parishes stay. Catholics move. Such transformation is not isolated to Catholicism, either—"There are no traditional, fixed, and bounded cultural worlds from which to depart and to which to return: all is situated and all is moving," geographers tell us.[31] As Catholics act less on residence and more on feelings of inclusion, they re-conceptualize their parish home. Bishops need a way to draw boundaries around what individual Catholics share socially as well as territorially.

Institutionally, personal parishes reconcile the canonical stipulation of a parish home with Americans' aspatial religious agency. Personal parishes intentionally detangle parish and place through their exceptionalism: they do not adhere to the rule of territoriality. No lines map their catchment area. But neither do they undermine Catholicism's tradition of territoriality. By contrast, they solidify it.

What happens to boundaries when personal parishes detangle parish from place? Unlike earlier national parishes whose enclaves (albeit often made, not found) matched parish with neighborhood, today's personal parishes rarely mirror the neighborhood in which they sit. The Polish parish at the start of this chapter is no longer in Polishtown; Poles no longer reside in one area. Parish, church, and neighborhood are no longer trifocal. But territorial parishes in this scenario deviate from the rule. Personal parishes conform to it.

Traditional Catholics desiring the Latin Mass readily illustrate this. There is no neighborhood ecology that organically generates a Traditional Latin Mass parish. Their minority status across a diocese means that they do not share an area. One pastor explains:

> The reality is that there are people interested in the Latin Mass scattered all over the place. So, it can't be territorial, because then you'd be asking people to move. Which is impossible, sometimes, or difficult other times. It seems to me that the personal parish is simply the Church's way of conforming itself to the needs of the people. The people are spread out all over the place, and a territorial model just doesn't work. We can't force people to move, you know?

Personal parishes reconstitute neighborhood across a diocese. A pastor of a personal parish devoted to Hispanic ministry describes the strategy behind personal parishes as somewhat "artificial": "We're setting up a parish some-where, and everyone just comes."

Personal parishes are an institutional strategy. Neighborhood is both everywhere and nowhere. Personal parish attendees drive in from outside the immediate surroundings of the church. "Be prepared to spend a lot of money on gas," says one pastor of an Anglican Use personal parish. Most attendees will pass one—if not a dozen or more—churches en route. This same pastor tells his attendees that "Even if [Anglican Use] gets going like gangbusters in the United States, it will never be playing at a theater near you."

In constituting parishes this way, the American Catholic Church is at once rooted and wholly disjointed from its physical surroundings. Inhabitants across the street—unless their identity or preference coincides with the personal parish's focus—are neither the registrants nor the responsibil-ity of the parish. Both the neighborhood in which parishioners live and the neighborhood in which the personal parish physically sits belong to another parish—a territorial parish. Sociologist Omar McRoberts noted a parallel dynamic among churches serving Boston's inner city, where adher-ents commute in to participate and congregations exhibit little connection to their surrounding neighborhoods.[32]

One pastor talks openly about the challenge of negotiating this alterna-tive conceptual space:

> Right across the street here—I see [the territorial parish's assigned community] all around me. We're surrounded by [that community]. We still owe it to the community to get out there. If the Catholic Church is supposed to do anything, it's supposed to be incarnational, and it's supposed to have this holiness, and goodness, and then radiate out into the community.

Traditional pastoral responsibility for the proximate community is out of sync with the translocal home of personal parishes.

Place and parish are not synonymous for personal parishes—at least, not in the expected sense. Vietnamese Catholics drive into predominantly Hispanic neighborhoods to worship at their personal parish; wealthy whites commute into low-income black neighborhoods to attend personal parishes with a social outreach focus. Older personal parishes once symbi-otic with the neighborhood (and an earlier Catholic era) look out-of-place in changed environments.

A pure territorial model of organizational Catholicism stipulates that a parish adapts to its surrounding ecology, because the parish is its surround-ing ecology. "When the people preexist the parish, the parish has to kind of conform itself to the reality of what exists," says a pastor. Neighborhood residents are parishioners. Neighborhood concerns are parish concerns. This logic also guards against the homogenizing tendencies of parish selection. But the reality is that today's parishes are hardly a mirror of their immediate ecologies. Increased mobility, lay choice, divergent preferences, parish options, parish mergers, consolidated schools, and arbitrary or ambiguous catchment areas render boundaries invisible. "People are choosing where they're feeling the most connection, the greater sense of belonging, where they're getting the most for themselves and their family as far as faith enrichment" says a diocesan multicultural director.

Some are wistful for a bygone model: parishes immersed in residential communities walking to Mass. "There's something to be said of the church, the building standing right in the middle in the heart of the culture, of the community," shares a pastor. "Here in the United States, that's not quite as strong anymore." Lay Catholics now move across space to worship and contribute where they feel at home. The Church is forced to respond.

CONCLUSION: RECONCILING TERRITORIALITY AND MOBILITY THROUGH PERSONAL PARISHES

A tension plagues modern American Catholicism: the phenomenon of mobility versus the Church's traditional, organizational focus on territoriality. Catholic leaders face the reality that while organizations (including parishes) can have boundaries, individuals cannot be contained therein. When American Catholics increase their freedom of movement and choice, who belongs? Who is bound? Institutions rely upon authoritative control to enforce organizational boundaries. Blurred boundaries signal loosened authority: "When the boundaries of an organization become blurred for an observer, it is probably a sign of change in the relative power of the organization vis-à-vis its population," say organizational scholars. [33] This power play makes Catholicism's tradition of bound parishes (and parishioners) more visible.

A neighborhood model of American Catholicism reliant upon territorial parishes is in decline. A "home" model that carves space for personal parishes is in ascendance. "In an era where more parishes are closing than opening, these market forces may be putting pressure on some parish leaders," notes political scientist Mark Gray. "The phenomenon may also be eroding some of the neighborhood culture of Catholic parish communities."[34] This institutional challenge entices new forms of organization (arguably, as a way to reassert control over American Catholics).

When parish and residence decouple, churches act increasingly as specialized, homogenizing spaces that may or may not resemble the constituency in domicile. A transient experience of belonging creates parishes in, but apart, from their immediate ecologies. The late Francis Cardinal George surmised rather disdainfully of parish choice that "the fact that, in the last thirty-five years or so, such a situation has come to prevail in practice, is a clear indication of the extent to which a congregational mentality has taken hold of our people's attitude."[35] If people now bind parishes more than parishes bind people, then people are less bound by the institution. This unsettling of parish boundaries lays the groundwork for the emergence of personal parishes in the modern US Catholic Church.

Personal parishes help the Catholic Church resolve this tension between mobility and territoriality—between ascription and achievement—by enacting a canonical, organizational form that can be legally chosen, socially bound, receptive to mobility, and simultaneously inscribed by institutional authority. They pair symbolic boundaries with legal-rational ones. Lay behavior may smear parish boundaries, but thicken diocesan ones—a phenomenon that returns in later chapters. Personal parishes help (re)bind the organizational experience of Catholicism locally. This is not a story of American Catholicism's disestablishment. It is a story of American Catholicism's institutional response.

Deciding precisely when, why, and for whom to establish personal parishes constitutes the focus of the next chapter. The implications of these decisions play out in chapters following.

CHAPTER 3
Decisions

The walk is a half mile or so from my hostel to the Mass of dedication for Christ Our Hope, Seattle's new personal parish with a social mission to serve downtown. En route, I pass a mix of retail, corporate, and condominium spaces, coffeehouses, boutique stores, and urban street dwellers. Revival on the block mixes old and new. Closer to the church, I cross paths with others dressed in semi-formal attire. My hunch that they, too, are headed to the dedication is confirmed when they pass beneath the awning labeled "Josephinum."

A middle-aged white man wearing a suit greets us with a printed guide to the ceremony. Dozens mingle and chatter loudly while waiting for the main event. Excitement is palpable. The space is striking—a 1907 hotel, renovated to showcase its ornate open lobby, multiple levels, marble floors, and high-reaching columns. A large crucifix and oversized flower arrangements lay against one wall, by two tall stained glass double doors. Priests and deacons adorned in white mingle about the room. The crowd snaps pictures. A woven basket invites donations. The space smells of flowers.

Once seated in a white folding chair along the room's perimeter, I strike up a conversation with a woman in her mid-sixties. Her eighty-something mother, sitting at her side, lived in this building back when it housed apartments. The Archdiocese of Seattle purchased the space in the mid-1960s, originally conceived as a residence for retirees. When the need for low-income housing emerged as a more pressing priority, it was converted into apartments for downtown residents. Today, the former dining room (then chapel) would be dedicated to yet another purpose. Her family played an instrumental role in envisioning a personal parish here, she says, supervising youth groups with paintbrushes and pondering how to fit a baptismal font through the doors.

The new parish, the woman tells me, is "a response to a groundswell, really." Although Seattle's cathedral is a mere seven blocks away, the needs of downtown residents remain unmet. Our conversation is cut short when all are summoned to gather near the stained glass double doors. Seattle's then Archbishop Joseph Brunett and the personal parish's new pastor, Father Paul Magnano, stand surrounded by white-robed deacons and priests. They adjust their microphones, preparing to speak to a crowd that by now has blossomed to more than 200.

"This is a personal parish . . . " begin the Archbishop's brief words of introduction. Soon thereafter, the doors swing wide to applause and cheers. The crowd floods slowly through as the choir sings "All Are Welcome," parted by the large baptismal font. Trumpets sound; Archbishop Brunett and Father Magnano shake people's hands as they enter.

Ceilings in the brand new (and very old) worship space boast ornate antique patterning. A faux balcony and railing draws my eyes to the back wall. Stained glass accentuates the front of the worship space. Sun pours through two clear pane windows, warming the right side of the room. Downtown Seattle looks back (see figures 3.1–3.3).

"Thanks be to God" resounds loudly from the crowd, amplified by the exceptional acoustics of the space. "We haven't dedicated a lot of brand new churches lately," Archbishop says during his homily. "Christ Our Hope is a beacon of hope for people in the inner city." People sitting near me are teary-eyed. During the Lord's Prayer, it's unclear whether to hold hands or not . . . both the space and the community gathered still feel new. Archbishop walks the perimeter to offer a blessing, stepping to the side of an African American man in faded sweats and jeans swaying with emotion in the moment.

Toward the conclusion of the service, Father Magnano walks up to the podium and says "Archbishop Brunett." Long pause. "We did it." His voice echoes pride and resolve. The words are met with boisterous applause. "I am a pastor without parishioners," he says, "in a parish without boundaries." "Thank you, Archbishop Brunett." All stand and applaud, enthusiastically.

* * *

Personal parishes appear anew amid the landscape of American Catholicism. New parishes signal an official, institutional move: a decision on the part of a local bishop to accommodate special purposes apart from the typical rubric of territorial boundaries. While canon law sets the parameters, exactly how, why, and which purposes or people receive personal parish status is not assured. This chapter looks at the underlying institutional processes and rationale surrounding bishops' decisions to establish personal parishes (or not).

FIGURE 3.1 Christ Our Hope personal parish celebrated its first Masses in downtown Seattle in 2010.

Innovation in parish organizing can be traced to the top (to the Vatican, the US Conference of Catholic bishops, and diocesan leaders)—and to the grassroots (where lay Catholics themselves mobilize and advocate for personal parish status). In this way, the process is participatory. But whether a given Catholic community achieves personal parish status depends ultimately on a bishop's approval and formal parish decree.

FIGURE 3.2 Christ Our Hope personal parish celebrated its first Masses in downtown Seattle in 2010.

ON BECOMING A PERSONAL PARISH: FROM THE TOP

When, why, and for whom or what are personal parishes created (or not)? Given the formal polity of the Catholic Church, these questions are necessarily couched in the power dynamics of diocesan leadership and management. Establishing any parish is a serious and (at least for the foreseeable future) long-term decision, with impact on the entire diocese.

FIGURE 3.3 Christ Our Hope personal parish celebrated its first Masses in downtown Seattle in 2010.

Asked in the National Survey of Personal Parishes (NSPP) if their arch/diocese has a formal policy in place for determining whether and when to erect a personal parish, virtually all dioceses (98 percent) responded "no." One diocese responding "yes" stated that: "The diocese does not permit personal parishes. Parishes are required to unite the different ethnic groups into a single parish." This same diocese later noted, however, that "we simply do not have the clergy necessary to establish personal parishes"—suggesting that resources, rather than policy, explained their initial response. Of the few other dioceses that responded "yes" to the personal parish policy question, survey respondents describe their diocesan stance as follows:

> Only canon law and, if we need one, their own statutes/canon law.

> * * *

> Only to follow canon law.

> * * *

> Nothing more than the Chancellor consults with canon law. The bishop consults the Presbyteral Council.

> * * *

> Depends on the bishop—no policy.

In short, even dioceses with a personal parish policy don't really have one. What was true a century ago is still true today: "In the United States, where many national parishes exist, there has never been general legislation providing for their erection."[1] Canon law is the sole source of polity informing personal parish establishment.

I affirmed this in subsequent interviews, such as one with a diocesan planner who said, "I don't know. . . . It really depends upon the situation. I think every situation is unique. We didn't have any kind of broad-based policy. We look at every situation uniquely, because—to be honest with you—many of these decisions were not black and white decisions." Another diocesan planner admits (with a similar dissatisfaction) that "it's all ad hoc."

Even canon law presents minimal instruction. Only the bishop's authority is clear, entrusted with pastoral care for all in the particular church (i.e. diocese). Per canon 515 (emphasis added):

> Can. 515 §1. A parish is a certain community of the Christian faithful stably constituted in a particular church, whose pastoral care is entrusted to a pastor (parochus) as its proper pastor (pastor) *under the authority of the diocesan bishop*.
>
> §2. It is *only for the diocesan bishop* to erect, suppress, or alter parishes. He is neither to erect, suppress, nor alter notably parishes, unless he has heard the presbyteral council.

"Parish" finds life only in so much as the local ordinary—the bishop— approves it, and formally acts accordingly. As one diocesan staffer wrote in an email reply to me, "Regarding your question on how the decision is made, I am told that there is not a "standard" process, but it's the bishop's decision, beyond question." Canon law informs protocol; bishops adjudicate from there.

The code cements a diocesan bishop's status as the sole decision-maker in parish choice. Canon lawyer James Coriden writes, "Only the head of the diocese and chief minister of its governance, the bishop, can take such an action, and he can do so only after consulting his primary collaborators and advisors, the presbyterate."[2] A presbyteral council serves as a consultative body of advisors. Their advice is required, but non-binding. The presbyteral council's role may be instrumental in swaying the bishop . . . or it may be merely formulaic and ultimately inconsequential.

One canon lawyer summarizes the consultation process as such:

> There is what we call the priests' council—it's called the presbyteral council, the council of priests. They're supposed to be [the bishop's] advisors with regard to pastoral matters that are affecting the diocese. And, obviously, one of the monumental things would be to establish a parish, or to suppress a parish, or to notably alter a parish. The diocese's bishop has to assemble the priest council. And normally, it would be a manageable group—let's say maybe 15–20 priests. And he's supposed to, first of all, place this before them, and say: "Alright. I'm thinking about altering the nature of Our Lady of Guadalupe parish. What do you think about that?" So, he needs to receive their input. That's consultation, alright? And there's a pretty high premium on—he really needs to listen to what they say. So, if everybody on the priests' council says "No, don't do that!" and he does it anyway, he better have a darn good reason.

Most dioceses (four in five, or 78 percent) report in the NSPP that the diocesan presbyteral council must be consulted prior to establishing a personal parish. The less-than-unanimous citation of consultation (which is canonically required) likely hints at the lack of a guarantee of council influence. As one personal parish pastor put it in our interview: "The bishop only had to come to his presbyteral council. They are merely a council body, not a decision-making body. Canon law requires it. In the end, it was still his decision." A bishop may veto or contradict any suggestions made by the presbyteral council (or any other consultative processes preceding). Canonically, the requirement is for the bishop to hear but not to adhere to their recommendation.

"(Arch)bishop support and/or advocacy" ranked highest among all factors listed in the NSPP as potential influences on personal parish decisions. Eight in ten dioceses report that a bishop's support is somewhat or highly influential in determining whether a personal parish is erected in the diocese.[3] The majority (60 percent) cite his role as "highly" influential. Bishop support is also prominent among a list of criteria that must be present before establishing a new personal parish. Three-quarters (74 percent) of dioceses say that "the arch/bishop must provide written approval" for the personal parish.

This is not to say that Vatican influence does not remain the pinnacle of authority in the institutional Catholic Church: it does. Nearly two-thirds (64 percent) of dioceses ranked "papal statements allowing for or encouraging the use of personal parishes" as at least "somewhat" influential in personal parish establishment decisions. But a full third of dioceses indicate that these are "not influential" at all—a sign of subsidiarity in action. The Vatican sets the stage; bishops enact it locally.

Vatican Influence on Personal Parish Decisions

Statements from Rome lay the broadest conditions for personal parish outcomes. The 2004 document *Apostolorum Successores*, for example, mentions the canonical option of personal parishes should local conditions necessitate. Within a section called "Persons in need of particular pastoral attention," the document affirms that "in order to provide pastoral care for certain dispersed groups present within the diocese, the Bishop may establish a 'personal parish.'"[4]

Vatican statements helped incentivize personal parishes dedicated to the Traditional Latin Mass (TLM), in particular—a necessary allowance for an uncommon liturgical form in the post-Vatican II Church. The 1988 papal document *Ecclesia Dei* permitted bishops to grant requests for the Tridentine liturgy of 1962 (the pre-Vatican, Traditional Latin Mass). Stronger still, a 2007 Vatican apostolic letter *Summorum Pontificum* written by Pope Benedict XVI motu proprio (which translates to "on his own impulse") offered bishops the latitude to create personal parishes specifically dedicated to celebrating the extraordinary form of the Mass. Its instruction read:

> Art. 10. The local Ordinary, should he judge it opportune, may erect a *personal parish* in accordance with the norm of Canon 518 for celebrations according to the older form of the Roman rite, or appoint a rector or chaplain, with respect for the requirements of law.[5]

The document also advised that "in parishes where a group of the faithful attached to the previous liturgical tradition stably exists, the parish priest should willingly accede to their requests to celebrate Holy Mass according to the rite of the 1962 Roman Missal," albeit "under the governance of the bishop."[6] In other words, bishops need to allow the TLM, and could allow TLM personal parishes, as desired.

An accompanying cover letter by Pope Benedict XVI suggested further that:

> I very much wish to stress that these new norms do not in any way lessen your own authority and responsibility, either for the liturgy or for the pastoral care of your faithful. Each Bishop, in fact, is the moderator of the liturgy in his own Diocese. ... Nothing is taken away, then, from the authority of the Bishop, whose role remains that of being watchful that all is done in peace and serenity. Should some problem arise which the parish priest cannot resolve, the local Ordinary will always be able to intervene, in full harmony, however, with all that has been laid down by the new norms of the Motu Proprio.

In this, Pope Benedict laid out an expectation of openness to special purpose parishes, while still subsumed under the authority of the bishop. One diocesan planner shared in an interview that their diocese began offering the Latin Mass because "we saw the handwriting on the wall" but that "if Rome tomorrow said, 'We withdraw that,' we probably would, too."

Similarly, Anglican Use personal parishes—which date back to 1983 in the US Catholic Church—found enhanced livelihood via a 2009 Vatican pronouncement entitled "Anglicanorum Coetibus," also delivered by Pope Benedict.[7] Anglican Use personal parishes use a liturgical form that incorporates elements of the Anglican tradition. Most are founded by former Episcopalians who wish to maintain Anglican features in their Catholic practice. The 2009 Vatican pronouncement encouraging Anglican Use personal parishes included the following:

> VIII. §1. The Ordinary, according to the norm of law, after having heard the opinion of the Diocesan Bishop of the place, may erect, with the consent of the Holy See, *personal parishes* for the faithful who belong to the Ordinariate.[8]

The structural arrangement of Anglican Use personal parishes got somewhat more complex when they were subsumed under a dedicated, US Anglican Use Ordinariate (similar to a diocese, but national in scope) in 2012.

Personal parishes also appear intermittently in Vatican documents related to migrants and travelers. For example, a 2004 Vatican paper entitled "Erga migrantes caritas Christi" (The love of Christ toward migrants) written by the Pontifical Council for the Pastoral Care of Migrants and Itinerant People had the following to say regarding personal parishes (emphasis added):

> A *personal ethnic-linguistic parish* or one based on a particular rite is foreseen for places where there is an immigrant community that will continually have newcomers even in the future, and where that community is numerically strong. It maintains the typical characteristic service of a parish (proclamation of the Word, catechesis, liturgy, diakonia) and will be concerned above all with recent immigrants, seasonal workers or those coming by turns, and with others who for various reasons have difficulty in finding their place in the existent territorial structures.

Elsewhere, the document clarifies that "when it is deemed necessary to erect a *personal parish*, in view of the number of migrants or the opportuneness of providing them with special pastoral care corresponding to their needs, in doing so the diocesan or eparchial bishop shall clearly establish the confines of this parish and the rules regarding the parish books."[9] Phrasing the condition as "when it is deemed necessary," with administrative oversight, reiterates the authority of a local bishop.

Personal parishes also find a place among myriad options for students proposed in Vatican documents. The previously mentioned *Apostolorum Successores* offers that:

> The apostolate among university students requires special attention on account of their particular needs and milieu. Either on his own or in collaboration with Bishops of other dioceses, the Ordinary will attend to the pastoral care of university students, perhaps by establishing a *personal parish* on the university campus or nearby, with residences and other centres which offer the students constant spiritual and intellectual assistance.[10]

Here, again, the Vatican presents the personal parish option if local bishops see that circumstances warrant it.

Vatican statements can lay fertile soil for personal parish formation . . . always contingent upon a local ordinary's (bishop's) own judgment. Allowance is different than advocacy, of course. Vatican documents present personal parish avenues, but do not mandate them. Asked in the NSPP to identify criteria that must be met before establishing a new personal parish, only two in ten dioceses say that "the Holy See must encourage, promote, or require the personal parish" for their diocese to proceed with establishment. Rome guides, introduces, and occasionally regulates—but does not compel or clearly circumscribe personal parish decisions locally.

National-Level Influence on Personal Parish Decisions

Looking to the national level, the United States Conference of Catholic Bishops (USCCB) offers "appropriate assistance to each bishop in fulfilling his particular ministry in the local Church." Bishops in the United States do not answer to the USCCB, per se. They report to the Pope and to the Vatican, but not to the US body of bishops in any binding way.

On the topic of personal parishes, the USCCB offers neither specific encouragement nor restriction around personal parish establishment. One bishop describes the relative absenteeism of personal parishes as an agenda item for the USCCB:

> I do not remember the question of personal parishes being brought up as some-
> thing that needs our attention because there's an important aspect that's not
> being fulfilled, or there's something going wrong. . . . At this moment, it's not
> seen as something requiring attention. This is something that basically belongs
> to each diocese.

His assessment implies that local bishops, not the USCCB, contemplate and enact personal parish decisions.

The USCCB's Committee on Cultural Diversity writes of how "Catholic parishes are moving from mono-cultural patterns to ones we call 'shared,' that is, to parishes in which more than one language, racial or cultural group seek to celebrate the Eucharist and embody Christian community." Historian Timothy Matovina observed almost two decades ago that "the reluctance to grant the canonical status of a national parish is fairly wide-spread among contemporary U.S. ordinaries."[11] Some casually presume this to still be the case. A handful of pastors or diocesan staffers I interviewed, for example, allude to a generic spirit among American bishops against the philosophical idea of personal parishes, but none could identify a formal policy as such.

My exchange with one priest is typical on this front:

> In the United States, I think that the policy of the bishops is not to
> create national parishes.
> *TCB: You mention a policy. Is there a place that you would point to, to iden-
> tify that actual policy coming from? Or is it more of a feel, a sentiment?*

I think it's mostly the experience of the local bishops to see what is the best way of serving that immigrant group, at the same time giving them the freedom to organize themselves to be in their own language, in their own church—or in other occasions, they can be just a part of a regular church, regular community.

TCB: *Okay. So when you say policy, you're not necessarily referring to something that's been codified, or written down?*

No. It's up to every bishop to decide that.

TCB: *Subsidiarity?*

Yeah, to decide about the creation of a national or local parish.

While such perceptions are important in guiding behavior, they do not rise to the level of written policy.

Bishop interviewees in myriad regional locales present neither a widespread nor consistent reluctance toward personal parish establishment, nor the opposite. Variation, judiciousness, and cautious (even creative) application better describe bishops' attitudes toward personal parishes today. More dioceses have granted personal parish status each year since 1983, a fact that itself contradicts the notion of unified disallowance. Personal parish "policy" circles back to complicated assessments of merit under the authority of local bishops.

THE SUBSTANCE OF SUBSIDIARITY

Taken together, canon law, the Vatican, and the USCCB all privilege bishop discretion in determining when, whether, and for whom or what personal parishes are created. The result is a highly localized, multifaceted, and bishop-dependent process of diocesan-level discernment. Decisions privilege subsidiarity, or the Catholic principle that decisions are first and best made locally. This idea counters older canonical regulations that put "a heavy, heavy emphasis on centralization," in the words of one canon lawyer. Referring to current code, one bishop summarizes:

> That [personal parish] clause in there is to give the diocesan bishop very wide parameters in which to establish any type of community that he sees fit. And this is going back to a legal principle that was basically touted at the Second Vatican Council and that was also highlighted in the law, and that is the principle that we call subsidiarity.

Subsidiarity lessens the power of higher order authorities in the Church and heightens that of the local bishop. As one canon lawyer put it, "it's very broad, and it's to allow ... basically, it gives the diocesan bishop carte blanche with regard to his diocese, as far as any reasons that he would see that are necessary to establish such a place."

Subsidiarity breeds diverse outcomes for personal parishes across dioceses and regions in the United States. Some dioceses have many personal parishes; others have none. Amidst differing local contexts characterized by numbers of foreign-born Catholics, population size, parish density, priest resources, finances, and so on, bishops decipher how best to respond for their particular church. One bishop tells me, "You know, canon law is universal, but the way I run a diocese ... and the United States might be different than it's running in Nigeria or Portugal or the Samoan Islands ... you have to adjust. And it's all a little bit different." Another bishop says: "Every diocese is unique, and every bishop has unique challenges. They're not always easy to—for me to look at some other diocese and say, 'Well, you should do this, or do that.'"

Absent a formally articulated stance on personal parish establishment, some bishops opt to not deploy the personal parish at all. Others simply follow past precedent in the diocese. Still others navigate an ad hoc approach influenced by resources and subjective assessments of "need." In all scenarios, the bishop sets a tone for personal parish receptivity or resistance.

Not deploying the personal parish at all is a common choice: 56 percent of dioceses established no new personal parishes in or after 1983. Some may have older national parishes that remain open (strategically, even), but no new personal parishes were decreed in recent decades. Bishops accommodate difference instead through other forms of purpose-driven activity (such as irregular Masses, or missions in territorial parishes), sans the canonical status of personal parish. The absence of new personal parishes does not imply that no lay requests for personal parishes were made during this time period. If such requests were made, they were declined.

Hearing why some bishops and dioceses do not create personal parishes can shed light on why others do. Nothing in church law requires their establishment. Personal parishes are proportionately few among all parishes. Not all bishops use them to organize Catholics in their dioceses. Sometimes no rationale is provided: "The bishop didn't want it. And no real reason given. 'We don't want that here' was the only excuse given," says one priest. Another long-term lay advocate for the Latin Mass describes "fifty excuses" from bishops denying his TLM personal parish requests.

Even so, there are common themes behind explanations for not starting personal parishes. One explanation come from past practice, or what economists and historians would call path dependence. The NSPP shows that dioceses with personal parishes established pre-1983 are more likely to have established them post-1983. One bishop whose diocese has no new personal parishes, for example, explains that their diocese has never used personal parishes. The more recent arrival of nonwhite Catholics to the area has only recently pressured territorial parishes. He explains:

> One of the big reasons is, first of all, there had not been [a need]. The phenomenon of multiculturalism in [our diocese] is relatively new—about 15 years—and so the community here is adjusting. [. . .] There's a different dynamic.

Introducing the idea of a personal parish from scratch can feel like an entrepreneurial leap.

Bishops also make future predictions in their rationale to decline personal parishes. While a group needs a parish today, will this always be true? One shares:

> To be honest, I think the Koreans, especially, have wanted me to establish a Korean Parish. And I have resisted that. Not that I don't—I'm not discouraging ministry to Koreans, or in Korean, but I'm thinking about the experience in other places where—after several generations—the immigration stops. And then you have an infrastructure that nobody can support.

The chance of future closure trumps the expression of current need. This reasoning is especially common in dioceses where older national parishes are closing. Some opine that this rubric is unfair to apply to the needs of today's Catholics, though ("Some bishops deny that. I think it's cruel to people. You cannot say that 'Okay, what happened to the European Church?' and then you deny the people; at this particular moment, you know?").

Another reason commonly offered by bishops for not starting personal parishes has to do with current availability of ministry in existing parishes. A bishop describes:

> People of that group are more integrated into their local parish. And they're not going to drive from all parts of the area to the center that their parents or grandparents did. I really want to make it theirs, and make sure that we do have ministries to those . . . but that we don't make them into ethnic parishes.

His logic pairs a long-range vision, predicting different needs for younger Catholics, with the hope that a territorial parish can adapt. He doubts that dispersed populations would even be willing drive to a personal parish; thus, better to task territorial parishes with embedding specialized ministry. Expanding upon this, some bishops reason that non-parish organizational options can serve specialized purposes, too, and are a better use of limited diocesan resources. Catholics' tendency to choose parishes, canonical non-compliance notwithstanding, provides for special needs already.

This line of thinking gets at two related notions that help to explain organizational emergence more generally: density and carrying capacity. How many parishes are there already (density)? And how many can the diocese support (carrying capacity)? Theories of organizational emergence would suggest that density encourages new organizational forms (e.g., personal parishes) to a point, but saturation does the opposite.[12] If there are already enough parishes to meet needs, if priest resources are maxed, or if the Catholic population is not sufficiently large, then incumbent organizations are expected to adapt to new needs. Dioceses saturated with numerous territorial parishes see lower urgency to start personal parishes.

Taken together, the reasoning used by bishops who do not start personal parishes considers historical precedent, future need, alternative ministry options, parish density, and carrying capacity, among other locally specific rationale. An overarching theme in personal parish reckonings—seen on the path to "no" as well as the path to "yes"—is that decisions are made at the diocesan level. A single personal parish is not determined in isolation. Broader diocesan context matters. Bishops read the demographics and capacity of their diocesan population. They consider the history of parishes in their area, and the availability of resources to meet specialized purposes. This underscores the embeddedness of personal parishes (and all parishes) within broader networks.

Asked directly why some communities of Catholics are denied their requests for personal parish status, one bishop says:

> Well, they don't have the right circumstances. Personal parishes demand a certain amount of factors, and all those factors to be present in a certain proportion. And a bishop judges that they don't have that. He's not necessarily saying, "I have a group of x country or x language that it might be useful on occasion to worship in their own language"; no, he's not saying that. He's saying "I don't have the combination of all the circumstances of a parish." I acknowledge the value of a personal parish. I acknowledge the difficulties of a personal parish. I acknowledge the fact that not everything is easy. So the establishment of any parish, but especially a personal parish, requires the supernatural gift of prudence, which is virtue.

Recognizing that decisions may not align with what Catholics in the diocese desire, this same bishop adds: "There is another level of seeing things. Not everybody sees everything in the same . . . not everybody has the same judgment on whether—Somebody has to make a decision regarding personal parishes." That somebody, canonically, is the bishop. Another bishop admits: "Well, it makes sense to me, but it doesn't always make sense to them."

GETTING TO "YES"

Forty-four percent of all US dioceses have established at least one personal parish since 1983. Clearly, "yes" is a popular answer—today—to the question of whether to establish new personal parishes. Citing the endurance of principles that inspired personal parishes in years past, one bishop clarifies that "personal parishes are not 'out' and shouldn't be rejected by some kind of little preference on our part. No, no, no, no." Bishops see personal parishes as an option to deploy as they see fit. Canon law provides the parameters, and bishops act entrepreneurially therein.

Revealing bishops' decisive role in personal parish outcomes, sometimes decisions to establish personal parishes come as a surprise. The "top-down" origins of one new personal parish led one priest to say "It was a surprise to everybody here that we got that designation." In another example, a bishop came to dedicate a packed new worship space and, during the service, to the surprise of the presiding priest—designated it a personal parish with the presiding priest at its helm. The priest, now retired, recounts the turn of events:

> [The community] kept growing and kept growing. We had started two Masses, because one was not enough. The day the bishop came to dedicate the church— giving his talk, he says, "I now make this a personal parish, and Father [ ] is the pastor." Which—he had said nothing to me! Never asked me! And I almost fell off my chair when he said it! And the parishioners were . . . they couldn't believe it. [TCB: You didn't know before that?] I did not know before that he was going to make it a parish. Nobody did.[13]

The decision came from the top.

What moves bishops to establish personal parishes? What is the origin of support or advocacy for this model of parish building from the top? One bishop says it all comes down to need:

> It's always the same question. Here is a significant group of people, and how can we help them the best possible way? Now a personal parish, there's a lot in the background. There's a lot of reality to be taken into account, a lot of ecclesial

reflection to be done. . . . But the thing that is so important is the *need*. It's the need—the pastoral need—and the pastoral advantages that come from this. And that brings us to the birth of a parish. And then, not everything is solved there . . . No; it's only the beginning of the challenge. But it is a very beautiful step. Because it brings with it this great joy of finding—in their own culture— the blessing of the Church.

Bishops, in other words, arbitrate lay Catholics' needs.

The NSPP offers some clues as to what needs bishops prioritize in granting personal parish status. Table 3.1 shows what criteria dioceses nationwide identified as being necessary before establishing a new personal parish for a specific population or purpose.

Two of the most common criteria have been discussed already: presbyteral council consultation and bishop approval. Dioceses' prioritization of the remaining criteria highlights four themes: access to a priest, enough people, a church, and finances. I explore each in turn.

A Personal Parish Needs a Priest

Three-quarters of dioceses report that "a priest must be made available to pastor the personal parish" prior to its establishment. This is the second most common criteria, after presbyteral council consultation. Per its canonical definition, a parish needs a priest to act as pastor. Priest shortages, however, make

Table 3.1 CRITERIA REQUIRED PRIOR TO PERSONAL PARISH ESTABLISHMENT

Criteria	Percentage of Dioceses
The diocesan presbyteral council must be consulted	78
A priest must be made available to pastor the personal parish	74
The arch/bishop must provide written approval	74
The special population must constitute a certain number in the diocese	65
Physical space for the personal parish must be secured	62
A certain amount of funds must be raised	54
A feasibility study must be conducted	52
Local Catholics must petition the arch/bishop	47
The Holy See must encourage, promote, or require the personal parish	20
Other	6

Note: Dioceses were asked, "Which of the following criteria would likely need to be met before establishing a new personal parish for a specific population or purpose?" and could select multiple responses.

this challenging. If a given community can identify an available priest (perhaps through international ties, or a proposed partnership with a community of priests), this may sway a bishop to consider the personal parish option.

One bishop affirms this in his own decisions, saying that:

> Absolutely; they have to have a priest. You don't manufacture priests. We have enough to take care of what we have. But we have lots of priests who come from Korea or Vietnam. . . . These communities are very strong. And they've grown and developed. It's phenomenal what they've done. . . . They want to move ahead, and they have everybody in place. Their local bishop or cardinal agrees that they could be appointed pastor of that parish. So it works very well, I have to say . . . so far, it's been beautiful. Wonderful.

Networks with international priests explain, in part, the higher incidence of personal parishes for Korean and Vietnamese Catholics in particular. Korean American Catholics, a substantial portion of whom prefer Mass and sacraments in Korean, are more likely to express the need for specialized ministries, to identify and bring in an international priest, and to advocate for personal parish status. This paves a convincing path toward personal parish status for communities who may otherwise feel insufficiently integrated into territorial parishes.[14]

A personal parish pastor from a Traditional Latin Mass parish also speaks to the persuasiveness of finding a suitable priest:

> It takes away the burden of appointing a local priest (an archdiocesan priest), because they're happy for us to be here. Because we're not priests of the archdiocese. And we're in here, and we're doing this, and as long as we do what's acceptable to the archdiocese—right—or we do what we *should*—no problem. They appreciate having us, because we're taking a load off of them, they don't have to appoint a new priest. So I think that's one thing: that they appreciate having outside groups come in, and take a burden off of the local priests.

Finding a priest outside the diocese reduces competition on existing, limited diocesan resources. Just as not having an available priest can be the first rationale for "no," having one can set a path to "yes."

A Personal Parish Needs People

Two-thirds of dioceses agree that personal parish establishment necessarily requires that "the special population must constitute a certain number in the diocese." In other words, the population of Catholics must be large enough to support a parish on their own.

One bishop shares how much the numbers matter:

> One of the natural factors that immediately comes to mind is the number of the people to be served. A parish is a vibrant group of people. And the vibrancy depends, to some extent, on how many people there are. So, it's one thing to have a sufficient number to have a particular Mass on a particular Sunday, to help these people cling to their beautiful traditions and to get help that they need. But that doesn't mean that we're able to do that, or that it's the right thing to do. So, a great deal depends on the number of people and who they are—what their needs are.

The prospect of personal parish status may even draw Catholics who do not otherwise claim a parish. Bishops are also mindful that siphoning off parishioners from their assigned territorial parish could harm that parish's financial standing ("I hate to say that the collection basket is what's counting, but for a lot of people—it is," evaluates one pastor). While growth does not dictate personal parish outcomes, it is high among the needed criteria.

Moving into specialized parishes can also be used strategically to shore up resources at parishes with a shrinking attendance base. A new personal parish designation can save an otherwise dying territorial parish. Combining communities of Catholics—particularly those desiring personal parish status and/or otherwise itinerant in the diocese—lends needed human (and financial) capital to salvage a parish that otherwise warrants suppression.

One parish whose roots extend deep into Midwestern Catholic history, for example, faced assured closure until it found renewal as a personal parish for Korean Catholics. A long-term parishioner explains, "I grew up in this parish. I grew up before it was ever built, because it was in the church basement. And the Korean people—they needed a place." Another parish leader explains how adding personal parish status—and its accompanying critical mass of Catholics—was their best (and only) option:

> I think at the end of the day, the [parish] originals understood that if they were going to stay single-focused on just being an American-only parish, that the bishop certainly has the right to say, "You're a mission parish," and we are going back to a chapel status, and you will end up being nothing! So, you'd better . . . essentially: "You need to recognize you have this Korean vibrant community here that is living with you. Don't ignore them. Accommodate. Not only accommodate, but assimilate with them, and together, you can grow as a single parish."

Bishops manage parish structures across diverse Catholic populations. Personal parish decisions consider all populations interdependently. At times, this displaces communities of Catholics (often minority Catholics) from long-term church homes when they are invited (mandated) by diocesan leaders to relocate into new personal parishes elsewhere. In this aspect, personal parish establishment parallels patterns of neighborhood gentrification.

A Personal Parish Needs a Church

In addition to a priest and people, a personal parish also needs somewhere to physically gather. A church. More than six in ten dioceses say that "physical space for the personal parish must be secured" as a personal parish prerequisite. While a personal parish does not require a bound territory, it does need a church. This motivates a powerful rationale for personal parish establishment: matching lay needs to empty churches.

Like with relocating parishioners, the personal parish option can help bishops preserve churches in areas where declining Catholic populations no longer justify a territorial parish.[15] A territorial parish market over capacity (meaning too many parishes ... but in beautiful buildings the diocese wants to keep) can be good news for an aspiring personal parish. Unused churches of suppressed parishes must be sold or repurposed (see figure 3.4). This can generate entrepreneurial opportunities for personal parish establishment.

For example, the storied cathedral near the St. Louis Arch—once the largest parish west of the Mississippi River—closed when the downtown Catholic population shrank. This created a problem (a beautiful cathedral with no parishioners) looking for a solution. "It is a historic church," said an interviewee familiar with what transpired. "It was a church that was going to be retained no matter what, because of its history as the oldest cathedral west of the Mississippi. And it's right by the Arch." The solution? Establish it as a personal parish "for reason of its history and sacred architecture," per its 2005 decree. Figure 3.5 depicts this transition-in-progress.

Bishops' decisions to suppress territorial parishes can breed new personal parishes. One diocesan planner conveyed how in his diocese, closures provided an occasion to meet specialized needs. He explains that they "had to figure out what to do with these buildings" and the bishop "found a reason to keep them. It was intentional/non-intentional, keeping them." One bishop comments on this, saying "the saving of a building is not a justifiable means for inventing something that is not true ... but it could be a providential occasion." Catholics can move. Churches cannot.

FIGURE 3.4 Dioceses throughout the United States have sold church and school property during times of restructuring.

Seattle's Christ Our Hope parish—whose dedication was detailed at the start of this chapter—reveals this dynamic. The archdiocese owned a building with historic value in a prime downtown location. They needed people to occupy it. A leader familiar with the process explained:

> We've had a church down there—a chapel in an old building called the Josephinum. This building goes way back—it's an historic building. . . . The two bottom floors are leased out by agreement with the contract on low-income housing to create funding to pay off the building. . . .. Building a church down there, we create something for low-income housing, for the day-care, a shelter for women—But also it gives us a place to be located to handle the people in cruise ships, and things of that nature.

FIGURE 3.5 The Parish of the Basilica of St. Louis, King of France, gained personal parish status for its unique service to tourists and "for reason of its history and sacred architecture," per the parish decree.

In such cases, a bishop's "yes" to personal parish status may derive as much from the desire to preserve diocesan property as it does from the desire to serve particular constituencies.

Matching available church homes to known pastoral needs explains why bishops are especially likely to establish personal parishes during times of diocesan restructuring. Restructuring raises questions about carrying capacity: how many parishes a population warrants. Excess territorial parishes are suppressed; but some of their churches survive through newly decreed personal parish status.

A Personal Parish Needs Funding

Securing a priest, people, and church often acts as a proxy for a community's ability to support and maintain themselves financially. "A certain amount of funds must be raised," report 54 percent of dioceses. One bishop says: "There's a certain evolution, you know, before you create a parish. You have to see if it can stand on its own feet, because that's what's expected of any parish that doesn't get entirely subsidized by the larger diocesan church." One pastor likens it to maturation, saying that a community at first "might not be self-sufficient," but in time, it becomes "like grown children—big now, and maybe the need is to have your own parish."

Finances play heavily into bishops' personal parish decisions. One pastor of a Vietnamese parish, for example, explains:

> The way that the Archdiocese operates is—more and more—you need to be financially independent. You need to be able to pay the pastor. You need to be able to maintain the building. You start from scratch, meaning that you need to buy land and then build a church. But when you prove to the Archdiocese that you are able to be financially independent, then, I think, you are already halfway through. Because there is a need there. But—if you are not capable financially to maintain that—forget about it!

Several interviewees allude to the persuasive power of finances for convincing a bishop to start a personal parish. Here, a pastor of a Traditional Latin Mass personal parish states plainly how much resources matter:

> Honestly, I think bishops tend to be pretty practical in what they allow. They can be ideological, but they can also be—they tend to be forced to be very practical. Money talks, because money makes the world go 'round. And so, if a group can afford their own building, and if they can afford to support a priest, and if they can find a priest and the bishop doesn't need that priest, then there's no reason in the world why the bishop isn't going to be willing to say "Okay, you guys go do your thing." But those are some heavy conditions—to have the resources to

support a building, to have a priest that the bishop won't need or want, and to be able to support that priest.

Charged with managing a diocese, bishops necessarily make parish calculations for the financial health of the whole.

In one example, a wealthy, white male lay Catholic donor offered an archdiocese the funds to do whatever it saw fit for pastoral need. Since Hispanic Catholics were not being welcomed into existing territorial parishes, the archdiocese opted to build a personal parish for them. One diocesan representative familiar with the history tells the tale:

> You had this tremendous population that was drawn there for work. You have six parishes who were not equipped to handle this great influx of people. You have two priests and a couple of sisters who start to work as a pastoral team, to address the needs of Catholic Mexicans in that area. So what they did was: they set up a mission. It was ministry in all six of those parishes, doing outreach to the Mexican Catholic community, inviting them to have Mass in those parishes, inviting them to have religious ed . . . all their programs and activities in those parishes. Even coming up with a bussing system to get people to those churches.

But, he says:

> What you have there is an Anglo community that's not receptive to outsiders; they're not receptive! And are saying things like, "Why are they using our school for religious education? When are they going to get their own place? Why are they using our church for Mass? And why did they put up all these decorations? Can you tell them to take them down? Because, don't they know this is *our* church?" So, constant messages being sent that—"You don't belong here. This is not your church. You're just using our space, you have to rent. You're a renter. You're not an owner. When are you going to get moving?" So, you have that environment. Some of it's unspoken, and some of it's not. And pastors—Catholic *priests*! Which, you would think . . . ?! But no, saying it.

Territorial parishes were not fulfilling the pastoral needs of the area's growing Hispanic Catholic population. This was the extant diocesan need, when the following occurred:

> So, showing up on the scene is a man with a lot of money. Who is looking to do something good for the church. He says, "I'll build you a church. You won't have to worry about all of this." And so, then you're thinking, "I'm struggling right now. We're in six churches, and we're trying to hold this up. And we're not

getting to that place where we're seen as equals. We're not getting to that place where we're seen as we're members of the parish. So, what do I do? And what does the archdiocese do?"

They established a personal parish. They built an impressive, expensive new church for it. He concludes the story:

> So, I think—if the money hadn't shown up—it would have been an interesting thing, just to see how all of that would have progressed. Because parishes would have *had* to deal with it. And they would have to say, "Okay; they're here. Let's work on it." But, the money showed up in a very generous man—and [the personal parish] was born. And now they have registered 12,000 parishioners.

Money talks. Finances can compel a bishop to start a personal parish to solve an institutional dilemma that may have social roots.

MANAGING THE FLOCK

This kind of institutional strategizing—balancing priests, people, place, and funds, reiterates how bishops' decision-making is diocesan-oriented. It sees parishes as interlocking, as opposed to narrowly focused on single groups or purposes. Bishops wield a high level of control over their "flock." Even while the Second Vatican Council empowered Catholic laity more than ever, parishes still fall under the jurisdiction of the bishop. One pastor says on the power of the bishop: "It simply overrides it, it overrides all of that—it puts the 'O' in 'ordinary.' If the bishop thought [a decision] was hostile, he'd never allow it, not over his dead body."

One bishop plainly affirms this power to override lay Catholics' personal parish advocacy, in the interest of the wider church:

> In many cases, it's reasonable for people to want a parish. But the final decision has to be for the church. Somebody has to look at it with as much objectivity as is humanly possible, to see if—at the time when there are the resources to make this a parish—is that a propitious moment? Is it going to be a moment where they can embark on this second phase of being a parish? So, it's a beautiful thing. The dedication of a mission is a day of joy and celebration. But there will be those who look forward, and rightly so. Let people look forward.

His positive spin on centralization is that bishops are best positioned to see the big picture, to know and respond to pastoral need across a diocese. Decision-making is embedded in subsidiarity. Another bishop surmises, similarly:

The Church leaves all of these decisions in the hand of the local church: the bishop, the people that know the situation. They have to decide. It's true there are these factors that we're talking about now—How many people are there? How necessary is it? Who is available to assist them? How long will this endure? What are the other factors around them in the city in which they live? How successful do we think this will be in another five years? Etc. So—all of that is the subject of a particular judgment.

Bishops exercise their power to respond structurally to the organizational needs of local Catholics.

Without personal parishes, bishops risk losing some of this power. One diocesan planner acknowledges that his bishop's personal parish decisions were about "justifying a reason for control of it. I think that was part of the reason for almost all of these parishes." Another diocesan leader affirms this motivation: "Yeah ... 'maintaining' may be a better word, a kinder word. I think that's why it was done."

Control, of course, can also squash dissent. Bishops wield the power to excommunicate Catholics and change parish status. One (now former) diocesan priest recalls painfully the day a letter from the bishop arrived, suppressing the personal parish he led and excommunicating him ("It was waiting on my desk when I arrived"). A canon lawyer described another instance of this:

We did have a case where a group just formed their own parish, so to speak, without the bishop's approval. And they got excommunicated. We defended them, and won the case: the law overturned the bishop. [*TCB: Meaning that they now have parish status?*] Well, um, ah ... [*TCB: Or meaning that they aren't excommunicated?*] Yeah, well—they're not excommunicated.

In yet another example of conflict, a community of Vietnamese Catholics lobbied heavily for decades to secure personal parish status. "It was a cold war," one leader recounts. "We called them the dissidents—that was what they were known as, the dissidents." The community eventually won approval from the bishop for a personal parish of their own.[16]

ON BECOMING A PERSONAL PARISH: FROM BELOW

A bishop's authority is instrumental in personal parish decisions. Even so, top-down tactics fail to explain the entirety of personal parish origins. Organizational innovation often finds its social sources at the grassroots.[17] Lay agency also matters for personal parish outcomes.

Table 3.2 FACTORS INFLUENCING PERSONAL PARISH ESTABLISHMENT

	Percentage of Dioceses		
Factor	Not Influential	Somewhat Influential	Highly Influential
Arch/bishop support and/or advocacy	20	20	60
Unmet need among a particular population of Catholics	23	36	41
Growth of a particular demographic group in the arch/diocese	15	51	34
Financial resources made available for ministry to specific populations or purposes	28	45	27
Papal statements allowing for or encouraging the use of personal parishes	36	46	18
Formal petition from a group of people in the arch/diocese	28	55	17
Multicultural office support and/or advocacy	35	56	9
Conversations with interested lay people in the arch/diocese	40	53	7
Conversation with religious groups (e.g., priests from the FSSP)	54	41	4
Other	27	27	45

Note: Dioceses were asked: "Many factors may influence whether or not a parish is erected for a specific population or purpose. For the ten factors listed below, please indicate their likely influence for your arch/diocese."

The NSPP offers clues as to what factors on the ground influence personal parish establishment decisions. Table 3.2 shows the percentage of dioceses indicating no, some, or high influence for each factor in whether or not a parish is erected for a specific population or purpose.

Two related criteria dominate: "unmet need among a particular population of Catholics," and "growth of a particular demographic group in the arch/diocese." More than three-quarters of dioceses say that both factors are "somewhat" or "highly" influential in personal parish establishment.

While population growth offers a more objective measurement—explored already among factors weighed by bishops—unmet need is interpreted subjectively. No personal parishes are needed by the territorial constitution of the local church. Every inch of a geographic diocese is covered by a territorial parish. No Catholic goes unserved. Thus, lay Catholics must convey that their specialized need supersedes (or coexists with) what territorial parishes are already accomplishing in the diocese . . . or, perhaps, that it compensates for what territorial parishes are not doing well.

How do Catholics convey and justify need to their local bishop? Some use formal petitions. One pastor recalled how Catholics "bugged" and "harassed" the bishop through letters and local Catholic media. A sizable majority of dioceses nationwide (83 percent) suggest that a formal petition from a group of people in the arch/diocese was at least somewhat influential in decisions to erect personal parishes.

TLM personal parishes illustrate this. Local chapters of "Una Voce"—a movement with international branches committed to increasing access to the TLM—solicit signatures in support of new personal parishes. This 2012 petition from a Los Angeles chapter provides one example:

> We, the undersigned faithful of the Archdiocese of Los Angeles, support the desire of our Holy Father, Pope Benedict XVI, to promote the Extra-Ordinary Form of the Mass of the Roman Rite.
>
> In accordance with His Holiness, we respectfully request that you invite the Priestly Fraternity of Saint Peter to assist you in establishing and staffing a personal parish centrally located in the greater Los Angeles Archdiocese to be dedicated solely to the Traditional Mass of the Roman Rite, now known as the Extra-Ordinary Form of the Roman Rite, as stated in the provisions of Article 10 of his motu proprio Summorum Pontificum:
>
>> Art. 10. The ordinary of a particular place, if he feels it appropriate, may erect a personal parish in accordance with can. 518 for celebrations following the ancient form of the Roman rite, or appoint a chaplain, while observing all the norms of law.
>
> We make this appeal to you in order to most effectively satisfy the legitimate needs and desires of the faithful who wish to live a locally-accessible, constant, full and integrated parish life according to the traditional Roman rites of our One, Holy, Catholic, and Apostolic Church and the spirituality of the Roman Missal published by Blessed John XXIII in 1962. We thank Your Excellency for your consideration of our request.

Networks of Anglican Use Catholics have taken a similar approach, distributing newsletter summaries of how to best make a case to a bishop for a personal parish.

Lay Catholics petitioning for personal parish status must make a convincing case that the shared, territorial parish (or another organizational form) is not enough. They emphasize is that a single Mass time cannot build and support a specialized Catholic community. While a full 80 percent of dioceses report that they offer Latin Masses, for example, TLM proponents relay to bishops that one Mass is insufficient. This pastor's comments illustrate:

The big thing about this is having a parish with Latin Mass *only*, versus a parish that *has* a Latin Mass. For us, the Latin Mass is integral to the parish life. It's not ornamental, it's integral. It's a very big thing, and there's a very clear distinction. That means there's a whole flow. We use a different calendar. We do things differently.

Similarly, a pastor of a personal parish that serves African Americans says that he had to convince his bishop that the symbolic value of his parish goes beyond what one Mass offers:

> If you just have a Mass someplace else, to me it's like going back to sitting in the back of the bus. But to say "We have a parish" is to say there is some authority, or there is some recognition. Yeah. I don't know how to say it other than that. But I think people know that the focus is on African American ministry here, as opposed to an afterthought: "Oh, well, we'll throw in a Mass for the African Americans to come to."

The desire for real and symbolic meaning mobilizes Catholics for personal parish status from the grassroots.

An extended look at the Archdiocese of Seattle illustrates the kind of grassroots labor that can catalyze establishment decisions made by bishops. Five new personal parishes were established between 2008 and 2010 by then Archbishop Alexander Brunett. While the archbishop's rapid establishment of parishes may imply a top-down, expedient organizational response, Seattle's personal parish origins must be understood in context. All came a quarter-century after changes to canon law in 1983. No personal parishes were established under the leadership of former Archbishop Raymond Hunthausen (1975–1991), nor under Thomas Joseph Murphy (1991–1997), nor even under Archbishop Brunett until the years just preceding his own retirement. Some of the affected communities began gathering decades prior. Other factors were clearly at play. The eventual decisions marked a receptive and, for some, long-awaited response to requests from area Catholics.

Seattle's Korean and Vietnamese Catholic communities were the first to inquire about the possibility of personal parish status, having organized in the mid-1970s. The response from the archdiocese had always been "no." The legacy passed along from former Archbishop Hunthausen—at the helm of the archdiocese when the new canon law came to pass—discouraged ethnic parishes. His fear, those familiar relay, was that new personal parishes would one day go the way of older national parishes, no longer serving their original population or purpose. Seattle's Korean and Vietnamese

Catholics were instead given the label "faith communities," loosely linked to a territorial parish. They leveraged this organizational status to raise funds, recruit willing priests, create ministry offerings, grow in size, and even build large worship facilities. All of this was done without formal parish status, despite their desire for it.

For years, "faith community" attendees traveled from miles away in and around the city to participate in shared worship and community. From an outsider's perspective (even an insider's perspective, for that matter), one could assume that their churches were parishes. A diocesan representative described them as "very large communities that have experienced a number of major shifts of location, buildings, waves of immigrants, leadership, etc. They are national parishes in everything but name, but have no real canonical standing." "They've been operating *like* a parish for many years," said another in the archdiocese. But they had no parish staff. Prior to 2010, they were not parishes per canon law.

Decades after their initial development, personal parish status was granted simultaneously to St. Andrew Kim, St. Paul Chong Hasang, and Vietnamese Martyrs. Why were they finally elevated to parish status? Catholics there were the first to request it, the first to gather as de facto congregations, but not the first to receive it. Understanding Seattle's Korean and Vietnamese personal parish decisions means seeing how they connect to Seattle's social mission personal parish and TLM personal parish. Both illustrate successful lay mobilization and entrepreneurial priests with elite access.

The space renovated as the personal parish with a social mission to downtown Seattle (whose dedication was detailed at the outset of this chapter) had been in archdiocesan hands since 1963. A converted dining hall acted as a chapel. After twenty-three years staffed by the Sisters of Saint Joseph of Peace (the building's namesake, "The Josephinum"), shifting demographics led the archdiocese to turn the building over to Catholic Housing Services. While "St. Joseph Chapel" continued to offer Mass (staffed by the Redemptorist priests of a nearby territorial parish), in time, attendance declined.

The underutilization of this space first provided an opportunity for a group of Seattle's lay Catholics devoted to the TLM. They had for thirteen years "worked in trying to urge, cajole, convince, lobby, etc. and through a succession of three archbishops" for a regular Latin Mass. Traditionalist leaders urged the laity to send local bishops "as many requests as possible" to prove demand for the TLM. National TLM advocates reached out to Seattle's diocesan leadership in support of local petitions. Upward of two hundred area Catholics met under the name "Ecclesia Dei of Western

Washington" (referencing the 1988 papal document supporting the Latin Mass) and, in 1997, became an original charter group of Una Voce America.

As with the requests from Seattle's Korean and Vietnamese Catholic communities, for years, the archdiocesan response to requests for the TLM (a personal parish) was "no." Speculating on the assorted reasons why bishops in Seattle and elsewhere resisted efforts to offer the Latin Mass, one lay insider relayed:

> Well, probably a complex series of reasons that they said no: their own personal opinion ... that they had moved on from the Latin Mass ... that that Mass had been abolished and was no longer viable ... that they're divisive ... no one understands Latin ... everyone's forgotten ... none of my priests know the Latin Mass ... I'll ask my presbyteral council, there's no support there ... etc., etc. So—a number of reasons. Some legitimate, some not so much. I've heard them all from various sources around the country as well as here, locally. The main thing was just trying to get the understanding and appreciation for what we, as laypeople, desired to be nourished by.

But in 2001, matching the underutilized downtown space with long unrequited requests from this group, Archbishop Brunett agreed to a single Sunday Latin Mass in St. Joseph's chapel. A key lay leader in this effort later reflected on this "tremendously gratifying" decision:

> [Archbishop Brunett] felt that these folks had been asking for a long time, here's a location ... we'll see whether or not it works. Allow them—under difficult circumstances, in terms of its location, and only a single Mass as opposed to a parish—and then see where it goes. And then, we'll see after that. . . .. It was tremendously gratifying to have that initial Mass, and then have the benefits from it. It was tremendously difficult for us, having a location without a parking lot in a bad part of town, at that point, and coordinating it all without any other staff. But it was, again, very gratifying. And spiritually fulfilling.

And so, for seven years, Catholics met in the Josephinum chapel for a TLM celebrated by a willing Jesuit priest. In time, "starved for the other sacraments," they shifted their attention to the goal of a personal parish.

Steady requests from Seattle's traditionalist Catholics—by then numbering in the hundreds—were bolstered by the apostolic letter *Summorum Pontificum* in 2007 and relationships with Una Voce and the Priestly Fraternity of Saint Peter (FSSP). The latter was founded in 1988 to train and send out priests who offer Mass according to the traditional Roman rite. FSSP priests have worked exhaustively to build the presence of TLM personal parishes throughout the world. Seattle's Latin Mass approval made the archdiocese prime grounds for personal parish activism.[18]

Archbishop Brunett described the conundrum he faced when this small but persistent group of Seattle's Catholics requested the Latin Mass, and why, eventually, a personal parish offered the best solution:

> We don't have a lot of people in the diocese [who want the TLM]. And with all the priests, I couldn't find anybody to volunteer to do this! And so the only way to provide—as the Holy Father asked us to provide ministry for those people who are still making transition into the more contemporary liturgical celebration— we wanted to provide an opportunity. . . . If we are going to be able at all to fulfill that responsibility, we need to establish a personal parish, not a geographic parish. It brings people from all over.

The readiness of an FSSP priest was pivotal in the Archbishop's decision to move forward with a TLM personal parish. Persistent lay advocacy from Seattle's traditionalist Catholics established the need. They had the people, the priest, the (temporary) place, and the funds. Archbishop Brunett invited the Priestly Fraternity of Saint Peter into the diocese to establish and staff a personal parish for the TLM. The move signaled formal, archdiocesan approval of traditional form of liturgy in response to Seattle Catholics' long-stated requests.

North American Martyrs was dedicated in 2008 as a TLM personal parish. It was Seattle's first personal parish to be established since the 1983 Code of Canon Law took effect. The parish's 34-year-old pastor, ordained just four years prior, arrived with experience having already served in two TLM personal parishes elsewhere. North American Martyrs' initial "quasi" parish status reflected the initial absence of a dedicated church building, an issue that continued to trouble the Catholic community as the young pastor lobbied for a space with a parking lot and out of the "bad part of town." As an archdiocesan leader later put it:

> [The new pastor] didn't like the place, nor did the people coming. Because being downtown—and numbers of them obviously not from here, or from nearby—saw the place as dangerous, and dirty, and so forth. It took a couple of years to find a suitable place for them. We moved that community out of here, up to another parish in north Seattle. And when it was moved, it became our first personal parish: North American Martyrs. It was established by Archbishop Burnett as a personal parish for those who were attracted to or drawn to the old Mass.

Seattle's first personal parish found life after thirteen years of petitioning for Mass and another seven to get a personal parish: some twenty years in the making. Una Voce announced their success proudly on its webpage, their goal finally realized:

> The establishment of a personal parish has been our (Una Voce of Western Washington) organization's prayerful goal for over twenty years and we offer our sincere thanks to Archbishop Brunett for his granting of permission to invite the FSSP into the archdiocese. . ... We are blessed, and so very grateful.[19]

Lay Catholics had convinced a bishop to make their vision a reality.

Seattle's TLM community's success in getting a personal parish set a new precedent in the archdiocese. Theirs was a pioneering organizational option to accommodate specialized communities of archdiocesan Catholics. The laity (albeit with support from a national, well-organized, and well-resourced community of priests) had converted a long-time, multi-bishop "no" to a "yes." The success of TLM Catholics in Seattle, moreover, enabled further mobilization with spillover effects. More personal parishes.

When Seattle's TLM Catholics moved to a new location in northern Seattle, coterminous with personal parish establishment, they left the Josephinium's downtown chapel space empty. Archbishop Brunett expressed new ideas for the space as a center where business people could gather and dialogue on church and culture. The area's religious orders—limited in human and financial capital—could not take the lead. But with the support and entrepreneurial spirit of the archbishop's vicar for clergy, conversations began for an innovative, diocesan, downtown parish. A lay leader described the entrepreneurial priest (and eventual pastor of the social mission personal parish) as follows:

> [He] did his doctorate in psychology on hope. He's known of the need for a parish in central downtown for a long, long time. He's been the vicar for clergy for a great while. The occasional planting of seeds was a long part of his patient ministry in that regard.

This priest's position in the diocese offered a strategic platform from which to plant seeds, in synergy with Archbishop Brunett's own vision.

Once the idea moved forward, the first question was what the new parish's boundaries would be. The targeted space (the Josephinum) was not far from a thriving territorial parish. The archbishop consulted canon lawyers to learn what his options were, in light of the recent TLM personal parish establishment. Archbishop Brunett shared that "the concept, or the definition of a personal parish kind of appealed to me" as a way to meet specialized needs. Describing himself as "not an expert in canon law," he consulted canon lawyers. "Anybody that I talked to said this was a perfectly legitimate process. I wanted to use it. I think it's done a lot of good." Another insider to the process summarized the negotiation:

> Rather than take on the issue of boundaries, the archbishop then said, "Well, we'll just make it a personal parish." Personal, of course, meaning just that it's anybody that might live, work, pass through, is connected to downtown Seattle.

A personal parish offered a creative and canonically sound solution to create a parish that would fall inside another parish's boundaries. "It's an idea that's in canon law. It's a good idea," said the archbishop.

Personal parish designation resolved the question of territoriality and boundaries, explained the named pastor:

> [A personal parish] had never been a part of my mind. I had assumed it'd be the downtown church. And [the archbishop] brought up this whole notion of personal parish, and it made sense. It was a little bit different.

The next step to grassroots action was financial, given the need to renovate the space. As the pastor recollects: "Once we got our first one million dollar gift, the archbishop determined the place was viable, financially. He had no question about its viability as far as parishioners, and the need for ministry downtown, particularly with the population growth down here." Christ Our Hope celebrated its first Mass in 2010.

Once personal parishes were established in Seattle to serve Catholics who wanted the TLM and to meet the social needs of downtown, it was difficult to continue to deny similarly justified requests from Seattle's longtime ethnic "faith communities." As a diocesan staffer shared: "The question came up: If the archbishop established a personal parish for an English-speaking parish in downtown Seattle, then what about the Koreans, and the Vietnamese?" The faith communities had experienced exponential growth and were financially viable. They, too, had the people, the priest, the place, and the funds.

Evidence and rationale in hand, the archdiocese's director of the Office of Multicultural Communities, himself Vietnamese, presented a convincing case for ethnic personal parishes. If a mostly white social mission and mostly white TLM community were granted personal parish status, what rationale could prevent the equal treatment of nonwhite ethnic communities who had long been meeting in a similar, non-territorial fashion?

Convinced, Archbishop Brunett expediently and simultaneously granted formal parish status to three more personal parishes: two for Seattle's Korean Catholics, and one for the area's Vietnamese Catholics.

The Seattle case showcases institutional decision-making in today's American Catholic Church. Clearly, the bishop, acting within the limits of canon law, formed the linchpin of approval (or denial) of personal parish status. The hinge moved one way. Top-down decision making mattered immensely, both in the long-standing "no" and in the eventual "yes." At the grassroots, Catholics convened for years around specialized purposes, absent parish status. The need was there. Local and translocal advocacy (as high as the Vatican) mobilized a case for personal parish status. Entrepreneurial leaders and priests with elite access and positions in the diocese brought forward the needs and desires of lay Catholics.

What mattered more? Hierarchical decision-making by the bishop, or Seattle Catholics' grassroots mobilization? When I asked one insider this question, he conjectured that it was both "top-down and grassroots, and on different timelines"; that the archbishop had offered "a very attentive response of graciousness to murmurings." But power and privilege matter in this narrative. The first personal parish successes enjoyed comparative advantage: they were overwhelmingly white Catholic groups, wielding substantial financial capital as well as social capital through extant networks. It is not insignificant that Seattle's Asian communities began asking for personal parishes decades prior to anyone else, but were granted parish status last.

The mixture of Seattle's personal parish types also suggests that getting to "yes" for any personal parish, as opposed to "no" for all personal parishes, is the most important first step. Once one personal parish is established, future appeals hold an increased likelihood of success. This signals that the route to new organizational forms is more about institutional process than it is about particular ideological bents.

STRATEGIZING PERSONAL PARISHES FROM ABOVE AND BELOW

Personal parishes reveal institutional determinism and its limits. A bishop's authority is a necessary but typically insufficient factor in predicting parish establishment. Lay and ordained Catholics' activism, organized movement, and entrepreneurial efforts inject agency into diocesan decision-making. Catholics make claims. Bishops adjudicate those claims through an interlocking rationale for meeting diocesan need. While the process is both top-down and bottom-up, the success of the latter is wholly dependent upon the route of the former.

Individual personal parish origins reveal an intertwined path of authority and lay input. Personal parish decisions are indelibly linked to a wider web: the diocese, with a bishop at the helm. As the Seattle case reveals, a single Catholic community's path to personal parish status (or not) intermingles with that of others in the diocese. Individual Catholics (priests, too) focus narrowly on with their own communities. This outsources, or upsources, management and strategic thought about pastoral planning to a higher, meso-organizational level: the diocese, not the parish. Bishops view all pieces in the game simultaneously, their moves contingent upon every piece therein.

Lay Catholics and individual priests don't typically strategize at this level. Exemplifying this is the somewhat surprising lack of knowledge that many pastors have about other personal parishes in their diocese. The following exchange is fairly typical on this front:

> TCB: As the pastor, do you see [your personal parish] as having anything in common with other personal parishes in the archdiocese? [Names of parishes]—do you see any commonality there?
> [Name] is a personal parish, it's not territorial? I didn't know that.

Strategizing parish decisions on the whole falls to the bishop. Bishops centralize decision-making to determine how to deploy (or deflect) personal parish requests. One bishop articulates his holistic mindfulness about parishes:

> I think [the personal parish option] prepares a diocese to be responsive to the needs of the church. I mean, I think it says "Here is how we are ready and·willing." And canonically, this is something we can do. So, it gives us a real strategy. Then, second: it allows for those of us who are on the administrative side, in the leadership part, to make decisions that are, say, appropriate.

Diocesan strategy regarding parishes emerges through deliberation and practice in subsidiarity, if not via formal policy.

To the extent that local Catholics understand this dynamic, their petitions may bear more fruit. One Vietnamese personal parish pastor describes diligently voicing a need until finally the right moment—a church closure—presented the opportunity. "Two things happened at the same time: they saw the need, we also expressed this to them, and then they saw the opportunity open." A lay leader from a social mission personal parish lauds "administrators being open to the needs of the people," compared to "a bishop that isn't receptive to a personal parish, or lets these [needs] go unheard."

Consolidated decision-making that rests mostly in elite diocesan leaders' hands results in unpredictable personal parish outcomes. Some question this ad hoc approach. One multicultural director in a large New England diocese, for example, wonders whether a recent personal parish was "a mistake," admitting that "it was an easy way out of a difficult situation." Another diocesan leader exalts strategic planning whenever possible, "to implement some of our best practices," particularly when it comes to serving minority communities of Catholics. This will "ensure that the local church understands the big picture."

A diocesan planner voices the goal of an explicit policy on personal parishes. Current practice leads to uncertainty (or unfairness):

> If you're able to develop a strategy, do so! Going ad hoc doesn't work! I say, we're doing it, but that doesn't mean I'm proud of it. You have to be able to image what kind of a church you want in 50 years. And if you want a Church that's segmented, and divided, then you may get that. On the other hand, if you build into this certain protocol/criteria/litmus tests—whatever—of where things are in the life cycle, and you deal with it before the death cycle comes. . . . The people know from the beginning that this is a pastoral response to a current pastoral need, and that that pastoral need may not always exist. And therefore, this is, perhaps, temporary. Because once you canonically establish a parish, it's very hard to destroy it, really.

The lack of a coherent strategy toward personal parishes is not necessarily born of a lack of desire for one.

CONCLUSION: THE SOCIAL SOURCES OF INNOVATION AND POWER OF INSTITUTIONAL ELITES

Absent a policy beyond canon law—and with foreseeable turnover in bishop leadership—American Catholic dioceses will continue to grapple with whether, how, and for whom to establish personal parishes. Demographic changes beg new needs and conditions. Non-parish lay collectives act as incubators for eventual personal parishes.[20] Entrepreneurial activity may convince bishops to try pioneer organizations unlike previous forms.[21] Once a bishop responds in the affirmative—and once a diocese has a new personal parish—the likelihood of future ones increases. Personal parishes thereafter are path-dependent: linked in rational and subjective process to earlier parish decisions. Prior foundings signal an opportunity structure that local Catholics can then use to legitimate future requests. While not guaranteed, they may benefit from what social movement scholars call spillover effects.[22]

The logic behind bishops' personal parish decisions is grounded in subsidiarity but also a meso-level, interorganizational (as opposed to congregational) needs and resource assessment. Institutional decisions—not unlike those made by CEOs at the helm of multisite corporate entities—consider multiple moving parts, serving dispersed and heterogeneous needs. Sociologist Martin Ruef suggests that the emergence of new forms of organization depends upon: (1) the organizational field within which they sit; (2) existing forms (new forms must mesh with preexisting cultural beliefs); (3) the density of organizations; and (4) the demands of constituents.[23]

Mapping this framework onto what we have learned in this chapter: (1) personal parish decisions depend upon an interlocking diocesan landscape serving changing lay needs; (2) past deployment of personal parishes predicts future deployment; (3) a higher number of parishes (or excess churches) encourages personal parishes to a point ... but having "enough" parishes discourages them; and (4) lay Catholics and priests influence decisions through networking and mobilization at the grassroots.

Through all four factors, the Catholic Church exerts institutional pressure over how local believers organize. Emergent forms require institutional leaders' action and approval as a regulatory marker. The authority of the local bishop matters immensely for personal parish outcomes.

CHAPTER 4
Difference

There is such racial diversity in the Catholic Church, and that's one of the great gifts of the Church: that you can celebrate that diversity in a liturgy that is attentive to your culture. That speaks to you. That allows you—in essence—to have full, complete, total participation. Isn't that what liturgy is about? Full, active, and conscious participation. And so, it allows one who is African American to come here and to celebrate that . . . to truly worship in a way in which they can fully, actively and consciously participate.

—Pastor, African American Personal Parish

* * *

They had this huge celebration [for the Feast of Our Lady of Guadalupe]. The next day—December 13th—[the pastor] goes to the parish, and everything is gone! All the flowers, everything—just gone! He's like, "This is weird." All the decorations in the church, flowers, and everything. Well, this was their first celebration [in the new personal parish]. Whenever they had a celebration in another parish, they weren't allowed to leave their things. They were told that, "If you don't clean up, you're going to have to pay to have people clean up." They didn't get that this [new parish] was theirs. They cleaned up everything, because they thought, "No, we've always had to clean up. We were never allowed to leave anything, because it wasn't ours." So [the pastor] had to actually tell people, "This is yours! You can leave the flowers as long as you want! You can leave Our Lady's picture up as long as you want! You don't have to clean up." That will tell you what they were living in those parishes: "You're renting here. And after you have your party, clean up, and get out."

—Diocesan Multicultural Director

* * *

Were each American Catholic parish a 100-person microcosm of today's adult Catholic population, 59 parishioners would be white, 34 Latino,

3 black, 3 Asian, and 2 of mixed/other racial backgrounds. Roughly 27 of our hypothetical parishioners would be foreign-born, another 15 with at least one foreign-born parent. Compared to the US population generally, our hypothetical parish is less white, more Latino, less black, comparably Asian, and more heavily first- or second-generation immigrant. American Catholics are a racially diverse lot, and increasingly so.[1]

Local religious organizations are a harbinger of institutional responses to racial heterogeneity. How Catholic leaders respond to the needs of diverse and diversifying local adherents outlays a modern approach to accommodating difference. Introducing purpose-based (personal) parishes alongside place-based (territorial) parishes demonstrates an institutional strategy that formally balances generalism and specialism. This chapter walks through the unrealized ideal of the generalist, place-based, territorial parish as an integrated, welcoming, multicultural home for all. Seeing this helps to explain the corresponding emergence of specialist, niche-constrained personal parishes that deemphasize assimilation. While the social responses to diversity are many, this book's focus is structural: how America's largest religion is reshaping local organizations in response to racial and other kinds of difference.

THE TERRITORIAL PARISH AS GENERALIST ORGANIZATION

Enculturation—rather than uniformity—marks the Catholic Church's move into modernity and globalization, post-Vatican II. "Catholicity" is the term used in the Catholic Catechism to describe how "the mystery celebrated in the liturgy is one, but the forms of its celebration are diverse."[2] Jesuit theologian Cardinal Avery Dulles writes that the idea "is a unity among individuals and groups who retain their distinctive characteristics, who enjoy different spiritual gifts, and are by that very diversity better equipped to serve one another and thus advance the common good."[3] Cultural diversity need not be minimized or shunned in favor of assimilation, but celebrated for enriching the whole.

The territorial parish would seem to be a good starting point for generating the kind of multiracial, multicultural spaces envisioned by some as "an answer to the problem of race."[4] If a church can effectively meet the needs of all residing in its catchment area, then surely it would encourage interaction, communication, networking, and friendship across lines of difference. Theoretically, territorial parish assignment offsets the racial partitioning that may otherwise result from congregational, preference-based belonging. A narrative of parish-as-home evokes a sense of comfort and welcome: a place where diversity is celebrated, bridged, and mitigated. As a community built among fellow Catholics, diverse expressions need not be at odds with unity: in the parish, all have a place. [5]

Serving its heterogeneous, geographically bound Catholic population, the territorial parish is a *generalist* organization.[6] One size fits all. Decreed by place rather than purpose, the territorial parish operates among a wide range of conditions, serving the spectrum that is the local Catholic populous. In our hypothetical parish (further diversification notwithstanding), this means that it adapts to the needs of those 34 Latino parishioners, integrates the liturgical celebrations of those 3 Asian parishioners, aids the incorporation of those 27 first-generation immigrants, and so on, making sure that everyone gets along in the process. In short, the territorial parish as generalist organization is tasked with meeting a tremendous set of diverse needs.

This pastoral challenge has spawned a veritable cottage industry of practitioner-oriented guides for intercultural competency. "Building Intercultural Competence for Ministers" and "Best Practices for Shared Parishes" are among the training titles published and promoted by the US Conference of Catholic Bishops. Learning a second language is now standard in seminary. Parish supersizing means that priests who are mostly white and all male wear many hats to serve their increasingly multicultural lay clientele.[7]

Sociologists of religion find that Catholic parishes are more likely to be multiracial when compared to their Protestant counterparts. Nearly a third of US parishes offer Mass in a language other than English. Using a common sociological rubric for "multiracial"—that no single racial group comprises more than 80 percent of the congregation—15 percent of Catholic parishes nationwide are multiracial (the other 85 percent, not). Catholic parishes are three times more likely than Protestant congregations to classify as multiracial. The "80 percent" rule stems from the idea that a second racial group achieves critical mass and influence at 20 percent. This predicts greater likelihood for contact among individuals from different racial backgrounds.[8]

But typical classifications for multiracial congregations can be misleading when it comes to Catholic parishes. Common space does not imply common community. Catholic parishes are much larger, on average. They have many more service times. Compared to racially integrated spaces described in other denominations,[9] Catholic parishes are often better described as separate communities sharing the same church building. They constitute what Brett Hoover calls the "shared parish": "parishes with two or more cultural groups, each with distinct Masses and ministries, but who share the same parish facilities."[10] Different cultural groups worship apart from one another.

This means that, for example, Latino parishioners might attend the noon Mass in Spanish, play in their choir, frequent the post-Mass social time, and congregate for special feast days in the parish hall. White parishioners from the same territorial parish, meanwhile, might attend the 7 a.m., 9 a.m., or 11 a.m. Mass in English, sing in their own choir, send their children to special programming, and gather for post-Mass social hours. It is quite possible—probable, even—that the 7 a.m. English-speaking white Mass attendees have no idea that Mass is offered in another language at "their" parish later that day, let alone know or interact with any parishioners who attend then.

The high odds of interracial interaction predicted by sociologists' multiracial congregation definitions seem nearly absent in this context. Interaction between parishioners of different cultural groups—distinguished here by race and language—would be limited to exchanges in the parking lot, if at all. Minority Catholic groups, in particular, may be rendered invisible, given the "worst" Mass times, forced to compete with larger groups for space, and underrepresented on parish committees. Fellow parishioners may worship in the exact same pews . . . unseen, unheard, and unknown to the dominant parish populous. For this reason, predictions of integration in multiracial Catholic parishes are often distorted, if not wholly false.[11]

The territorial parish frequently unifies Catholics more symbolically than practically across racial and ethnic lines. Parishes containing multiple racial groups may operate more like "parallel parishes" or a "community of communities," to use the phrasing of former Pope John Paul II. Different group of parishioners—separated by Mass time—retain their cultural distinctiveness. Maybe, suggests religion scholar Kathleen Garces-Foley, this counts as a success. US bishops tacitly promote a "community of communities" vision for American parishes. But interviews with personal parish participants (territorial parish refugees, if you will) lend a more skeptical conclusion. While the notion of catholicity does not imply uniformity (or even integration, apparently), it certainly cannot be meant to imply structural inequality, or institutional racism.[12]

THE UNREALIZED IDEAL OF THE TERRITORIAL PARISH

The unrealized ideal of integrated, territorial parishes represents a core reason why personal parishes exist at all. Most personal parish pastors and diocesan representatives view the territorial parish as ideal for organizing local Catholics and accommodating difference. Interviewees, by and large, do not wish to replace the Church's principle of territoriality with one of pure congregationalism, where all Catholics can pick a parish right for them.

Take, for example, one proponent of the territorial model, a Hispanic ministry director for a northeastern diocese. He expresses his vision:

> Basically, we want the parish to be a whole community, a comprehensive community. Not just the English-speaking, or the Hispanic. Some of the parishes we have are being heavily populated by Filipinos, or Koreans, or people from Haiti. We want a parish for everyone. We are baptized Catholics, and this is our home.

Another pastor of a Vietnamese personal parish offers a similar vision of the territorial parish ideal:

> I want the church to have all kinds of people in one church. That's ideal. That's perfect, and in the image of the Church. All people speak different languages, but we worship one God. Together, together, around the other. The priest says Mass, and different backgrounds, different ethnicities get together in one language. That's the ideal. That's ideal. That's the perfect image of a church. And I think, one day when the people feel . . . Maybe the fourth generation.

The territorial parish—diverse, welcoming, and shared—is the parish "on the hill."

In this idealized form, territorial Catholic parishes model an integrated, multicultural space. Ethnicity and other forms of difference matter in that they add value to the shared experience. They don't separate groups holding different levels of power. They extend equal access to church facilities, to representation on pastoral councils, to authentic inclusion in all parish activities, and to meaningful friendships. Differences need not be rendered invisible, but incorporated proportionately across parish structures and leadership.

But if so many uphold territoriality (the generalist organization), why establish personal parishes, with specialized purposes? If territorial parishes are the solution to cultural accommodation, why do personal parishes grow in number across dioceses in the United States each year? And why would lay Catholics petition for them as their preferred parish home?

Unfortunately, the envisioned ideal of a territorial parish merging a community of communities is often artificial at best, hostile at worst.[13] This is the lesser-told story of territorial parishes, but one to which numerous personal parishioners bear witness. One pastor, having previously led a mission for a community of Chinese Catholics within a majority white territorial parish, tells of how the parish felt like it was "not yours at all." He expands:

You're always somehow in another people's place. And you feel that *all* the time. For instance, we were using the classes and it was communicated there was a change of the keys. So I'm trying to find the principal . . . I was told that she was going to give me a key. In the Easter celebration, we didn't have enough room. You try to keep good relationships with everybody. This is not your place. You want to respect—have special respect for these people. They allow you to be here, and so you want to keep the relationship.

The Chinese community had worshipped there for thirty years: hardly a new or itinerant group. And yet still, it felt "not your place." No parish sign displayed Chinese characters: "If they were trying, you'd see Chinese. 'They are welcome'?! If this is home for them, *Chinese characters* is home! We need to be more welcoming!"

Another pastor from a personal parish observes that "If you're sharing the same church, it can be kind of cumbersome. Because, well, to be honest, not everyone looks at the other benevolently. They have an ideological . . . I don't know . . . I wouldn't go so far as to say "hatred"—I haven't seen any foaming at the mouth, but. . . ." Interactions among groups in a single parish are often fraught with tension—a "permanent crucible of grief where resentments and frustrations dominate the scene over time," observes Hoover. Meaningful integration remains minimal in Latino-serving parishes, too, generating Mass isolation.[14]

Differences in parishioner needs—especially language—necessitate different skills. But when more than one priest serves a territorial parish, this can exacerbate a feeling of separation. Interviewees describe this as being particularly acute with international priests. Parishioners who speak one language will go to one priest; those who speak another will go to the other. "The risk is to create a parallel church," warns one multicultural director in a southern diocese, "And that doesn't work." This can "create a division. It is one body, but is divided in two. So, that is not good."

The more diverse a population, the more difficult it is for a generalist organization to appeal to all. The territorial parish cannot be everything to everyone. But the challenge of living as the consistently underserved or invisible exception—the special request, the culturally different, the linguistically isolated, the late or leftover Mass time—can be particularly acute among racial and ethnic minorities. Code switching to fit into predominantly white Catholic spaces can also be taxing. One Latino pastor explains how minority Catholics carry this special burden:

> The opposite extreme of niche Catholicism is, just, everybody's all alike. "You're welcome: leave your culture at the door." Well, we're not! We come with our culture, and asking people to do that is a disrespect! It's like you have to put on other clothes to come in. You have to stop being yourself. There's an inauthenticity about it, which is why I think a lot of Hispanics are drawn to evangelical churches. Because they're Hispanic churches—Different religion, but they're allowed to feel at home in their culture.

One African American pastor echoes the plight of racial minorities in predominantly white Catholic spaces:

> You know, when I was at a conference [of priests], there were like a thousand people—and four blacks. You know, that's all I need to say. That's standard: being Catholic, and being the only black person in the place. You don't have to say anything else. Just say that. But that's not something you're going to get at another church. A white person's not going to stand there and say that. A priest, he's not going to necessarily . . . Too often, they don't appreciate it! You know, they can have a black parishioner that's been coming to their church forever and just *not get* how they might feel.

In our earlier hypothetical of a representative territorial parish of American Catholics, black parishioners would number just three in 100.

Time and space emerge as central points of contention in shared parishes. Interviewees frequently describe having been given secondary consideration in decisions about facility use. This usually translates to accessing main spaces only during off-peak times like Sunday afternoon, when the parking lot and sanctuary space are not otherwise occupied. As one Vietnamese pastor put it, "They give the Vietnamese people the spare time that they [the white, English-speaking parishioners] don't use." Comparing their experience in a shared parish to what they now have in the personal parish, another pastor shares:

> It's different, in the sense that we can plan our schedule ourselves. Because when you come to an American Church, it's kind of like random choice: you don't have a first choice in terms of schedule. But here, you have a first choice! You can pick whatever time is the best for you. In other instance, you have to usually have permission from the pastor when you say 'Okay, I want to worship at this

particular time,' or if you want to use the facility the same day. I mean— it's not prioritized for your community.

Decisions in territorial parishes regarding which group gets which Mass time are most often not made by minority groups themselves. Their proportionately smaller status dictates their deprioritized facility use. Specialized groups take what's leftover.

Even parking lots can start battles, as one Mass ends and another begins. A personal parish pastor reflects:

> You have all the conflicts that come up just sharing the same spot. Like, you have limited parking, so that means the next Mass people are just driving around until they give up their parking spot, and the other ones are taking their time. And then there's even some nastiness, where they basically look at the others as intruders.

In one example, a Chinese Catholic group—in the minority at their parish—volunteered to park at a public transportation station miles away then ride public transport to the church, so as not to occupy limited parking spaces. They did so in gratitude for use of the church, but one leader quietly expressed her displeasure about it.

Beyond leftover Mass times and parking lot traffic jams, Catholic communities in the minority may also have trouble accessing other needed facilities. Belonging to a parish means accommodating different youth groups, religious education, celebrations, and so forth. One pastor recalled a conflict that arose in his shared parish: "The Spanish Youth Group wanted to meet there on Sunday afternoons. Would it be possible—could they unlock the basement of the parish hall so that they could use the bathroom?' . . . 'No.'" In another example, a pastor shares how his community quickly outsized the facilities available to them in their shared parish:

> We kept growing. And of course, we had then started religious education classes. . . . We had to rent the schools, the classrooms, but we only could use them on Sunday morning. And when they were being used by [the larger parish community], we couldn't use them.

Clashing communities of Catholics may view each other as the "other" and may figure that the situation is temporary. For some, it is. Absent personal parish status, a community may move from parish to parish to accommodate their specialized ministry.

Even while finding ways to operate in the interstices of an otherwise packed church schedule, some express dismay at persistent outsider treatment. One priest recalls a poignant moment of discrimination:

> I remember sitting with the maintenance man one day in the parish, and he was complaining about a party that was in the school hall, and he had to clean up some stuff. And I said, "I understand. We'll talk to them, and make sure they clean up better next time." And he basically said, "How long are these people going to be hanging around?" And I said, "Do you realize that if these folks weren't here, this parish would be closed?" And he said, "Well, we could use the chapel for Mass." Now, the chapel is a small room that seats about thirty people. In his mind, that would be *better*. So, this idea of being separate—of having our own place—is really ingrained in people.

Minority Catholic communities in shared parishes risk becoming a disempowered "them" against an empowered "us." Language, generational, cultural, and class differences materialize in intra-parish social division. Partitioning reifies in ways more harmful than just Mass times.

Minority disadvantage may also play out financially in territorial parishes, particularly with uneven contributions across racial groups. If attendees from one Mass time contribute less, others may conclude that they are owed less in parish decision-making. One diocesan director of Hispanic ministry criticizes this, sharing that:

> In some places, the English-speaking community says, "We are the ones who donate the money, and we don't want that need there." We are a church! We are Christian! It's not just for my group! It's for the body of Christ.

Financial disparities also matter in parish staffing. One leader in Hispanic ministry said (with dismay) that parishes share responsibility and leadership, "but for the Spanish speakers, it's all volunteer, and for the English speakers, it's all paid." This finding is confirmed by Hosffman Ospino's national study of parishes with Hispanic ministry.[15]

Pastoral councils, required after Vatican II as a means of ensuring lay input, can also represent parishioner voices unequally. Election ballots with English instructions exclude parishioners with limited English-reading abilities. Some parishes create entirely separate pastoral councils for each parish community. One pastor at a shared Latino/white parish described how their voting long disenfranchised Spanish-speakers:

We started making ballots, and the secretary said, "How many ballots should we make?" I said, "Well, you need this many at the 5:30, you need this many at the 8:00 . . ." And she just looked at me, and she said, "But Father, we don't vote at the Spanish Masses." And I just . . . ! I said, "This year, you will."

This same pastor surmised that "if [shared governance] is not reflected in the finances of the parish, it doesn't work."

When minority parish groups grow in number, strengthening access to decision-making and parish resources, others may perceive the parish as being "taken-over." Scholars of race describe this dynamic as the minority-group threat effect.[16] This also conjures what sociologist Korie Edwards has observed in multiracial congregations: they work, so long as minority groups surrender to white advantage.[17] Pastors take care to avoid sending the message that white Catholics are "losing their parish."

One African American parish even felt this tension as its ministry to Latino parishioners grew. The pastor describes:

[Latino newcomers] weren't interacting—especially the adults, who were not fluent in English. So, they couldn't interact with the African Americans. So, the African Americans think, "Well, [Latinos'] numbers are increasing, they're taking over the church." That's the common phrase—"taking over." And the Spanish are like, "eh? . . . You know . . . What's that"? It's just because of the numbers— the numbers have grown and grown. And, because of the growing numbers, then you sort of have to cater to some of the needs of the growing numbers.

Unfamiliarity with cultural practices can further exacerbate this disconnect.

Just as minority Catholic groups occupy the "other," white parishioners and white parishes emerge colloquially as the mainstream, the default, the "American" parish. Invariably, every reference to the "American" parish made by interviewees—both white and non-white—worked as a code word for the white, English-speaking parish. Predominantly Latino parishes were not called American parishes. Vietnamese parishes were not called American parishes, citizenship or long-term residency notwithstanding. The discursive default among American Catholics is a predominantly white, Novus Ordo parish. Worship practices elsewhere are filtered through the dominant habitus of white, non-immigrant social groups.[18]

This social construction of a mainstream parish embeds what sociologist Eduardo Bonilla-Silva calls the "racial grammar of everyday life."[19] The hegemonic assumption, the standard, the default is whiteness. This presumption is especially problematic for a Catholic Church comprised increasingly of Latino Americans and a growing number of Asian Americans, not to mention black Catholics, long excluded from the US Catholic Church. When more than a third of Catholics are Hispanic, constructing white experiences as the default reproduces racial privilege.

Difference drives division in American parishes. Division drives inequality. When difference, division, and inequality fall along racial and ethnic lines, they produce injustice and discrimination in even the most well-meaning congregational scenarios. Descriptions relayed here do not represent all territorial parishes, or even the majority of them; most interviewees belong to personal parishes for a reason. But their stories are too-often silenced or overlooked when presenting the ideal vision of the multiracial, multicultural, territorial parish—and discounted when advocating against personal parishes in contemporary American Catholicism.

THE PERSONAL PARISH AS SPECIALIST ORGANIZATION

Given the unrealized ideal of the territorial parish—and given that some 85 percent of Catholic parishes in the United States consist almost wholly of one racial group—Catholics' lived practice suggests that a sense of unity may not always cross racial lines. The vast majority of church-going Catholics in the United States attend a parish where nearly everyone else looks like them. In a Church whose adherents are more racially diverse than the United States overall, territorial parishes fail to embed such diversity. This sets the stage for alternative structural responses to accommodating difference via the local parish.

Unlike the generalist organizational approach of territorial parishes, personal parishes are *specialist* organizations. They explicitly focus on a more narrow subgroup of American Catholics, whether by way of ethnicity, liturgical style, or otherwise. Specialist organizations cater to a segment of the whole: a niche audience or purpose.[20] Rather than aiming to meet everyone's needs, they intentionally target certain needs. One pastor summarizes how personal parishes differ:

> A geographical parish is generic, in some respects. I don't mean to describe the faith lives of Catholics as generic, but diocesan ministry is not necessarily specific. It is meant to carry . . . the Catholic Church mission to a certain area, whereas a personal parish has the ability to focus on a particular area.

Sociologists of religion note that niche specialization reduces competition with other congregations, thus increasing survival odds.[21]

This organizational model makes room for diversity in novel ways. First, personal parishes are formally decreed with a certain purpose. Their specialization is made explicit by name, not merely through choice or reputation. Personal parishes mark an accepted canonical deviation from the still-extant (and more common) territorial rule of local Catholic organization. They are purpose-based, not place-based. They are unabashedly focused on a more narrow set of parishioners.

Second, diocesan authorities regulate this specialization. This means that organizational forms are as much structural as they are cultural, determined by institutional elites rather than simply emergent of religious actors' agency. Personal parishes are closer to what sociologist Michael Emerson calls "mandated" multiracial congregations, formed "not from internal decisions, but from decisions made by an authority structure outside the congregation."[22] Rather than outsourcing specialization beyond the congregation,[23] personal parishes are designed to meet niche needs as parishes.

Third, personal parishes exist alongside territorial parishes in the same diocese. The presence of both generalist and specialist organizations demonstrates what organizational scholars call *resource partitioning*.[24] A heterogeneous market with heterogeneous tastes opens up pockets for concentration. Personal parishes serve needs unmet by territorial parishes. In this, specialist organizations capitalize on what Glenn Carroll and Anand Swaminathan call "resource space that lies outside the generalist target areas."[25] Generalist organizations need not crowd out specialists, but can actually enhance their vitality. The two organizational forms work interdependently.

Pushed and Pulled into Personal Parishes

Both "push" and "pull" factors lead Catholics into personal parishes. Discomfort or discrimination within territorial parishes pushes some Catholics out, stymied by attempts to fit in or gain power. Personal parishes can create a safe space—a parish home—where others understand; where Catholics need not "transcend" race to feel included.[26] One personal parish pastor shares how this motivates some black Catholics' personal parish belonging (first-generation black Catholic immigrants, in particular):

> Well, I think for the Africans, they chose this place because they saw African Americans. The same color skin. So, I think that was the first attraction. But then, later on, there was some conflict in the city. Because there was some news in our local paper about—you know—Africans' homes being stoned, and all that kind of stuff. So, there was some tension. Those first years, I think, are tough for the Africans.

Another pastor adds on this theme that "microaggressions are less [here in the personal parish], you know, from the other communities."

Cultural and social needs may pull Catholics toward specialized ministry only available within the context of a personal parish. Factors that attract Catholics to a personal parish supersede logistics, musical taste, and Mass times. What may look like pragmatic subtleties in fact reveal meaningful differences in how Catholics approach their faith and their Church. Put simply: different Catholics do Catholicism differently. These differences frequently fall along racial and ethnic lines. Ethnic exclusivity may operate as a consequence of being "who you are," surmises one diocesan multicultural director: "It happens because you believe you are who you are. . . . I don't think that they are, on purpose, excluding whites—but they are nurturing their identity. And it's a good thing." Similarly, a Vietnamese pastor states:

> I would say [uniracial parishes] are not a problem. It depends on the situation—
> the people, their background. It's not meant to divide out like, the white color,
> the blue color, the poor. No; we don't want to do that. And, at the same time . . .
> go where you feel comfortable! You're not being a racist; that's not what I'm try-
> ing to say. But, go where you feel more comfortable.

Cultural expressions of Catholicism, realized through individuals' identities, pull people into personal parishes that specifically serve them and others like them.

In the case of personal parishes that serve specific ethnic and national groups, their uniracial composition is neither happenstance nor wholly self-selected. It is intentional, known, decreed by the diocese, and integrated into the parish's explicit mission. Personal parishes are born of a similar spirit as the idealized territorial parish: the desire for a space where all feel welcome. Where Catholics feel at home. But they are *named, specialist organizations*, explicit in promising welcome and inclusion for a minority Catholic community.

By claiming and naming space, personal parishes convey the sentiment that minority Catholic communities are not a second-class citizens. That resources belong to you, rather than being shared or lent temporarily until someone else needs them. One diocesan director of Hispanic ministry says this makes people "feel validated and affirmed," "important," and that "the Church is honoring them."

Specialization manufactures a sense of formal welcome by identifying a parish's purpose. A name, a sign, a mission statement, a statue in your likeness . . . these are intentional markers of inclusion, suggesting that this is your place (see, for example, figures 4.1–4.3 depicting Virgin Mary statues encountered in visits to personal parishes).

FIGURE 4.1 Ethnic personal parishes integrate symbols meaningful to Catholics served there.

This can especially matter to first generation Americans. The majority of new personal parishes—three out of four—cater to ethnic populations, many heavily immigrant. One priest from a Polish parish and another Vietnamese multicultural director describe this specialized function:

> That's the reality of immigration—that the first generation needs that link with the old country. Denying that has been inhumane. You cannot take someone out of your tribe, and make him or her deny the reality of his or her tribe. And it does end up being mono-racial, but it's not the purpose! It's the side effect. Because you nurture your identity.

***

FIGURE 4.2 Ethnic personal parishes integrate symbols meaningful to Catholics served there.

> If we move to a city, we want to have our own house! We live, get comfortable, and then we can go to our neighbor and say "Hey, I'm a new neighbor." If you have to move in with a new neighbor right away, you sort of feel uncomfortable. I think it's the same thing.

Religious congregations can facilitate immigrants' welcome in a new society.[27]

Leaders express that ethnic personal parishes reconstitute a "home away from home" through shared identity, food, architecture, and language. Several interviewees echo this theme:

FIGURE 4.3 Ethnic personal parishes integrate symbols meaningful to Catholics served there.

We call that coming home. After working outside, people want to come home. People want to see each other. I think that's a welcome therapy—how to help people. They miss their home in Vietnam, their homeland. So, the parish not only fills a spiritual need, but also, they feel a piece of the land—a piece they can see they belong to.

* * *

To come into a church that's called "national," it's more than that: it feels like entering Portuguese country, Portuguese territory, so you are in Portugal. Because this church, if you look at it and see it, it was built exactly like the ones we have in Portugal. And so, it reminds us everywhere that we are Portuguese.

This is part of our background and part of our blood, brought to us—because it was built for people to feel at home.

*   *   *

There is a sense of identity for them. I think that's the mindset of immigrant: when they come here, they want to find a place where they can call home. Home is with their own people, and so they feel very comfortable.

Particularly for recent immigrants, these social, familial, and cultural orientations sustain connections to the native country. As one Korean pastor shares about his Korean parishioners, "they are really Korean at the beginning." American culture shock elevates the desire to be around others in the diaspora.

Language—itself a carrier of culture and religion—presents the most apparent and pressing rationale for a specialist religious organization. One Vietnamese pastor points out how "language helps the Vietnamese people, parishioners, hopefully, feel a bit more at home." Personal parishes can offer language-specific Masses every day of the week and multiple Masses each weekend.

Catholics frequently desire sacraments (Mass, baptism, confession, etc.) in the language they understand best. Intelligibility and participation underscores Vatican II's emphasis on the vernacular.[28] Catholics first learn to pray, connect to God, and embody meaningful rituals in their native language. "They feel more comfortable worshipping in their own language," says one Vietnamese multicultural director on the West coast. A Polish pastor shares similarly, "They tell me, 'Father, We speak English, but we cannot pray in English. We cannot go to confession in English.' Even with the children—they learn to pray in Polish." While first-generation immigrants build bilingual proficiency, the native language persists as the way many speak to God. One multicultural director shares:

> We will always need Spanish Masses, even if people are very fluent in English. Because people pray in the language of their heart, and the heart language is the language that you learn when you're growing up.

This idea underscores a rationale for personal parishes despite predicted linguistic assimilation over time.

In preserving language, personal parishes preserve culture. Evidence of this can be found even in personal parishes where English is predominant—for example, those serving black Catholics. Although these parishes also serve a variety of immigrants with distinctive linguistic needs, even the English Mass embeds specialized culture. One pastor of an African American personal parish tells how:

The use of language is different. The metaphors, the similes, the cadence, the innuendo, the body language, you know. ... There's a whole range of things that go into it. It's not necessarily as obvious—maybe you won't necessarily pick it up immediately, but it goes into it. So, yeah, we speak English. But we speak it differently, and we have different emphases, which gives a different meaning.

This pastor's own exuberant two-hour Mass affirms his description.

Personal parishes, moreover, offer a rare place where Catholics can fuse their ethnic and religious identities. An African American deacon, for example, describes how his parish's focus on African American culture and history enables black Catholics to be simultaneously black and Catholic:

Now, you have to remember that this Archdiocese is predominately Hispanic. Anglos and African Americans are minorities. So, if you're the majority, a lot of the focus is going to be on that culture. What happens to a race of people is— they have nowhere to go to really celebrate their culture, the richness of their heritage—what it means to be black and Catholic. *This* is the place that they can do that. Doesn't mean that they can't take part in any other liturgy, but here, they can come and know that they are home.

Language mediates understanding. In personal parishes, it reclaims a place for racial diversity in the American Catholic tradition.

A Parish Family

Personal parishes blend individual identities with collective experiences. Co-ethnic congregations enable groups of similarly-situated Catholics to convene, socialize, network, and build critical structures for social success and religious retention. To many parishioners, belonging to a personal parish means belonging to a family.

One Vietnamese pastor describes the sense of community forged in his personal parish, contrasting this to the dispersed Vietnamese population at the territorial parish of his youth:

Being a personal parish—we can do more. For example, we have weekday Masses, and then we have the different groups, or committees. We have our own Vietnamese Parish Pastoral Council. It gives us more chances to practice our faith, and to have a sense of what we call "big family," larger family, rather than just seeing each other once a week. Growing up as a member of a small community where we just gathered once a week on Sunday, just being a community within a parish. . . . It's not the same.

Interviewees use the family metaphor frequently to describe fellow parishioners, as this pastor of a Korean personal parish does:

We are like a family, because they need many things: to read a letter, to translate something, they need many information for life . . . So they get information from here. Social time is very important for us. Not only Mass. This is a social time. They exchange the information and help each other.

The communal experience of Catholicism builds connections with others to whom parishioners can relate. Bonds solidify parishioners' shared identity as Catholics and co-ethnics.

Sociologists as early as disciplinary founder Émile Durkheim have credited collective worship with this kind of communal power, coalesced even more so through shared ethnicity. Being together engenders a collective power or collective conscience, as Durkheim calls it—a strength in numbers, a whole greater than the sum of its parts. One Chinese priest summarizes how vital this collectivity is to faith retention:

Being together is an energy. If not, they just dissolve. In fact, some of my people that prefer to be, kind-of, more quiet Catholic life—they just go to an American community. They don't need to do nothing; they just go just to listen. You are here all the time, you are called to the sacristy! It's kind of . . . it is a high level commitment, yes it is. So, it is a powerful church.

The collective energy of the personal parish can elevate individual participation. Personal parishes afford the chance to convene as the majority in both numbers and power.

Using this collective strength, ethnic personal parishes incorporate a host of activities focused around cultural traditions, music, food, language lessons for youth, religious education integrating culturally specific variations of Catholicism, and social services most pressing to parishioners. Rolling carts sell Mexican treats just outside parish doors. A veritable farmers market transforms the parish hall of a Vietnamese parish. A roasted pig brings joy to the Mother's Day celebration of a Korean personal parish. The smell of tamales, rice cakes, or pho infuses the parish hall. Wigilia and Simbang Gabi Masses receive first scheduling priority. While possible to celebrate these traditions within the context of a territorial parish, they pressure limited resources within shared space that is not "ours." Personal parishes ensure space, inclusion, and a sufficient crowd.

The scale of these activities distinguishes personal parishes (whose decree is oriented to a single ethnic community) from shared territorial parishes. A comprehensive ministry can, in turn, enhance the overall quality of the parish experience for minority Catholics. One diocesan director of Hispanic ministry expresses this:

> There is a noticeable difference in terms of just the number of pastoral services that are available—the catechetical, the spiritual direction, the follow-up, the pastoral visits with the family, the one-on-one pastoral conversations—all that is a very rich pastoral experience. I hear from other feedback, from other parishes where there is that desire to have more opportunities to do that—to have a priest that they can talk to after Mass for a period of time, to have more catechetical programs through a priest, or other services. The difference is in the quality, in terms of the pastoral services. And also, it responds to the needs of the community. I've noticed that's the big difference.

Specialization enables personal parishes to better target needs. Personal parishes tailor priorities to a dedicated population. Parishioners find a safe place from which to bring their own and their families' needs to the table. The parish is an extension of Catholics' identity, person, family, nation, heritage, and legacy, even. Parishioners belong.

Personal Parishes and (Non-)Assimilation

Working to preserve culture, personal parishes today operate as a *non-assimilative form of religious organization*. Like a shared ethnic enclave, personal parishes fill a quintessential role of providing sanctuary and cultural preservation among co-ethnics.

In some ways, this function is similar to that of their erstwhile (mostly European) national parish counterparts. A diocesan pastoral planner explains:

> The church for [new immigrants] is taking on a role that the church may have taken on in the '50s and early '60s for other people. The church was the center of social life, the center of academic life, the center of spiritual life, of course—and any outreach or anything that was related to that.

But older national parishes were strategically isolationist, shoring up Catholics' capital and institutional capacity in a heavily Protestant America. This facilitated generations of social mobility and "Americanization."

Today's personal parishes operate in a context less hostile to Catholicism, but nonetheless demanding in social pressures to embrace dominant

American norms (whether for immigrants or any Catholics of color).[29] Personal parishes intentionally act as a counterforce against dominant cultural narratives. One Korean pastor describes how "traditions and cultures are shared here. Whereas, if they were a fish in somebody else's water, they wouldn't have the same community." Personal parishes do not require Catholics to blend or integrate into shared spaces where non-whites may be in the minority.

The importance of a non-assimilative space is acknowledged especially when it comes to younger Catholics, whose exposure and choices will carry on ethnic culture (or not). One diocesan director of ministry to black Catholics describes how assimilative pressures leave his parishioners fearful that their language and traditions will not survive beyond the first generation:

> [Fear of culture loss] is the primary reason why the African Catholics are very, very focused on worshipping together as a community. They are terrified that their children who are first-generation American-born are going to completely lose their language, lose their culture, and become completely assimilated. That is one of their big fears.

Another pastor expresses a similar urgency to ensure that both parents and children can "maintain our identity as Vietnamese American, even though we've become American. We still want to keep the root, retain the root." As specialist organizational spaces, personal parishes facilitate social and religious formation that does not come at the expense of distinctive ethnic culture.

The counterargument is that dedicated, co-ethnic personal parishes undermine racial integration and Americanization. If Catholics build separatist organizational worlds, does this not stifle their success in plural environments? Such arguments ebbed the growth of national parishes a century ago. A pastor of an older Italian personal parish articulates this logic:

> If you have typical Hispanic ministries, you are not going to have any kind of assimilation at all. The community is insulated. They insulate themselves, and the church assists in that insulation, I think. And, thereby, does itself and the people a disservice. Now, there's good assimilation, and there's bad assimilation. Good assimilation is: you preserve your identity. You preserve your customs. You preserve your language. But you still, you live in this country. So you have— one of the things is language. You have an obligation to speak the language of the country in which you live, and in which you work. I think ministries in other parishes do not foster that. They'd rather work against that.

The insulation of personal parishes, by this reasoning, may predict both "good" and "bad" forms of assimilation (or lack thereof).

But assimilation is a complicated reality for immigrant Catholics today, and in particular for immigrants of color. Race mediates immigrants' adaptation to American society.[30] The vast majority of Catholics in ethnic personal parishes are people of color. Unlike for white Catholic migrants a century ago (some of whom experienced intense discrimination, to be sure), today's nonwhite Catholics encounter limited agency in electing whether or not to embrace their ethnic identities, as Catholics or otherwise.[31] Their paradigmatic path to assimilation is balanced by transnationalism and ethnic resilience, whether elected or imposed. Paired with the realities of inequality in the United States, differentiating between "good" and "bad" assimilation does not fall entirely in the hands of new Catholics themselves.

In this, the story of today's personal parishes does not replicate that of past national parishes. Racial and ethnic identities mediate the experience of Catholicism in both non-assimilative, specialist personal parishes and generalist, territorial parishes. This complicates the question of whether personal parishes, in reifying protected spaces for linguistic and cultural distinctiveness, work against new immigrants' likelihood to "blend" into their new American environments. Personal parishes may in fact level the playing field, offsetting in small measure the steamroll of subtractive assimilation to Americanization.

Cognizant of the imperfect resonance between a diverse America and persistent realities of racism, personal parish pastors frequently deemphasize assimilation and instead help parishioners more comfortably balance the two-ness that comes with being an American Catholic of color.[32] Pastors convey a mix of approaches to the supposed goal of Americanization via the personal parish:

> To still be Vietnamese, and practice their faith within the United States, a different culture ... there's a sense of identity, their own identity. A sense of, hopefully, enculturation to it. Somehow, it's up to the priest to be the leader somehow—to guide and direct like that, together. I would say that's the goal.

* * *

> I would say the personal parish here is to help them to practice and increase their faith. Not necessarily to Americanize them.

Sometimes these identities clash, as one Korean pastor notes: "After time go pass, [newly arrived Korean Catholics] become Korean-American, and then become more Americanized. Eventually for children, they become American-Korean. And, the interesting part is, they don't go all together."

The personal parish provides a space where his parishioners can navigate these contradictions as they adapt to their new social environments.

Most see the non-assimilative approach of personal parishes as nonetheless compatible with Americanization and an ethos of multiculturalism. Personal parishes simply provide a specialized vehicle for a market expansion, of sorts, rather than a competitor with generalist, territorial parishes. Personal parishes retain and sustain strands of ethnic Catholicism. Territorial parishes risk threatening and marginalizing minority Catholics.

SEGREGATED (PERSONAL) PARISHES?

The specialization offered by personal parishes carries with it two equal and opposite consequences: establishing place, and establishing a place apart from other places. These are mutually exclusive outcomes: one cannot have a parish that is fully "ours" without being segregated from other parishes and other Catholics who are not "us." This is a structural and social boundary. A question that follows is whether specialized personal parishes, and co-ethnic parishes in particular, are equal within the landscape of all parishes.

One diocesan pastoral planner, for example, warns that:

> One temptation that may not be as helpful in one way, but helpful in another, is that you begin to isolate Catholics. The overall goal, after all, is not to say "That's for the Hispanics; that's where they do their thing." So, to the degree that we isolate, or that it creates an isolating effect or a disjointing of 'We are one church,' I don't think that's very helpful. And to the extent that the parishes begin to see those parishes as perhaps 'less than,' or second class, I can see that being problematic.

His caution—similar to that expressed by others—is that separate spaces for certain Catholics have a place, as long as they do not imply inequality or disrupt unity. Do personal parishes segregate Catholics into spaces that are separate and unequal?

Personal parishes serving black Catholics offer a useful space from which to consider this question. Black Catholic personal parishes disclose origins different from most white European national parishes: namely, the legacy of racially segregated churches. As historian Timothy Matovina notes, "For African Americans, who were not immigrants but predominantly slaves and the descendants of former slaves, the general pattern of the national parish as a mediating institution for assimilation did not hold."[33] African

American parishes empowered black Catholics and protected them from discriminatory treatment elsewhere, while being simultaneously segregationist and discriminatory in and of themselves. Later moves toward integration, fueled by civil rights, met mixed receipt among African American Catholics. Critics mourned the closure of scores of black parishes. Black Catholics had to join desegregated parishes (likely led by whites), or leave Catholicism altogether. Parish closure also meant redrawing parish lines in predominately black neighborhoods.[34]

One pastor recalled this history in his diocese, saying that:

> In the '70s, they closed an African American church, a personal parish, and they merged it with [a white parish]. Took them a long time to come together. I heard that people did not feel welcome, initially. But it was one of these things where they thought the time of separation has passed, and we need to all worship together. What, unfortunately, they ended up doing, not just [here] but in a lot of places, was they destroyed very vibrant, vital African American communities—Catholic communities—in the name of trying to do integration. Well, what happened was: "You go to the white church." Well, the white church was not really interested in having them, in a lot of cases. Most cases. And in their own parishes, they ran everything. All of a sudden, they were guests.

Black parishes—in their origins and in their closure—"did not facilitate integration but intensified African-American despair at the refusal to accept them as equals in U.S. church and society," writes Matovina.[35] Black parishes signaled not (just) cultural celebration, shared heritage, and a path to integration . . . but inferiority, prejudicial judgment, and a lack of acceptance in the wider Church.[36] They were separate, and unequal.

The small number of new personal parishes serving African American or black Catholics today—just six parishes, or 3 percent of all new personal parishes—reverberates this painful history of exclusion. Dioceses remain reticent to officially mark a space for black Catholics, even those serving first-generation immigrant black Catholics from Haiti, the Dominican Republic, and elsewhere. This is not forced segregation: it is, arguably, forced multiculturalism. As Catholic historian Gerald Fogarty has noted, when it comes to blacks, Puerto Ricans, and some Hispanic immigrants, "by and large there seemed to be a determined effort not to establish separate parishes for them, as had been done for other national groups."[37] This pattern of black exceptionalism remains true today.

On my visits to case study dioceses, I would often encounter one or more parishes well-known as black Catholic parishes, but lacking a personal parish designation. I asked a diocesan representative why one such parish didn't have personal parish status, despite the presence of personal parishes for other purposes in the diocese. He replies:

> That's an interesting question. Because really, [that parish] serves the smallest geographic territory of any parish in the archdiocese, and there's very few houses there anymore. It's a very impoverished area. There's just not much left there. In effect, all of our primarily African American parishes are really—for all practical purposes—personal parishes. But they are territorial parishes.

While few parishes are canonically designated to serve black Catholics, a far larger proportion of dioceses (44 percent) report having dedicated territorial parishes without personal parish designation, or dedicated ministries at shared parishes. Some of this can be explained by the fact that residential segregation generates black territorial parishes in predominantly black neighborhoods. But it also reflects how personal parish designation bears a negative connotation here: Church leaders hesitate to formally label separate black parishes. Doing so harkens back to a painful era of segregated Catholic parishes.

By implication, black Catholic parishes today are more precarious and less stable. Recall the African American pastor's words from chapter 1 regarding personal parish status—"it doesn't matter until it matters." One diocesan planner relayed how a task force charged with studying the question of whether to designate a parish for black Catholics was divided into two camps: those who wanted to integrate into territorial (and predominantly white) parishes where they lived, and those who wanted to worship with traditionally African American style liturgies. Given that the latter already had access to the kind of de facto parishes I have described, the task force ultimately recommended against the designation of a new personal parish for black Catholics. Structurally, this lays less stable ground upon which to enact specialized ministry.

One African American pastor predicts that denying personal parishes for African and African American Catholics risks losing them altogether:

> In terms of African Americans, my fear is that if [the personal parish] disappears, the African American Catholics are going to disappear. African American Catholics are going to disappear, or Africans are going to become African American Catholics, which still means African American Catholics are disappearing.

To this, the pastor shakes his head, assessing that "the African American Catholic that I am is disappearing, and nobody really cares about that. I've got to say it. Nobody really cares about that—that we're disappearing. Nobody cares."

The story of black Catholic personal parishes diverges from that of other new personal parishes. Naming a "black parish" carries different connotations in light of American Catholicism's problematic history of race relations. Dioceses today may discriminate against black personal parishes to avoid the perception of discrimination against black Catholics more generally. Black immigrants, who move from immigrants to ethnics in America's racialized context, follow patterns of belonging that more closely resemble African American Catholics than other immigrants.

These are difficult questions. Sociologists of religion Michael Emerson and Christian Smith consider similar questions in their book *Divided by Faith*. Examining white evangelicals, they find that multiracial social ties in congregations enable access to things like jobs, wealth, and power. In-group ties assure privileged access for some, while limiting it for others.[38] Racially homogeneous congregations heighten racial boundaries, reduce interracial ties, and, therefore, perpetuate racial inequality.

Catholic leaders present a nuanced view of personal parishes when it comes to racial justice in the Church. One priest expresses concern that personal parishes deny Catholics a faith-context in which to work out their differences with others. If Catholics surround themselves only with others like them, the Church misses out on its key function as "a mediating institution," preparing people to live in a diverse society. A pastor of a Hispanic personal parish admits that "there's something good about it, and there's something ill-conceived about it." Two personal parish pastors state:

> I mean, that could turn into a very bad reason. "Oh, let's have a personal parish
> for blacks, so that we can sort of separate them."

* * *

> I also think that there's a danger, and the danger is that it might facilitate the
> breakup of the church.

Interviewees generally call out the limit as the point at which separation supersedes unity, however difficult to ascertain.

The irony of this argument—that personal parishes do a disservice by denying parishioners' sufficiently diverse interchange—is that many personal parishes are established for the very reason of acknowledging and accommodating diversity. But, in specializing on certain people and certain needs unmet in the territorial parish, personal parishes do segregate Catholics and, therefore, risk doing more harm than good.

CONCLUSION: DIVERSE PARISHES IN A MODERN AMERICAN CHURCH

How do religious institutions structure local organizations to incorporate racial and other forms of difference among adherents? Talking about religion as an answer to the "problems" of diversity too often frames the discussion in terms of already-privileged voices and already-dominant histories. Solutions, moreover, tend to overemphasize the role of individuals acting within individual congregations (e.g., training for intercultural competency and effective leadership, worship practices that bridge difference, or immigrants' entrepreneurial church-building). But undergirding any negotiations around difference are the very organizational structures in which they are lived out. Difference operates in context.

In the US Catholic Church, this means looking at how parishes are formally decreed by institutional leaders. Examining personal parishes shifts attention to this more structural, institutional view. Amidst an imperfectly realized, integrationist model of accommodating heterogeneity, some leaders in the US Catholic Church have introduced an alternative, non-assimilative model for organizing local religion. Put more sharply, personal parishes respond to the failure of territorial parishes to fulfill their guiding orientation of serving all. They openly serve only some. American Catholicism's institutional response to difference now includes both generalist and named specialist organizations, operating in tandem.

The oft-told story of Catholicism in the United States details how generations of European immigrant Catholics assimilated into the fabric of America, reconciling the seemingly irreconcilable tension between an American identity and a Roman Church. Few predicted Catholics' steady rise into the middle and upper class when viewed from their starting points in US history. But this was substantially assisted by national parishes and an extensive Catholic infrastructure that fostered Catholics' economic, social, and cultural success.

Today's immigrant Catholics are overwhelmingly non-European; today's ethnic personal parish occupants mostly nonwhite. "I would say that China is not Italy," admonishes one pastor. The racial grammar used to describe the contemporary American Catholic experience inconsistently includes a huge swath of immigrant and other Catholics of color, the fastest growing population of the Church. The expectation that generational change will eliminate the need for personal parishes does not erase the needs and expressed desires of many Catholics today. Nonwhite immigrant Catholics are most likely to seek ethnic personal parish status, in search of institutional protection, cultural safekeeping, and faith retention.

The story of Catholics today must be told alongside a story of race and intergroup relations, and organizational structures of accommodation. New immigrant Catholics' assimilation is less patently linear than that of their forebearers. New American Catholics, too, move from "immigrant" to "ethnics," subsumed within the racial hierarchy of the United States. Immigration scholars Alejandro Portes and Rubén Rumbaut write that:

> Assimilation to America has seldom taken place in the way recommended by nativists. Instead, the reaffirmation of distinct cultural identities—whether actual or invented in the United States—has been the rule among foreign groups and has represented the first effective step in their social and political incorporation.[39]

In this, the cultural and religious identities of new immigrants matter.

The question for today's personal parishes and the Catholics who inhabit them is: Will they, like personal parishes of old, build and bequeath a Church bearing their own cultural traits? Or will their cultural Catholicism get lost in generalist organizations that privilege already-privileged groups? Cultural erasure is a real risk, should dedicated structures not provide a balance against it. Assimilation is a powerful but not innocent signifier of progress.

Religious identity is lived out collectively through parishes—whether in choosing a territorial parish with co-ethnics, struggling through the tensions of shared territorial parishes, or opting out entirely through named specialist, personal parishes. Race and immigration are inseparable realities in the United States; so too are religion and race. The fact that several interviewees, including pastors, felt compelled to add a disclaimer that they were not meaning to act "racist" in creating uniracial spaces accentuates the sensitivity and absence of discourse around race and place in American religion. Seeing congregations without seeing ethnicity as a salient marker of identity, culture, welcome, and inclusion fails to account for the organizational functions of American religion.

Territorial parishes operate under the illusion that they work, and that they work ideally. Unnamed but nevertheless uniracial territorial parishes advance an illusion of multiculturalism and welcome. Responses to ethnic diversity that focus solely on integrated parishes insufficiently acknowledge racial salience and power. To forever be the special ministry, the asterisk offering, the renter, the exception, means that a huge and growing proportion of American Catholics do not constitute the American Catholic story. An integrated model of the parish, organizationally, requires minority Catholics to assimilate, conform, and bend to others' preferences and needs. Structurally, this threatens to extinguish an entire swath of the Church. Diverse Catholics require diverse parishes ... including personal parishes. Personal parishes fill a structural gap for those most deeply impacted by exclusion from a unified whole. Multiracial parishes are not the only option for organizing local religion amid racial diversity.

Personal parishes—as an alternative, emergent organizational form in the US Catholic Church—present a non-assimilative model for accommodating difference in local religion. At their inception, they name difference and its place. While still operating within the confines of institutional regulations, they present symbolic ownership for traditionally marginalized groups of Catholics. Personal parishes do not require sharing. They suggest that, organizationally, difference does not have to be dealt with in assimilative ways. While the integrated, territorial model still exists in the majority, personal parishes present an alternative, concurrent organizational form.

Named specialist organizations remain the exception in Catholicism today. Territorial parishes (themselves racially partitioned) are still the dominant model, evidenced by the vast underrepresentation of personal parishes for Hispanic and Latino Catholics as compared to their proportionate numbers among all Catholics. But an unrelenting commitment to a multiracial parish can distract from immediate and pressing realities. Personal parishes are reservoirs, not way stations. Generalist organizations, despite their well-intentioned desire to serve all, cannot erase persistent realities of division by language, color, and custom, or discrimination and inequality in modern America.

"Catholicity is never lacking to the Church," states theologian Avery Dulles, "but it is dynamic and expansive; it continually presses forward to a fullness and inclusiveness not yet attained."[40]

CHAPTER 5
Fragmentation

The whole history of the United States, we've had different groups coming which do not always get along in the same territorial parish. Sometimes they just don't get along, you know?
—Pastor, Traditional Latin Mass Personal Parish

* * *

Some people don't play nice with others. And sometimes it's best, if people care so much about one particular aspect of church life, particularly liturgic church life, and they're going to be annoyed all the time when they're at worship that it's not being done the way that they want it to be done, it can be best for all involved to accommodate them.
—Pastor, University Personal Parish

* * *

People want to be more separate than they want to be together, honestly.
—Diocesan Multicultural Director

American Catholics have a reputation for reconciling their dissent with Church teaching. The usually pejorative term "cafeteria Catholic" describes individuals picking and choosing what they like from theology and tradition. More generously, Catholicism is a "pluralist tradition" of discerning Catholics who trust their own judgment. In his book *Sense of the Faithful*, Jerome Baggett tells us that individual Catholics reappropriate the Catholic tradition together, in parishes, to resolve the dilemma of authenticity and authority. Parishioners negotiate. They reframe. They innovate. In short, they make the Catholic tradition their own through collective cultural work in parishes of their choosing.[1]

But how is this kind of pluralism dealt with from the top? We have some clues about lived religion on the ground, but what of "institutional" religion? How do Church leaders respond to individual Catholics' religious agency? Put another way, how does individual agency find structure through formally sanctioned organizations? The answer in the Catholic Church is through personal parishes. At the institutional level, personal parishes reconcile religious agency by creating an alternative organizational form to accommodate distinctive cultural preferences.

This chapter explores the ways in which personal parishes—in bringing people together under the rubric of shared mission, identity, and purpose—sort Catholics organizationally. Naming lines of difference, personal parishes sanction cultural divides, exacerbating what already separates individual American Catholics. Specialization finds justification under the rubric of personal parishes: a structural compromise in an authoritarian tradition to accommodate religious agency. Personal parishes consciously fragment American Catholicism.

Taking a cue from sociologists Fischer and Mattson, fragmentation can be thought of as "widening breaches among Americans, whether by demographic traits, ideology (core beliefs), culture (tastes or habits), or social ties."[2] Its expression may arise as either two stark, opposing poles engaged in ongoing "culture wars" as sociologist James Davidson Hunter depicted them, or as a multitude of smaller and distinct subcultures, à la Robert Ezra Park: "a mosaic of little worlds that touch but do not interpenetrate."[3] Personal parishes more closely evoke this second manifestation, separating individuals and communities into like-minded, similarly situated silos of identity and engagement.

THE HOMOPHILY OF RELIGIOUS PREFERENCE

"Birds of a feather flock together," or so goes the saying describing people's desire to join together with others like themselves. Sociologists use the term "homophily." Similarities in race, class, age, religion, education, politics, ideology, and occupation spawn networks that are overwhelmingly homogeneous. As H. Reinhold Niebuhr wrote in the *Social Sources of Denominationalism*, what distinguishes religious organizations from one another reflects social differences alongside theological ones.

Contact between similar individuals reinforces shared beliefs and behaviors. Homophily marks a line between "us" and "them." The primary structural/sociological roots of homophily lie in proximity (where we live), organizations (where we belong/participate), and the social roles we occupy (like our jobs and family positions). We live, work, worship, commune, befriend, and marry people like ourselves. American communities mirror these splits in demographics and culture.[4]

This partitioning, whether sought or bred, generates what journalist Bill Bishop calls the "big sort." Americans find themselves in homogeneous "tribes" in their neighborhoods, churches, volunteer groups, and the like, creating a "fundamental kind of self-perpetuating, self-reinforcing social division."[5] Separation occurs through Americans' socialization, structural embeddedness, and everyday choices. Our families, jobs, neighborhoods, and churches—tied together through social networks—create circles of connection and disconnection stimulated by shared identities. We live in a "partitioned city."[6]

Homophily characterizes local religion, too. America's religious landscape is a free and plural marketplace. Niches therein produce "market segments of potential adherents sharing particular religious preferences."[7] Subgroups of adherents display a homophily of preference in need, taste, and expectation. Religious groups make choices about when, whether, and how to cater to given niches. Specialized religious organizations, in this way, reflect both supply-side innovation and an institutional response to demand. American religion reacts responsively (or not) to the particular and changing needs of its consumers.[8]

In their widely read treatise on religion, *Habits of the Heart*, Robert Bellah et al. suggest that religious groupings of those sharing similarities are akin to "lifestyle enclaves."[9] These constitute "an appropriate form of collective support in an otherwise radically individualizing society ... the necessary social form of private life in a society such as ours." Their assessment is hardly a positive one, though, as Bellah et al. go on to call lifestyle enclaves a "segmental" social form that "celebrates the narcissism of similarity." The authors even avoid associating the word "community" with such gatherings of like-minded individuals. Homophily comes at a price.

Personal parishes formally sort Catholics into homophilous units. Vietnamese Catholics worship with Vietnamese Catholics. College students do ministry with college students. Traditionalist Catholics celebrate the TLM in pews next to others desiring the same. And so on. The definitional characteristic of the personal parish fragments the American Catholic Church into distinct subcultures as formal structure, not merely cultural byproduct.

Territorial parishes produce some of these same outcomes through the homophily that characterizes neighborhoods. The share of upper-income homes residing in predominantly upper-income census tracts has increased in recent years, for example, as has the share of lower-income homes in predominantly lower-income census tracks.[10] The wealthy live by the wealthy; the poor by the poor. Residential segregation by race is even more pronounced. And when wealthy, racially similar people live near one another, their assigned territorial parishes will look wealthy and racially similar. Poor, racially similar neighborhoods elsewhere in a metro area will likewise gather in poor, racially similar territorial parishes. This is the social sorting of America's territorial parishes working just as they "should," canonically.

Nearly all parishes—in a sea of congregations from all denominations—learn to maintain market relevance in a dense and competitive religious field. This market approach to religion, its awkward economic metaphors notwithstanding, reveals key dynamics of religious organization in an unrestricted and pluralistic American context. "Magnet" parishes attract a particular clientele. "Niche" congregations make identities apart from the neighborhood. Catholic parishes—often spearheaded by the pastors who lead them—embody particular varieties of Catholicism, distinguishing them in an otherwise indistinguishable field.[11]

But even while territorial parishes build distinctive cultures, personal parishes stand out in that they are labeled, canonically defined, and officially dedicated to the identified subpopulation and/or purpose. They are named specialized organizations. This sets personal parishes apart meaningfully from de facto constitutions of parish culture. Their purpose and identity, moreover, is what made it possible for them to secure personal parish status in the first place. The fragmentation that results is intended, done in the interest of meeting needs that do not logically trace territorial partitioning.

A pastor of an Anglican Use personal parish describes the benefit of partitioning parishes this way:

> Over the years, I have seen tremendous wisdom of these personal parishes in that it does enable people of a similar—it doesn't have to be a similar background, but just a similar philosophy and outlook on one's spiritual life and what it is that helps one in one's own expression of religion—allows you to kind of come together as a bona fide parish and actually belong to it. You don't sneak off to it or anything like that; it would really be your parish.

While liberating in its consolidation of like-minded Catholics, the personal parish is nonetheless limiting in specifying just who can belong. "When this parish was started, the terms at first were very, very limited. You had to be a convert from the Episcopal Church to have the right to belong to this personal parish." This kind of specification runs counter to the place-based model of a parish welcoming all who dwell in its midst.

Occupying their specified niche, personal parishes look to purpose as a compass. While a territorial parish is charged with hosting a diverse set of populations and needs, personal parishes prioritize with specific regard to their canonical purpose. One priest shares of this mission-narrowing:

> One of the things that I learned early on is that you have to know why it is you exist as a personal parish. You have to look to that, and then process the liturgy. And be very careful when others come in, that they don't attempt to change the ambience of the place.

Personal parishes anchor to a purpose apart from residential proximity. This is the point, as another pastor articulates:

> A personal parish has to—its first identity, of course, is Catholic. But after that, it has to carefully define its identity. Why do we exist as a separate parish? Because I mean, quite honestly, if this parish were to disappear . . . and our folks all live in some territorial parish . . . they would find some place to go. So we don't *have* to exist in order for people to receive the sacraments. They'd receive the sacraments in other places. So, why do we exist? Well, it's for the liturgy. That's the reason for our establishment. But I think that any personal parish has to define very carefully *why* it exists.

To this pastor's point: personal parishes are innately redundant. All Catholics already have a territorial parish, because the territorial parish system is structured to care for all. Personal parishes are supplemental organizations. Thus, they can exude unabashed claims of purpose, boldly stating what they are and why they exist.

For Catholics sitting on the extreme poles of ideology, this unabashed embrace of identity is a freeing premise. Otherwise marginalized within mixed parishes, they need not shirk nor silence deeply felt commitments to a particular variety of Catholic thought and expression. Numerically in the minority across a full diocese but emboldened collectively in a single parish, communities of Catholics can identify even more strongly with their chosen Catholic subculture.

Unmitigated identity, though, yields a hyper-fragmented American Catholic Church. Personal parishes solidify fragmentation. They create a named home (or a siphoned ghetto) for ideological and liturgical strands. This effect can be seen most visibility by examining two oppositional fragments of the Church, both denoted as personal parishes: TLM personal parishes and parishes with a social mission.

The extraordinary form [of the Mass] is in ascendancy, at the moment. It's getting more and more and more momentum. And I think that's a very good thing. . . .. I must say, in all honesty, that is what I prefer. That is what I want. That is what I love, and that is what I want to do for the rest of my life. If I never have to do another ordinary form again, that would be fine with me! If other priests don't like that—well, too bad for them! I don't have to do it anymore, because it's no longer expected of me. If I never have to celebrate the ordinary form again, that would be fine with me.

Catholics who choose to attend personal parishes devoted to the TLM celebrate Mass only according to the Roman Missal of 1962 (pre-dating the changes of Vatican II). They cultivate a community welcoming highly traditional, ortho-dox Catholics. TLM personal parishes number twenty-eight according to the NSPP and are most prevalent in arch/dioceses in the South and West. They are the most numerous non-ethnic based variety of personal parish.

Many TLM personal parishes are administered by the Priestly Fraternity of Saint Peter (FSSP), a community of priests established in 1988 with an exclu-sive focus on the traditional liturgy of the Roman Rite. While FSSP priests serve in various capacities, their preference and pride is to establish personal parishes that only celebrate the TLM. They have experienced impressive growth both in number of priests and number of personal parishes entrusted to their care. Two such parishes are shown in figures 5.1 and 5.2.

Once commonplace, celebrating the TLM was disallowed after Vatican II in favor of the vernacular and enhanced lay participation. But a sizable minority of priests and lay Catholics continued to prefer the more traditional liturgy. This meant celebrating Mass in secrecy from the end of the Council through the early 1980s, without formal Church approval. Then, in 1984, the Congregation for Divine Worship under Pope John Paul II issued "Quattuor Abhinc Annos," describing "the problem of those priests and faithful who had remained attached to the so-called Tridentine Rite." The document granted permission for the TLM on a case-by-case basis with approval from the local Bishop, who reported back to the Vatican. This "indult" offered a formal means to deviate from the common law of the Church. Subsequent institutional actions granted Catholics ever-more-ready access to the TLM.

The collective identity of Catholics attached to the TLM today bears this legacy of secrecy and precariousness. Priests and parishioners who prefer the TLM remain attuned to their potential for exclusion and are still not fully welcomed with available Masses or personal parishes in all US dio-ceses. Some fear that even the acceptance they have achieved is fleeting. One priest articulates the tenuous nature of the TLM in today's church:

FIGURE 5.1 Traditional Latin Mass personal parishes create a distinctive space for traditional styles of Catholic practice.

Originally [the TLM] was thought to be suppressed. It was gone. And there were a lot of people, clergy and all that, who would be indignant if someone wanted to have a traditional Mass. Okay, well, we've gone beyond that—but we're not entirely beyond that. It depends on whom you're talking to. . . . So you just have to watch that—because it's still precarious.

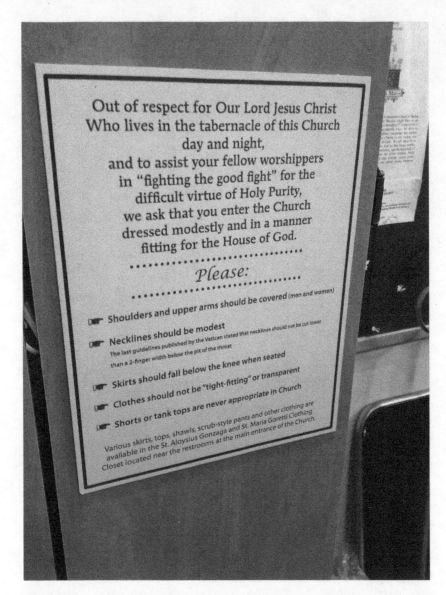

Out of respect for Our Lord Jesus Christ
Who lives in the tabernacle of this Church
day and night,
and to assist your fellow worshippers
in "fighting the good fight" for the
difficult virtue of Holy Purity,
we ask that you enter the Church
dressed modestly and in a manner
fitting for the House of God.

Please:

☞ Shoulders and upper arms should be covered (men and women)

☞ Necklines should be modest
The last guidelines published by the Vatican stated that necklines should not be cut lower
than a 2-finger width below the pit of the throat

☞ Skirts should fall below the knee when seated

☞ Clothes should not be "tight-fitting" or transparent

☞ Shorts or tank tops are never appropriate in Church

Various skirts, tops, shawls, scrub-style pants and other clothing are
available in the St. Aloysius Gonzaga and St. Maria Goretti Clothing
Closet located near the restrooms at the main entrance of the Church.

FIGURE 5.2 Traditional Latin Mass personal parishes create a distinctive space for traditional styles of Catholic practice.

The once-ostracized relationship to the Church solidifies a sense of apartness. Belonging to a TLM personal parish is deeply felt; beleaguered, even. Uncertainty builds pride, strengthening shared identity among TLM goers.

However tenuous, the ascendance of this older form of the liturgy signals a formal place for—and acceptance of—an especially traditional iteration of American Catholicism. Personal parishes that exclusively celebrate the TLM envelop Catholics with more orthodox values. One pastor of a TLM personal parish affirms this alignment of parish and person, saying that "we've got that charism of the Latin liturgy, and along with that, it goes hand-in-hand that they're going to be more traditional, more orthodox in their teachings." Parish selection maps onto (and maintains) parishioners' preexisting ideological commitments. TLM Catholics embrace an alternative Catholic positionality at the conservative pole of the US Catholic Church.

Visiting a TLM personal parish quickly corrects the misconception that Latin Mass attendees are all older Catholics who remember the Mass before the changes of Vatican II. Younger Catholics are in the majority, both in the pews and on the altar. As one pastor of a TLM parish describes, "One of the things that's been so interesting about it—and it's something that sort-of defies the stereotype among a lot of people—is that the parish is young, with a lot of families." Pope Benedict XVI affirms this counterintuitive appeal of the older form of the Mass, in his letter accompanying *Summorum Pontificum*, granting the possibility of TLM personal parishes:

> Immediately after the Second Vatican Council it was presumed that requests for the use of the 1962 Missal would be limited to the older generation which had grown up with it, but in the meantime it has clearly been demonstrated that young persons too have discovered this liturgical form, felt its attraction and found in it a form of encounter with the Mystery of the Most Holy Eucharist, particularly suited to them.

An older diocesan leader echoes this reality in her diocese, saying: "It is not all my age group that grew up with the Latin Mass. It's a whole different generation. And quite active, very much devoted to the parish."

One pastor at a TLM personal parish, himself a member of the post-Vatican II generation, describes his initial introduction to this liturgical form:

> I always went to Mass. My first Latin Mass was when I was 19 years old. It was just something that my father never liked; it wasn't his thing. And when I saw it, I couldn't believe it! I was dumbstruck! It was everything I had received; everything I thought Mass should be like. From that point on, I studied it, and then I became a priest.

For future priests and lay people alike, the Latin Mass appeals to a small minority of Catholics longing for a ritualized, past-looking, high-stakes variety of Catholicism only available via the TLM.

Comparatively younger attendees and a strict adherence to Catholic teaching also translates into a high number of children in TLM parishes. I observed this phenomenon throughout the country during my TLM personal parish visits. One pastor describes:

> [My parishioners] are mainly young couples who are home schoolers, interested in the Latin. These young couples, this is what they want. And they have large families—7 children, 6 children, 5 children—and the children are all at the Mass. We have lots of children at Mass. And those people like it. This is actually what the Second Vatican Council asked for: the Second Vatican Council didn't ask for the English Mass that we have today, you know? There's a whole history to that, which we won't go into . . .

The frequent breastfeeding I observed at TLM services offered further evidence of the Mass's appeal to young families. I asked one pastor about this directly, to which he responded:

> Yeah, [breastfeeding] is natural, it's normal, it's what God wants. I think people are rebelling against this whole artificiality of modern culture. I think there's a certain rebellion with that, too. The technological world, the technology, has usefulness but it doesn't define human beings. I think there's a certain, genuine rebellion there. There's nothing regal about it.

His response ties liturgical preference to worldview, here articulated as one that is rather suspicious of modernity.

Still in the minority nationally, TLM adherents have come to anticipate questions about why they prefer the Latin Mass to the more modernized, mainstream, ordinary form of Mass (the Novus Ordo). The younger average age of TLM parishioners dismisses, for most, a rationale based upon reclamation of childhood faith. One TLM pastor relays parishioners' myriad reasons for attendance:

> Well, I would say [parishioners'] reasoning is as personal and unique as each individual. . . .. Depending on when they've come, and how old they are, and at what point in their own Catholicism they are . . . I would say we could probably group them into groups and categories. It is definitely the case that some are nostalgic for a time that they considered to be a happier one in the church, and that being the '50s, '30s, '20s, you know. But really, the majority of our parish doesn't

have a chance to be nostalgic; we're simply not old enough! So what are our reasons? Well, they're really are personal ones. Some come for the sake of reverence. They don't really care much about the Latin language, they really could take it or leave it, but it's reverent and they seek that, they hunger that, and it's what they appreciate. And the fact that it's in Latin, well, they're willing to accept that.

He continues:

Some really do appreciate the Latin. Having a liturgical language is something that they see as valuable and useful: something good in itself, and something to be preserved. That—I would say—is probably a less common reason. Some have come as refugees, as those who have fought a war and are beat up in the battle. And they come here as a safe haven where they don't have to—you know— where they feel like they don't have to do battle with liturgical abuse, or doctrinal abuse, or whatever. For them, I suppose the reverence would be part of the package, but for them, it's a place of safety. And they don't have to watch things that they find really hateful in other places.

Several TLM interviewees share that their own devotion to this sacred liturgy is not merely preference, but is in fact an embrace of the truest, most historically accurate mode of liturgical celebration. Two advocates for the TLM state:

What motivates me (and has from the beginning) is the deep richness of the liturgy. It's more than human, it's so God-centered. And the sacrifice of the Mass is so directly apparent, hearing about Christ dying on the cross for our sins, and the powers of redemption. Those are the reasons of what motivate me, in response to the question, "Why the Latin Mass?"

* * *

That's a pretty basic question, and one that I even had from the Chancery, from the woman who was in charge of liturgy from the Archdiocese for decades: "What is it about this Latin Mass, while nobody speaks Latin?" It all comes down, for me personally, to the deep spiritual sacred liturgy, and the mysteries associated with it. When you read the translations of the Latin Mass and then immerse yourself in it. . ... It's the incense, it's the Gregorian chant, it's the deep solitude of the canon and the moving words that are contained in the liturgy that is so motivational. And it causes you to become, at least for me, introverted in terms of my spirituality. And quite moving, in terms of what it does in causing me to reflect, and to reflect upon the cross, and the basics of our faith.

TLM personal parishes are simultaneously a fragment of the modern Church and a world wholly apart, circumscribing orthodox (mostly white)

American Catholics through liturgy, community, and practice—apart from all others in the US Catholic Church.

FRAGMENTS: PERSONAL PARISHES WITH A SOCIAL MISSION

Our parish—we're very active in our faith. I would say we're not a conservative group, if you will. You mentioned you went to [a neighboring TLM parish]? Okay; that would be more of a traditional, Latin-type situation. That's not us. At all.

A smaller number of personal parishes hold as their core purpose a social justice orientation, or social mission devoted to meeting local needs. While many territorial parishes claim a justice focus in part, personal parishes maintain an explicit and holistic personal parish designation for this purpose.

A social mission varies in scope and rationale. The phrase here encompasses a category of analysis rather than consistent decree wording. Personal parishes with this purpose could operate as urban hubs—such as the case of the downtown Seattle parish described in chapter 3. Its ministry extends to the homeless, to urban workers and residents, and to tourists arriving on cruise ships. A personal parish with a social mission may explicitly commit to social justice in light of Catholic social teaching, with a central ministry to racial injustice or homelessness, among other structural issues.

What does it mean to be a personal parish with a social mission? Interviewees from parishes instilled with this purpose describe it in their own words:

> Well, it means taking care of the poor, and the homeless. We care for one another. There's more of a sense of family here than at a lot of parishes, even though we don't live in the same area, like other parishes would be. But there's just a sense of care for each other.

* * *

> It's a parish that—from its onset—has been there to provide hope. And fundamentally is rooted in the idea of doing redemptorous things for the downtown community, such as social justice ministry, advocacy. We've had so many requests: things that just don't happen in the sea of people in the middle of downtown. This is the thing that I think will separate us from the average parish, because people will seek us out in regard to being in the heart of the city. We're in the heart of that space where faith and real life is a physical window.

* * *

Tonight at 7:00, sixty homeless men will spend the night in the basement of our church. And then we have a meals program, and that takes place cattycorner, and various churches take a night of the month. So, for 21 days of the month, there's anywhere from 150 to 200 meals served by these various groups.

* * *

Their role is to be a living, vital force of the church down in that area. To take care of all of them. To take people living in the condominiums—there are younger people, there are secular people—we need to be down there. Be present to them, and not ask them to come a couple miles up the hill.

Personal parishes with a social mission are usually located in urban settings. Parishioners may or may not live anywhere in the immediate vicinity, and may or may not match the racial profile of the neighborhood in which the church physically resides.

Parishes with this canonical designation sometimes capitalize on the availability of historic downtown church spaces. Local bishops assert the merit and viability of this fairly unusual and rather creative parish decree. One bishop explains why it made sense in his diocese:

In the area of downtown, way down in the heart of things, there's a large flux of people, transient and otherwise. We have a lot of street people, we have a lot of people on drugs. We have programs for women . . . a whole variety of community things. We have to be down there, anyway. We are right on the harbor. We have a lot of cruise ships that come in here all the time, looking for Mass somewhere. So we have docks down there, cruise ships come in all the time, and then we have tremendous growth in condominiums. . . .. We figure that at least 10% of [condo residents] will be Catholic. Plus the street people, plus all the tourists that come here. We needed to have something down there in the midst of all that to serve and minister to those people—not geographic, but being able to serve the people who come downtown—whether it be on a daily basis, go to the office or whatever—that's convenient. That is able to reach out to them.

When Catholic populations do not warrant a territorial parish, social needs can warrant a personal parish with a social mission.

The explicit social mission of personal parishes attracts Catholics whose own faith and justice commitments align. This includes Catholics reared in Vatican II and 1960s modes of justice and transformation, as one parish leader describes: "The people in our parish have always been active in social justice issues, and on the forefront. Many of them were activists during the '70s and '80s, and still are activists to this day." Social justice personal parishes tend to attract Catholics with a more progressive ideology, certainly as compared to TLM parishes. Asked whether his parish may be viewed as progressive, one deacon responds:

> I can see why somebody might say that, or speculate about that. And there's some truth in that. I would say that some people would experience our liturgy as progressive. And I'm not sure what that means, but I think that that would be true.

A progressive orientation can translate into a fairly radical welcome at personal parishes with a social mission, extended to individuals whose inclusion in Catholic communities can be less forthcoming elsewhere. One pastoral associate describes this:

> Our focus on social justice is also justice *within* the church: breaking down those barriers between them and us. Because justice in the Gospel is talking about right relationships. And so, when we're talking about social justice, we're talking about justice between social groupings of people. Right relationships. And that means that we reach out to people of all types. You're welcoming to people of all kinds; we don't make these kinds of judgments between people on the left or the right, whether they're gay or straight or whether they're purple, or pink, or whether—you know? People are people.

Visitors to her parish, she says, describe it as overwhelmingly welcoming and energetic, engaged.

Others in personal parishes with a social mission describe a similar "open-door" philosophy, informed by their stated decree:

> We talk to the folks at [the parish meal] program. Not everybody is homeless that comes in, but a lot of people we talk to. We invite them to come worship with us, even though they're not Catholic. We say, "Come on over. We'd love to have you." . . . I would say our doors are really open to anyone.

The social mission of personal parishes bearing this designation enables them to clearly express a radical openness to all under the umbrella of the Catholic Church, beyond that expressed at other parishes without this named purpose. A parish decreed to serve the homeless, for example, can own and act on this charge without hesitation, to shape congregational priorities and funding.

While a personal parish with a social mission may display an openness atypical among territorial parishes, there are, nonetheless, limits to what gets canonically recognized via personal parish status. A parish may have a reputation for welcoming gay Catholics, for example, but there are no personal parishes officially decreed to serve gay Catholics. There are de facto ones, to be sure, including Most Holy Redeemer Parish described in Baggett's *Sense of the Faithful*. But these lack a personal parish designation. This exclusion is significant, shedding light on which communities of Catholics receive explicit pastoral structures via personal parishes and which do not.

As with TLM parishes, a personal parish's social mission decree shows up in patterns of interaction therein. Whereas formal hierarchy is esteemed in manner and practice at TLM personal parishes, shared leadership and heavy lay involvement characterizes personal parishes with a social mission.

Considering women's involvement, for example, one leader at a social mission personal parish shares that "our parish council is 50/50 male and female. Women are very valued in our parish. They lecture all the time; we have communion ministers. Women have a place here." I asked one female leader at a personal parish with a social mission what parish roles are available to her, to which she responds: "Everything! What don't I do? I don't say Mass. I don't hear confessions." Personal parishes with a social mission exhibit high levels of lay involvement and leadership, including expanded roles for women.

Personal parishes' leaders admit that they must walk a fine line to embrace the values of full inclusion and adhere to Catholic regulations. Personal parish status proffers crucial protection. Some try to stay under the radar to ensure their continued status in the diocese. One leader describes:

> I mean, we have lay preaching here, but we don't like to advertise that too much, just because we don't want . . . Our bishop right now is very open to letting us do whatever we want, within . . . as long as we don't make a big splash about it, and put him in the hot seat. Then he would almost have to come down, or do something. So, we walk a fine line between being as progressive as we can be, and still trying to be sensitive to him, too . . .

In this way, the same precariousness that characterizes TLM parishes also characterizes personal parishes with a social mission. Worshiping on the margins of the Church, their inclusion can feel tenuous even with canonical, personal parish status.

Personal parishes are edge churches. One leader puts this directly: "Our parish would be more—people who are on the edge, you know? But there's a home for them, too." Like in the emerging church movement beyond Catholicism, personal parishes provide a collective structure for religious individualization, or, further still, a "religion on the edge."[12] Edges—boundaries—continue to matter in this story. Both TLM and social mission personal parishes respond to adherents' nonconformist take on a shared tradition.

FURTHER FRAGMENTED

Beyond fragments of American Catholicism housed in TLM and social mission personal parishes, still other personal parishes facilitate places for any bishop-decreed purpose, in accordance with canon law's allowance for personal parishes "even for some other reason."[13]

As with most uncommon personal parish designations, Anglican Use parishes are accustomed to small numbers nationally and a fairly minimal influence on the US Catholic Church. In dioceses where they hold a presence, parishioners drive great distances to partake in the distinctive Mass, surrounded by others who also prefer it. Many once belonged to the Episcopal Church. Some enter the Catholic Church along with their once-Episcopal pastor, who—upon conversion to Catholicism—requests permission to celebrate Catholic Mass according to the Anglican Use. This was made possible through the "Pastoral Provision" of 1980, permitting the priestly ordination of married clergymen who convert from the Episcopal Church. The document also permits worship communities to integrate elements of the Anglican liturgy into Mass. Entire Episcopalian congregations have become Catholic after this change.

Among the men who took advantage of the provision was Father Christopher Phillips, removed from the ranks of his Episcopal diocese upon his stated desire to join the Catholic Church. Then in his early thirties, married, and with three children under five, he moved to San Antonio to serve a community of former Episcopalians aspiring to become a Catholic parish. Then Archbishop Patrick Flores welcomed Father Phillips and his small community into the Archdiocese of San Antonio. Theirs was the first Anglican Use personal parish, canonically erected on August 15, 1983: the same year that the new Code of Canon law was issued.

Reflecting on the occasion of his homecoming to Rome (as he refers to it), Fr. Phillips shared with me that, at the time, "I didn't realize the import of what we were doing. All I knew was that I wanted to be Catholic." Organizationally, they had pioneered a new path: a personal parish for the Anglican Use was both novel and experimental. New circumstances sparked the innovation:

When I first went to [the Archbishop], I think he was thinking in terms of "A parish, yeah, I know what a parish is. Sure." Then, when his chancellor finally had to look at the situation—"Okay, when we establish this parish, does it have boundaries? What is this?" I think it was probably then, I'm surmising, that they figured out, "Oh, wait a minute, we need to . . ."

The new Code of Canon Law enabled the bishop to exercise this creative option.

Anglican Use parishes today are most common in the South, and especially in Texas—not surprising, given their origins in San Antonio. Many Catholics join even without an Episcopalian background. One Anglican Use pastor attributes this to "the power and the appeal, to certain people, of this." The growing appeal of Anglican Use personal parishes led Father Phillips to write in 2011 that:

> More parishes, however, are needed, which means more willing bishops and a supportive structure within the Church are needed as well. There are people scattered throughout the country who are looking for guidance and help in forming the nucleus of an Anglican Use community, and Christ isn't pleased when his sheep are left to scatter.[14]

National-level organizing around this goal spawned additional Anglican Use personal parishes since that time.

Fragments "for some other reason" also include personal parishes serving colleges and universities. One in six dioceses (17 percent) report having a personal parish of this type, for a total of thirty-five personal parishes. Catholic ministry to US colleges overall expands far wider, of course, indicating that personal parish status is a less common route chosen by dioceses (or universities) for meeting this ministry need. College and university-serving personal parishes are most common in the Midwest.

When diocesan survey respondents describe the process behind establishing the most recent personal parish in their diocese, several mention college-based parishes:

> It was a university parish.

> * * *

> It was established to meet the needs of the Catholic student population. It grew out of a Newman Club.

> * * *

> Bishop [ ] saw a need at [ ] State University.

Several college-serving personal parishes pre-date the 1983 Code; many were founded in the 1960s. One at the University of Kentucky merged a Newman Center and parish to develop a prototype for other universities in similar situations.[15] College-serving personal parishes occupy a unique position vis-à-vis the wider landscape of personal parishes. While they specialize in serving college students, they attract a hugely diverse population in terms of liturgical preference, ethnicity, and other forms of difference.

One pastor of a college personal parish describes this dynamic and its challenge:

> It's a balancing act, because I've got people that want all kinds of different things. And without watering the whole thing down, I'm some sort of insipid common denominator. I need to be able to accommodate different expressions of Catholicity.

College and university personal parishes report to two bosses: the diocese and the university. They are, as one pastor put it, "like independent contractors with the dioceses that we serve. And so, whatever the policies they decide on, we end up working with." Some are exempt from setting diocesan fundraising goals during annual appeals. One pastor readily admits that personal parish status is less germane to his own work than the politics of university administration, or ecumenical efforts with other non-Catholic university ministries there.

Even more personal parish fragments serve deaf Catholics, charismatic Catholics, Catholics attached to the charisms of particular religious communities, tourists, and more. One personal parish has an ecumenical decree, uniquely ministering to a combined community of Catholics and Episcopalians. Personal parishes offer these and other communities a structural sanctuary for like-minded Catholic communities.

How far does homophilous Catholicism go? What specialized purposes and populations warrant personal parish status, and the consolidation of like-minded Catholics? Theoretically, personal parishes could make a dedicated home for every fragment of Catholics in the United States. They could replace the territorially bound model of parish organizing with a purely social one. Can it go "too far"? Where does the edge for edge churches lie?

Examining what does not receive personal parish status sheds light on this question. One personal parish pastor speculates:

> Can it go too far? Of course it can. I think all you have to do is look at some of the Society of Pius X chapels. Some of those are practically what's called *sede vacante*.

That's a term that means "vacant seats," which means that they don't acknowledge that there's any pope of St. Peter. There's always that danger.

His comment alludes to an ultra-conservative and politicized group—SSPX—whose break from the Church some years ago has as-of-yet gone without mend, despite numerous attempts (even by Popes). They lie outside the church, not afforded personal parish status. This example showcases the boundaries of personal parish fragmentation: TLM parishes are okay; SSPX parishes are not.

Several dioceses actually allude to the formation of TLM personal parishes as a way to reconcile orthodox Catholics' relationship to the official Church. The following NSPP comment is illustrative in this regard:

> The issue of offering/establishing a "Traditional Latin Mass" parish had been discussed for several years. A schismatic ecclesial community from the Society of St. Pius X is active in the area, causing a great deal of confusion among the faithful as to who or what was the proper Catholic parish. The local Latin Rite parish was unable to provide sufficiently for those who wished to return to full communion with the Church. A determination was made to allow an experimental chapel to be established within the Latin Rite parish boundary to see if the community could be self-sustaining. After a successful three-year period, and after proper consultations with local pastors and the Presbyteral Council, the bishop decreed the establishment of a personal parish for the Traditional Latin Mass Community.

Personal parish status can subsume fragments of American Catholics who may otherwise leave the Church altogether.[16] But Church leaders do not (yet) go so far as to label personal parishes for "progressive" or "conservative" Catholics, for gay Catholics, for young adults, for women, or for countless other specialized populations of American Catholics today. Even "some other reason" has its limits.

One bishop offered parting words on this in his interview: "Well, good luck to you. Just so that there's no craze on—you're not promoting a craze to make up personal parishes, and we don't have enough categories of them, so we have to artificially do them."

"US" AND NOT "THEM"

Personal parishes unify around a Catholic and another common identity. An explicit "us." Lines around who constitutes "us" and, correspondingly, "them," are definitional to the character of personal parishes. Personal parishes require a level of cultural compliance from their parishioners.

An Anglican Use personal parish pastor shares how these lines become quickly apparent to newcomers:

> Unless [new parishioners] really buy into the reason for our existence, then they're not going to be happy here. So I think that might be a danger: let's fracture society. I think one of the great things about territorial parishes is that you get a mixture of all sorts of people. Here, the folks that are attracted to this place are looking for very traditional worship. They're looking for a very traditional presentation of the Catholic faith. They're not into experimentation, or anything like that. In the whole existence of this parish—never once has a young girl asked if she can serve at the altar. We don't have altar girls, never will have altar girls. But the interesting thing is—not a single girl even asked. It wouldn't dawn on them to ask! So, it does tend to kind of homogenize people in that way.

As shown through his example, Catholics sort themselves into personal parishes. A labeled identity and reputation in the diocese lends efficiency to a sorting process already occurring via parishioner choice among territorial parishes.

Sorting also occurs when Catholics disagree with something at their territorial parish, leading them in search of an alternative. One pastor of a TLM parish explains this type of situation:

> I think that's the good thing about personal parishes: they can be very specific in the way they do things and, therefore, give people that option to go. . ... There may be people who initially go there not because they are gaga over the extraordinary form—they may have never been to one before—but they don't like something else, whatever it might be.

Feeling out-of-place elsewhere, personal parishes present another "us" that's better than "them" for Catholics to join and feel at home.

Personal parishes require Catholics to choose what component of their multifaceted identities and commitments is most salient to their faith lives. Is it their ethnicity? Their liturgical preference? Their commitment to social justice? Parish participation becomes an outgrowth of individual commitment. One lay leader in a social mission parish shares:

> If some of those people who go to [our social mission personal parish], let's say, were Hispanic, and now "Oh now, what do I do?" but they live in another parish; where's the allegiance? In a sense, it's unfair to have them have to choose—"Do

I feel more strongly that I am committed to social justice, or do I feel more strongly that I'm Hispanic?"

Unlike a territorial parish whose primary adhesive quality (canonically) is the neighborhood, a personal parish adheres around shared purpose or identity. One must be "us" to feel inclined, welcomed, and included. Given the parameters imposed by the specified mission, this means privileging certain facets of one's identity above others.

Taking this further, upholding us and our own can reach beyond surface-level preferences, into fundamentally different visions of Catholicism and the Church. A personal parish is different, apart, better, preferred. Pastors of TLM parishes echo this:

> Technically speaking, the ordinary form can be done in a church that's completely equipped for the extraordinary form without any changes. Because you don't need to face the people when you say Mass, and you can have a community rail. And so for the physical space, that wouldn't be too much of a problem. But I have to say—even though they're different forms of the same rite, they're still very different. It's almost like a different world.

* * *

> It goes down to a very philosophical point—the Traditional Latin Mass is very theocentric, whereas the ordinary form, even if it's in Latin, it's more anthropocentric. And that whole change in perspective of how you view the entire world, that makes a big difference. It does.

Another parish is not just preference, but (by this reasoning) a lesser form of Catholicism. Additional interviews hint at the disdain with which some TLM Catholics view the Novus Ordo Mass:

> Communion in the hand—I've always loathed it. I think it's disgusting! I think it's horrendous, hideous practice. It fosters—no one will be able to convince me otherwise—it fosters disrespect to the Blessed Sacrament and a lessening of the knowledge, a lessening of the belief, I think, in the true presence. So, there are going to be people that want that. They're going to want the hideous music, the dreadful happy, clappy music. They're going to want "Father Bob" up there making nice with them, and jokes, and smiling, and mugging. They're going to love the impromptu this and that that happens at the Mass. They're going to love—they love the sign of peace. There are going to be people that loathe to give that up. But there are a lot of people that *love* to give all that stuff up.

* * *

We're all dependent, ultimately, on the will of God, anyway. But, I think that God must have something to say about this, or else the Latin Mass wouldn't be in its resurgence, and there wouldn't be an upsurge of Catholic beliefs and identity among a lot of people. But as long as there's going to be Catholic churches that look like banks, or factories, and the happy clappy and things like that, it's going to be a long road.

Ergo, the rest of the church (beyond their personal parish) is flawed. Not only are TLM parishes more right, but others are wrong in how they embody their Catholic faith collectively. Another pastor critiques this attitude of fragmentation and disdain:

There's a tendency for the people in this [TLM] movement to be spiritually proud and, therefore, they come across as being more Catholic than the church— which gives the whole movement a big black eye, and it comes across as being uncharitable—and all that is true. As a priest, I'll always have to fight that. There's always that tendency to say, "That church down there—the people come in wearing bathing suits in the summertime, and they clap through Mass, and they're talking all through Mass, and it's not like here, where they're reverent and they genuflect. They don't have kneelers at this church, and the tabernacle is in a room down the hall . . ." So, there's a tendency to puff yourself with pride, and all. A lot of bishops know that; they've seen it. They're the ones that get to receive the letters, and this has all been known. It's unfortunate those things happen.

Personal parish structures separate the like-minded through institutional fragmentation. This kind of othering distances Catholics from each other, each side righteous in their stance vis-à-vis the wider US Catholic Church. In-group solidification begets out-group antagonism.

Out-group antagonism risks infusing diocesan culture as a whole, too. One pastor observes this, saying:

I was in a meeting where one of the key lay people in the parish looked at the people from the [other parish] and said, "We don't want your church in our Church." That's a direct quote. "We don't want your church in our Church."

Another relays a story from a diocesan barbecue, his own distancing embedded:

Bishop has dinner in the backyard. The priests, they come in groups of eight, or ten, or whatever. The [TLM] priest showed up in his cassock! That's normal for them. It's not normal for us. The bishop was wearing an aloha shirt, and he has one of his priests in a cassock. . . . ! That's not the right thing at the right time.

If I'm in Rome, I wear the cassock when I'm supposed to; when I'm here, if I'm chaplain to the bishop, I wear the choir robes and the purple thing and all that, and maybe on Christmas and Easter, I'll do it. That's it. I mean, it's called a house cassock! I don't walk around my house in it! I live in a condo. The people that live near me would think I'm very strange.

Personal parishes reify social boundaries. Some belong; others don't.

Personal parishes enable Catholics to choose their world. This carries positive effects, such as the idea of a parish "family" discussed in the last chapter. One pastor of a Vietnamese personal parish, for examples, uses the Vietnamese phrase "dai gia dinh"—extended family—to explain this intentional parish reality:

> For English, you call it like "extended family." For Vietnamese, the word large family, that same idea call—I'm going to say it in Vietnamese, okay? Dai, Gia, Dinh. Dai—that's the first word. The next word is Gia. The next word is Dinh. Notice Vietnamese are all monosyllable, just one syllable. The last two words mean family. The first one means larger family. Or, in English, we call "extended family." That's the idea. That somehow we feel connected, and know each other enough so well that I consider you my family member. Part of the family. And hopefully from there, guide them to a bigger family, we call God's family.

He playfully continues on to explain that, once a member of the family, "next time when you come to my house, you know where things are. Feel free to just open the refrigerator, get your own drink or food, something if you're hungry; feel free to do all that. You're my family member. I consider you my family member now."

Parishioners' notions of family illustrate the powerful way that personal parishes act as extensions of identity, ethnicity, and national heritage, even as they fragment some Catholics away from others. The family metaphor draws lines around who is in and who is out. It conveys that not all belong to the same bloodline; some reside outside the family. Ethnicity and ideology excuses exclusion. The symbolic work of personal parishes harkens back to their historic origins, which included parishes for families. The family bond adheres a group together while also fragmenting that group from others. It isolates and serves.

Pastors acknowledge the isolation that personal parishes foster. Two Korean Catholic personal parish leaders describe how, in their parish:

> They always say "Koreans first," so they are not really trying to involve with others outside than just Korean community.

* * *

They are becoming very isolated. One of the main problems with [the parish] is they are very—they get tight, very strong hold bonding together, but they are not really reaching out.

While isolation does not have to be synonymous with fragmentation, it is certainly compatible with it. Personal parishes deal with their own, not with the perceived other. One deacon warns that "as people, we can isolate ourselves, or become elitists, if you will." A bishop adds his own concerns:

> My fear is: when you set up some of these other churches, it's almost like setting up a segregated school—that everybody thinks like you, and everybody looks like you, and everybody agrees or disagrees with the institution. So, it's almost creating a segregation.

Importantly, each of these statements come from individuals who support—or participate in—personal parishes. Even support for these alternative, specialist organizational structures typically comes with a healthy critique. Personal parishes offer an imperfect model of ministry specialization.

INSTITUTIONAL CONTAINMENT

With the lines between us and them clearly established, specialization fuels a structurally enabled myopia: disjointed fragments focused inwardly on themselves. Personal parishes magnify shared concerns while minimizing the concerns of dissimilar others. Dioceses cultivate and reinforce this division of labor through personal parishes. One parish does one thing; another does another: cafeteria Catholicism, parish style.

One lay leader from a personal parish with a social mission, for example, knew nothing about parishes in the diocese that offer the TLM:

> I don't know. I don't know how—I mean, I don't know canon law or anything—but I don't know how you could make a parish out of something like Latin Mass kind of thing.
> TCB: *You can, actually.*
> You can?
> TCB: *Yeah.*
> Well, I don't know. I have no idea why . . .

TCB: 'I don't know' is a perfectly good and honest answer.
And I don't get into the politics of it, either.

The exchange reveals a Church fragmented in such a way that it does not know what other fragments may be doing, nor how all fit together into a whole. Specialization means boldly ignoring other aspects of Catholic life (and people).

Individual Catholics do some of this work themselves, sorting and appropriating a shared tradition to make "distinctive parish cultures that emphasize certain meanings within the broader Catholic tradition and de-emphasize others," Baggett tells us.[17] Others describe similar trends in Protestant denominations, where pastors carve out special-ties to avoid "sheep-stealing."[18] But personal parishes' strategic myo-pia is not solely the product of agency and discretionary culture work, either by pastors or lay Catholics. It is the product of strategic actions by institutional elites.

Personal parishes eschew other ways of being Catholic, outsourc-ing those tasks. The TLM personal parish can handle requests for the Traditional Latin Mass. The Hispanic personal parish can handle Hispanic ministry. This gives one leader in a social mission personal parish pause:

> I'm not convinced that having personal parishes with social justice is a good idea, because the Catholic Church needs to be every single Catholic Church. "This parish will be about the 6th Amendment, and this one will be about the 5th Amendment"?!

Other parishes now have a reason to deprioritize social justice. Organized, strategic myopia fosters tunnel vision. One Korean personal parish pastor and another bishop admit the risk that accompanies an overly inward-looking focus:

> That's the problem we've got to solve. We look at ourselves, and say, "We are so good, because we are ourselves"! But the Pope has said, "No, you need to be outside and reaching out to people outside." . . . You have that world that's just outside the door that we really don't have an outreach to, to draw them out, into the Church. So, you are missing out on being the fishers of those men and women, and bringing them into the Church.

* * *

If [personal parishes] are closed to everyone else than to me, that's not what the Church is about. The Church is universal. It's including people that you agree with, but maybe you might disagree with. That's the beauty of the world.

Fragmentation separates as much as it coheres Catholics.

The myopia introduced by personal parishes, of course, can be useful administratively. With an intentional, limited focus on a particular people or purpose, personal parishes are simpler to operate. Sociologists cite this as one explanation for uniracial congregations. A pastor shares how personal parish status makes his job easier:

From my point of view, it's nice. I have fewer problems here, of trying to keep all of these disparate groups happy. People are here because they like what we're doing. If they don't like it, then for heaven's sake—go find another parish! I've had to tell people that, once in a while: Either go to [a different] Sunday Mass, or go to another parish. We're not going to change what we are, and what we do, because of personal tastes or likes or dislikes or whatever. We are what we are.

Similarly, a pastor of a TLM parish states that "having the Latin Mass in its own church kind of avoids all that unnecessary conflict."

Management advantages appear especially at the diocesan level. Bishops may look favorably upon strategies that enable Catholics to find a community home that suits their Catholic faith expression, without bending or ignoring territorial parish boundaries. They can minimize intra-parish conflicts among dissimilar Catholics in the big tent. In the words of one pastor, "Sometimes they just don't get along, you know." Personal parishes with stated foci help bishops to achieve dioceses where good-fences-make-good-neighbors.

Thinking especially of Catholics sitting at the margins of orthodoxy or progressivism, personal parishes offer a containment strategy. They offer a rationale and means to separate given communities of Catholics from all other Catholics. "Those Catholics" can congregate in a single parish, rather than scatter throughout the diocese and (theoretically) wreak havoc, complain, or challenge pastors who must serve multiple constituents. Personal parishes excise troublemakers from generalist territorial parishes.

What this implies is that personal parishes let dioceses silo Catholics as a way to contain them within single parishes. "It's like, kind of, 'keep all the liberal people in with the crazy folks in one spot, so they can be contained,'" says one leader. Another pastor tells of how his former bishop did this with the TLM:

Take the folks who are very supportive of the extraordinary form: let's give them a personal parish that will keep the troublemakers separate over here. It is a way—in fact, one time, Archbishop said inadvertently—I mean, I know he didn't mean anything by it—he said, "I'm so glad that parish exists out there." He said, "Anytime a troublemaker comes along complaining about something in their parish, I say 'Why don't you go out there? You might be happy there.'" . . . Let's siphon all of our troublemakers off to that place.

Another pastor shares likewise how his diocese manages social justice dissenters via personal parishes:

Well, many people have a very good and wholesome dedication to the exercise of justice in society—social justice, social ministry. There are many people, earnest as they may be . . . who are not necessarily following all the doctrine of the Church. And, may be called dissenters. And, may be very open about being dissenters. And so, they claim to be Catholic, but in actuality are really not, in terms of following this doctrine. Alright, these people had been all over the place. [The personal parish] was created to bring all of them into one place, rather than all over. To keep everyone, sort of—here.

This pastor talks about it with a sense of relief, because, as he puts it, "It can be a bit of a headache, poor priests that we are; we've got so much to do, and we don't—there's always someone who goes 'Oh what about this, and what about that?'" A personal parish isolates "those" Catholics in "that" parish, with a sympathetic pastor.

What this suggests is that personal parishes fulfill an important political function in the diocese. They sift Catholics out of other parishes and into separate, contained spaces. Priest appointments are made accordingly, even politically. Intentional fragmentation is a structural accommodation for big tent Catholicism.

Some leaders justify this tactic with a variation on the family metaphor, this time applied to the diocese in its entirety. Within the larger family of the diocese, there will be natural points of unity among those similarly positioned. One personal parish deacon rationalizes fragmentation in this way:

I think we—as a diocese—are all welcoming. Everyone is welcome in a diocese, and they all belong; they're all part of the family. Like any family, the teenagers like to hang by themselves, and whatever. . . . It's good for the family to have their little groups that they feel most comfortable with. I don't see any problems.

He continues:

> Some people say, "We don't need these special pockets. Let's make sure that
> everybody knows that they belong to a parish." And, I can see some priests
> thinking that way, or maybe some bishops. I think, on a diocesan level, we *are*
> one big family, and everybody needs to know that they belong to the family
> church: the diocese.

The bishop oversees family dynamics, considering all parishes in a particular church ("particular church" meaning diocese). This strategic partitioning
reiterates that parishes exist in larger contexts, within structures of authority that supersede individual discretion. The bishop, as the pastor of the diocese rather than of a single parish, balances fragmentation with unity.

One diocesan planner relays that his bishop embraces an approach to
parishes that allows for fragmentation (and diverse expression) across the
diocese:

> Well, the bishop here calls the approach; he uses this a lot, he says, "Well, we use
> the Whitman Sampler." [*TCB: Like the chocolate?*] Like the chocolate. You know,
> there's different flavors for everybody. And people will go where they feel drawn,
> and parishes can offer different things.

Each parish embraces a given character; together, they serve all diverse
needs of a diocese. The diocesan collective means something more than—
and apart from—the sum of all parishes therein.

Viewed in this light, fragmentation is neither organic nor accidental,
but strategic. Bishops look at needs across the diocese as a whole, not just
needs within a single parish catchment area. One bishop echoes this kind
of intentionality:

> The challenge, of course, is to ensure that integration is happening; that they're
> not, they don't become this sort of—"Those people, those churches"—but that this
> is an integral part of the overall ecclesiology of a local church's understanding. And
> that that part is at the heart of mission and evangelization, of whatever language
> you want to use. But for practical purposes, I think it becomes very helpful one,
> strategically, organizationally, fiscally—it just makes it much more of a fair process.

Considering the host of factors explored in chapter 3, bishops act instru-
mentally in their use of personal parishes. They weigh how much fragmentation their diocese can withstand. Division is a tradeoff for keeping
the peace.

Personal parishes are named specialist organizations introduced and sanctioned by institutional elites. They are structural embodiments of difference. That personal parishes subdivide Catholics into like-minded spaces is not in question. They do. The question then becomes not one of condition, but of consequence: Does this kind of division fragment the US Catholic Church in problematic ways, catalyzing or deepening fissures among fellow adherents?

Interviewees' reference terms like "segregation" or "ghetto" to describe the negative, fragmenting potentialities of personal parishes. Words like "family" or "enclave" describe their more positive outcomes. Given that such terms appear also in urban studies, this literature offers a pertinent frame for analysis. Although usually concentrated on patterns of residential and neighborhood partitioning, the underlying tenets bear utility for parishes. Peter Marcuse, for example, puts forth a useful typology distinguishes between "ghettos" and "enclaves."[19] Both refer to majority racial minority residential arenas (and personal parishes are not solely for racial/ethnic groups). But the critical distinguishing dimension for Marcuse is that of election: whereas ghettos result from "the involuntary spatial segregation of a group that stands in a subordinate political and social relationship to its surrounding society," enclaves are a consequence of "voluntarily developed spatial concentration of a group for purposes of promoting the welfare of its members."

Adapting this typology here, personal parishes are fragmented spaces with the potential to exhibit either or both qualities: compulsory exclusion, and/or voluntary separation. Elsewhere, Marcuse (with Ronald Van Kempen) writes that "the critical question in each case is the relationship between the residents of the particular area of spatial concentration and those outside it: the residents of the ghetto are held in a subordinate position by the outside world, the residents of the enclave, although often newcomers and perhaps slightly 'different,' are entitled to equality with those outside in all legal, social, economic, and political matters."[20] Clustering takes on a different character by virtue of participants' agency and their equality to outsiders.

This implies that the fragmentation of personal parishes must be considered as both top-down structure and bottom-up culture. Do personal parishioners exercise agency? Do they feel forced out of territorial parish alternatives, disempowered among the Catholic majority? Have they been ousted, and thus lack a parish home? Or, do they congregate with a voluntary desire to be together, to bolster a shared identity and distinctive expression of faith? Do other Catholics respond with acceptance and equal-ity, seeing difference as part of an integrated whole? Or, do other Catholics view a personal parish and its parishioners as lesser-than, justifiably out-cast? Diocesan integration offers a measure of equality.

When asked, Catholic leaders generally privilege the spirit of a voluntary enclave rather than that of a forced ghetto. Personal parishes cannot divide the Church into wholly separate, mutually exclusive, or combative clusters of belonging. Parishes must not be ghettos. One Polish pastor remarks directly: "We say in the Society of Christ that we cannot divide people. 'Polish? You go here.' . . . But we cannot be a ghetto." Personal parishes cannot be the consequence of involuntary segregation and subordination. In this, institutional structures necessarily mesh with the individual cul-ture work of Catholics who prefer, choose, and enact distinctive spaces of belonging. Personal parishes represent institutional culture work.

Catholic enclaves can benefit "edge" Catholics through strength in numbers and power in mutual affinity. Elected and participatory, personal parishes enable Catholics to fuse individual identities and collective faith. One pastor describes the personal parish as a "mediating institution" or "enclave kind of style of parish, where it almost becomes a refuge from the difficulties that you have to face in the other style of parish." Personal parishes are a safe space.

The enduring challenge, then, is how and whether fragmentation can reconcile with a unified American Catholic Church. Further, what is the a risk of shifting the basis of local connection from territoriality to social identity? A bishop speaks to this conundrum and the imperative to retain unity. "The Church permits this," he says, but it requires "the willingness of the people of God to join with one another over and above their particular selection of friendship." He elaborates:

> We just don't go out and pick our own people. So, whereas the Church has left this open—to some extent—there has never been a word of encouragement on, "Dear people of God: What we want you to do for the next three years is to go out and divide up the world in the way you like it! And that's probably going to result in fantastic worship ceremonies, because you're all going to want to worship the same way and do things the same way!" That's a long, long cry from the fact that we are all brothers and sisters in Christ, and there's neither male, nor female, nor Jew, nor . . . etc. No, no. This is an unmet challenge. And in my estima-tion, the challenge has to be placed out there and have people—the importance of accepting one another, or worshipping together—not because we find it so exhilarating and "I just think the same way that this person next to me thinks!" and "We just all love to give the sign of peace in one way!" or, "This is neat!" . . .

Well, it may be neat; but it's not Catholic. So, I recommend the greatest amount of prudence in the application of the principle of worshipping together. And the origin of a personal parish was never understood in the history of the church as, in any way, opening the door to this type of . . . [fragmentation].

The concerns he voices regarding fragmentation are that (1) Catholics may find a parish that meets their needs; (2) but this does not grant open permissiveness to pick your own people (3) because worshipping together is Catholic. Fragmentation is not the goal; the goal is acceptance, inclusion, and unification.

Others echo a similar warning. Even while acknowledging the benefit of unabashed identity and vocal commitment to Catholicism, leaders recognize that personal parishes do fragment Catholics. A diocesan director of Hispanic ministry says:

To the degree that any—that the local church can honestly come together in terms of leadership and community and say, "These are the signs of our times: We need to be flexible, to allow those gifts to take place, and take root. To nurture the larger local church." To the degree that we do that in community and in dialogue and in mutual discernment, I think can be very fruitful. And I hope it never goes away. To the degree that it becomes an excuse to marginalize one another from that one baptism, one communion, one faith? Then, I think, we're in trouble.

Catholic leaders familiar with personal parishes do not discount the notion of separation. They acknowledge the value of linking collective identities to individuals' core notions of themselves. Culture unites with structure. Parishes do cultural work for the Church. The resulting individual parish pieces are rationalized through their mandated interconnection. This vision of catholicity is simultaneously diverse and cohesive. Lines drawn between parishes congeal Catholics to their parishes, and parishes to each other.

CONCLUSION: PERSONAL PARISHES AS A STRUCTURAL RESPONSE TO DIVERSIFICATION

American Catholics are a diverse and fragmented lot. Individually, they sift and discern within a shared tradition to make it their own. Together with other Catholics, they construct parish cultures through shared action and collective adherence. Not unlike what happens across virtually all social spaces, people make borders and boundaries to separate themselves from others. Parish cultures reify individuals' own notions of self and other.[21]

Explaining parishes through individual agency alone does not account for the prevailing role of authority and power in enabling (or inhibiting) parishes as organizations. Structurally, there are additional dynamics at play. The entire parish system in the United States depends upon codified fragmentation to define and divide Catholics. As early theorist of space and society Georg Simmel notes, "The boundary is not a spatial fact with socio-logical consequences, but a sociological fact that forms itself spatially."[22] The social divisions that partition Catholics reify in parishes. Catholic leaders mediate the cultural work of individual Catholics by defining (and binding) parish structures.

Personal parishes calcify the fragmentation already occurring in American Catholicism. Social boundaries are bred through homophily in networks, neighborhoods, class, ethnicity, and more. Personal parishes give them structural expression and enable them to flourish. In this way, personal parishes are less the cause of fragmentation than the institutional sanctioning of it. Whether or not personal parishes exist in a diocese may have little bearing on whether fragmentation does. The parish model itself implies the division of Catholics into smaller, manageable communities. Erasing personal parishes would do little to erase the divisions that already characterize chosen parishes or homogeneous neighborhood clustering. Personal parishes name it.

In using personal parishes to organize local religion, the US Catholic Church engages a parish structure that both empowers collective identity and perpetuates difference. Consolidate like-minded Catholics in personal parishes, and they may more readily engage in face-to-face discussion of matters impacting their lives and shared social milieu. But, nestled in their own utopias, Catholics will reinforce extant views among others like them. In personal parishes, this is not merely cultural reappropriation of a shared tradition. These are institutionally sanctioned organizations.

Catholic parishes differ from most religious congregations in that they are not constituted independently, but in relation to one another. Fragmentation in this light is not the sole consequence of attendees' own choice. Voluntary association and religious agency cannot explain the organizational structure of the US Catholic Church, nor the fragmentation it implies. Decisions regarding organizational forms to make room for diversity are made interdependently, considering all other parishes in a diocese. Catholic leaders' structural response is both spatially and socially oriented. Territorial parishes divide territorially; personal parishes divide socially.

This implies that any fragmentation among Catholics may be equally connective. Georg Simmel's classically dualistic view of social life as "Bridge and Door" foreshadows this: "The door represents in a more decisive manner how separating and connecting are only two sides of the same act."[23] Whether as door, bridge, boundary, or border—separation marks social differences subjectively, via shared understanding of self, and objectively in real and physical organizations. From Simmel: "In an immediate sense just as in a symbolic sense, in a physical as well as a spiritual sense we are, at each moment, the ones who separate what is connected and connect what is separate." Catholic leaders do not draw lines to separate parishes without assuming connections between them. This interconnectivity is inherent to the meaning of "parish" in Roman Catholicism, and to the notion of community explored in the next chapter.

CHAPTER 6
Community

At the corner of Philadelphia's 6th and Spruce sits a narrow strip of fenced-in tombstones inscribed with the names of once-parishioners of Holy Trinity, the first national parish in the United States (see figures 6.1 and 6.2). Cremation then disallowed in church law, Holy Trinity's German Catholics necessarily found their final resting place on parish grounds. High-rise apartment buildings now overshadow their stone markers, alongside plastic riding toys from a proximate daycare. The church itself remains; its parishioners and parish status do not. Holy Trinity reverberates reminders of American Catholicism's historic rootedness: tied by place and oriented by purpose.

Elsewhere in the archdiocese, soaring wooden doors welcome Hispanic Catholics for a Saturday vigil Mass. Scores of laity pass beneath a colorful Virgin Mary, her arms outstretched to the children of the world. Glass windows tender a thin barrier between jubilant liturgical sounds and the vast field within which the church sits. Most in attendance were drawn to the area by work in nearby *hongueras* (mushroom farms). Their new personal parish actualizes a thirty-year plea from Catholics whose culture and celebrations long moved itinerantly among territorial parishes. Donated funds made it possible to build a dedicated space and elevate the community's status from mission to personal parish. Annual baptisms now eclipse those of all other parishes in the archdiocese.

* * *

American Catholicism is a Church built from place and purpose. This chapter asserts that the US Catholic Church reconciles place and purpose through a higher-order outlook on community: one that is managed across

FIGURE 6.1 Holy Trinity, in Philadelphia, was the first personal (national) parish established in the United States.

dioceses, rather than within single parishes. Bishops focus not on parishes in isolation, but on parishes connected at the meso-level. Their interpretations of community envisage organizational interdependence across wider conceptions of space. Accordingly, personal parishes operate as an institutional tactic for managing community across difference, and difference across community. Parish matters, but so too does diocese.

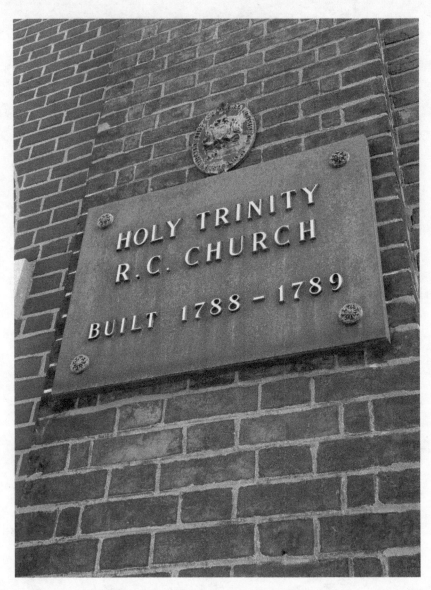

FIGURE 6.2 Holy Trinity, in Philadelphia, was the first personal (national) parish established in the United States.

Previous chapters predict this pattern. The evolution of "parish" in the American context reigned in religious agency by reasserting diocesan control. Tensions surrounding parish boundaries (brought by lay mobility and choice) resolve through personal parishes that eschew boundaries. Bishops' power and diocesan-wide assessments of need underwrite decisions to establish personal parishes. Dioceses make space for less assimilative forms of organizing difference, alongside integration. Fragmentation at the diocesan level responds to the cultural work happening among individual Catholics. In each preceding chapter, parish interdependence and diocesan-level strategizing lends institutional control, and helps to explain organizational responses to grassroots transformation. This chapter follows through on this line of theorizing, explored here as an institutional strategy for maintaining community across people, place, and purpose.

CONSTITUTED IN COMMON

"Parish" derives from both Greek and Latin sources, the former evoking the notion of a common dwelling. The word "community" also bears Latin roots: *com* (meaning with, or together) and *unus* (meaning the number one, or singularity). The two words are equated in church law: "A parish is a certain community of the Christian faithful stably constituted in a particular church . . ." Community, though, is ambiguous. By way of example, the word "communio" appears 285 times in the documents of Vatican II but, once translated into English, the documents interchange the words "fellowship," "community," and "fraternity." All reflect networks of relationships that go beyond domicile, each with slightly different interpretations.[1]

How does the Catholic Church structure community in practice, through parishes? Sociologist Jerome Baggett describes in *Sense of the Faithful* how parishes build "communal narratives" generating shared imagery of parishioners' relationships to each other and to the wider Church and society. "Hometown," "multicultural," and "oppositional" parishes construct different purposes and provisions of support.[2] Catholic community is actively produced, collectively construed, and reified through canonical structures. A diocesan multicultural director reflects this kind of thinking when she describes how Catholics build a sense of community through differing approaches to "the way we celebrate our faith." She illustrates by pointing to two parishes in the same diocese that are "fully Catholic—both of them . . . but, it's a different way of worship."

Others describe single parishes as home to multiple communities, indicated by the idea of the parish as a "community of communities." In this, "community" implies subsets of Catholics housed in relationship together in shared (usually territorial) parishes. Ever-larger parishes foretell ever-more communities therein. Pope Francis describes the parish as "the presence of the Church in a given territory" and "a community of communities, a sanctuary where the thirsty come to drink in the midst of their journey, and a center of constant missionary outreach."

A parish-as-community-of-communities denotes place, people, and purpose all together. One bishop speaks to this, saying:

> We also have to speak about the dignity and the importance of the traditional parish as it exists. It obviously is fraught with all kinds of imperfections, because it's made up of people, and people are imperfect. But they're in it together, and all the beautiful things that are happening in just the regular parish now embraces so many different people, different languages, etc. There's something beautiful in the United States, when we go to Mass and all the people are different.

The bounds of community may even extend beyond a single parish. This interpretation resonates with that of sociologist Stephen Cherry in *Faith, Family, and Filipino American Community Life*. "Overlapping community circles," Cherry writes, foster civic engagement even beyond the parish. Catholics' community-building incorporates but is not limited to individual parishes. For the Houston Filipinos at the heart of Cherry's study, community means immediate families, prayer groups, parish churches, and Filipino centers: together, "a larger family." It is the diocese (the "particular church") where Catholics work out and around differences to worship together.[3]

Parishes (should) unify diverse communities. The presence of personal parishes in the US Catholic Church implies that "community of communities" extends across a diocese. One personal parish pastor describes how American Catholicism allows for community on this broader level. He states:

> [Personal parishes] work with unique groups of people with distinct needs. I would never want to see the church become where everybody came in according to their own needs, their own desires. It's the best thing about Catholic churches: we're all in it together. It's unity within the diversity. And I think personal parishes can support and allow for that diversity in some unique ways.

A bishop likewise harkens to this "bigger picture" institutional strategy for community:

> If we're separating ourselves for a given reason, there's always a call to not forget the greater unity. Because we're all Catholics. So we always have to be called to a greater understanding. And any way we break this down, we have to make sure that we see the bigger picture, and acknowledge it, and in some way belong to it.

Viewed this way, personal parishes cater to different communities while forming a diocesan "community of communities" together, managed by a bishop.

Structurally, the American Catholic Church balances difference among individual Catholics and among individual parishes through interdependence. This theme runs through the earliest sociological theories of community, such as that posited by Émile Durkheim in *Division of Labor in Society*. For Durkheim, two forms of glue ("solidarity") hold societies together. "Mechanical solidarity" stems from shared beliefs, practices, and worldviews. Similarity (homogeneity) binds people. But dissimilarity, too, binds people. Heterogeneity requires interdependence, or what Durkheim labels "organic solidarity." Solidarity, Durkheim concludes, is not doomed by increased diversity of experience or specialization, but leads to a new form: reliance upon others.

One leader in Hispanic ministry alludes to this kind of interdependence when he says:

> The local reality is that, where there's a large number of other ethnic groups, that local church needs to develop those competencies, and find ways to integrate these national churches. Even though there's a purpose for their being separated—because I believe that there is an important role for that—there needs to be connections back to the entire church.

Personal parishes forge one form of community. The diocese then connects what individual parishes fragment.

Community among a diverse population of Catholics is as much about navigating difference as it is about finding commonality. Pluralism is inherent, writes community scholar Gerard Delanty: "No discussion on community can avoid addressing the question of multiculturalism, for community has become irreversibly pluralized as a concept. To speak of community is to invoke the notion of difference."[4] In *Congregation and Community*, Nancy Ammerman writes that while religious collectives tend to be sorted, homogeneous, and specialized, this need not threaten the general social order because they simultaneously build bridges to the community at large. Describing congregations as "connected communities," Ammerman suggests that isolation is offset through voluntary coalitions that "offer opportunities for going beyond the relative homogeneity of the individual, particularistic congregation."[5]

In Catholic parishes, such interconnection is not merely achieved voluntarily, but also ascribed authoritatively. Connectedness is mandated to exist as a parish in the diocese. This contrasts community definitions spawned primarily from the grassroots. For example, researchers in *Congregation and Community* asked interviewees to identify where their own community began and ended, subsequently matching responses to corresponding census tract maps. Catholics' community lines are not just socially constructed from below; formal boundaries encapsulate them. The very idea of a parish suggests that community is not merely the product of voluntary association, communal narratives, and chosen coalitions. It is also the outcome of religious elites' organizational decisions. Bishops ascertain how to organize Catholics in parishes through an interdependent, wider assessment of community.

BONDING PARISHES AND BRIDGING DIOCESES

A closer look at the idea of *social capital*, considered one key benefit of community, shows how this works in practice. Social capital refers to the advantages (such as friendships and opportunities) derived from one's social networks. People tend to do better when they are connected to others. As symbolic and real communities, parishes—like other local collectives—build social capital for their parishioners. Parishes sew connective threads to the cities, districts, and dioceses in which they sit. They are brick-and-mortar engines of "community-specific social capital," building relationships and networks that strengthen communities and residents therein.[6]

With their emphasis on similarity, personal parishes are particularly good at proffering what political scientist Robert Putnam describes as *bonding* social capital.[7] This kind of social capital is primarily inward-looking, bringing together others like "us." Homogeneous groups network through similarity. Bonding social capital solidifies current group identities and exclusivity. Personal parishes don a quintessential form of bonding participation where attendees form relationships with others like themselves.

Personal parish leaders frequently describe ways their parishes grant access to bonding capital and the economic and social benefits that provides. "The parish isn't only the place where you worship, it's where you socialize" says one Korean pastor. A Latino pastor says similarly that "people come from throughout the county plus beyond the county. They come for Eucharist, they come for social, they come for the educational. And so, they stay." Shared culture, language, and concerns unite fellow Catholics, building relationships through similarity.

Personal parishes issue bonding capital through dedicated spaces that generate a feeling of identity, ownership, and pride. Having one's "own" parish, dedicated to the needs of a particular group, is deeply meaningful to those who belong. As one pastor of a Vietnamese parish put it, "That's right, ownership. They want to own their place. That's the mentality of the Vietnamese people. They don't want to share; they want to own their place." A pastor of a Hispanic personal parish says similarly that "what it allows for is that, for these people: it's their parish."

In this, bonding capital brings with it another form of capital: what Pierre Bourdieu calls "symbolic capital," or "a form of power that is not perceived as power but as legitimate demands for recognition, deference, obedience, or the services of others."[8] The parish, in other words, supersedes individual identities to create legitimacy as an organization. A pastor expands:

> A personal parish can really allow people to be themselves in a way that a blended or diverse parish doesn't offer that possibility. It's just impossible for that to happen; they're not set up that way. And as good as a diverse parish can be, you're never going to ... especially if you have a large number of African Americans, or if it's Filipinos or if it's Hispanics—that minority group, for lack of a better word—is never going to be able to just realize their full potential. Even given the best of scenarios. I mean, you're going to have to sacrifice something. Now, maybe that sacrificing of something is—in a particular circumstance where it's a large, diverse parish—it's good for the whole. But for the target people, is that ... ?

Formal, personal parish status proffers a voice and place at the table in ways that shared spaces do not. A personal parish has a label and status from which to make demands. Symbolic ownership empowers otherwise disempowered Catholics.

The counterpart to bonding capital is *bridging* capital: connections, friendships, and opportunities individuals form with dissimilar others. While bonding social capital brings homogeneous groups together, bridging social capital describes social networks that expand across heterogeneous groups. Connections with those who are not like us, whether racially, economically, ideologically, or otherwise—have a profound impact on our ability to get ahead and to mitigate social inequalities. Sociologist Mark Chaves points out that Catholic parishes are more engaged in bridging activity than conservative and evangelical white Protestant congregations.[9]

Given the intentional homogeneity of personal parishes, they first appear stronger in bonding capital and weaker on bridging capital. The territorial parish as a generalist organization seems better suited to facilitate bridging. Designed to accommodate heterogeneity, territorial parishes prioritize outward-oriented social capital. But the lack of heterogeneity in practice, and imperfect welcome described in earlier chapters, can counter this. Bridging for minority groups of Catholics may look more like a one-way process whereby they must assimilate into extant parish norms.

Non-majority groups integrate by fitting into dominant Catholic culture. They learn to adapt as chameleons so as not to disrupt the status quo. The use of the phrase "American parish" as code for a predominantly white, Novus Ordo territorial parish marks this distinction. Insufficient bonding capital can undermine the capacity for bridging capital in territorial parishes.

This is where the vantage point of the diocese comes in, offering a wider view of community that incorporates parish interdependence. Bishops allow personal parishes to fulfill the prerequisite of bonding capital. Only then can bridging happen, across Catholics in the entirety of a diocese. Parishes are homogeneous alone, but heterogeneous together. Symbolic capital afforded by parish status—a parish for us—translates into bridging capital among wider and diverse others. These are both ordered and simultaneous functions managed across a diocese: bonding within parishes of similarity, bridging across parishes of dissimilarity.

Personal parish leaders talk about how the bonds in dedicated, more homogeneous parishes are what build tools for incorporation into other social contexts. This facilitates integration, as suggested by one Vietnamese personal parish pastor:

> It helps them to adapt to the way of how church is run in this country. It's different...It's, "Hey, I'm going to network in my parish to get a job," maybe, or things such as that. All of these things contribute to forging a strong sense of community.

Officially recognizing a parish home for a given population of Catholics opens avenues for incorporation into diocesan, city, and even national discourse and politics. One bishop surmises that "we're able to get better ministry to these cultural communities, because we deal with the realism of the situation," which in turn leads to "greater integration into the life of the archdiocesan church." One pastor of a Hispanic personal parish asserts the overdue urgency of this:

> We have a unique opportunity at the moment where the eyes of the nation are looking constantly at the Hispanics, at their importance in this nation. And I'm trying to get [my Hispanic parishioners] to understand how they play a factor in all this. No longer do you just—hat in hand—stand outside the door, and wait for the others to finish using the facilities while you just wait patiently. No; we have an opportunity here to make a bold statement that we are here. We are Catholics, just like you.

Older national parishes were hailed for their success in integrating past generations of Catholics. Today's personal parishes provide an opportunity to do the same.[10]

Bishops structure parishes to be interconnected, all the more so given increased diversity and constrained parish (especially priest) resources. Catholics belong to both their parish and their diocese. Leaders share resources. Sacramental preparation relies increasingly upon shared programming, such as engaged retreats and couples ministry. Young adult ministries draw in twenty-somethings from a wider geographic area for "theology on tap" or praise gatherings.[11] A territorial parish's geographic zone will not typically contain a large enough contingent of Catholics "like me." Bridging requires bonding.

Leveraging a diocesan vantage point means forgiving personal parishes for their failure to incorporate bridging capital alone, and territorial parishes for their failure to deliver bonding capital for all. It prioritizes interdependence across parishes, overseen by a shared institution. The diocese is structured to manage parishes organizationally, to build community among a diverse Catholic whole. Parishes bond; dioceses bridge. This kind of logic circles back to Durkheim's conception of community. Solidarity is forged not just through similarity, but difference, lived out interdependently.

RELIGIOUS COMMUNITY WITHOUT PROPINQUITY

If Catholic leaders organize community on a higher, wider plane, this has corollary implications for how local religion relates to place (or placelessness, as the case may be). Traditional conceptions of community (Catholic and otherwise) romanticize locality and territoriality: households that know one other, aid one other, bond and belong in spatial proximity. Adherents are propinquitous. Historian Raymond Gillespie describes this of early Ireland: "Parishes acted as a way of articulating senses of the local that bound people together regardless of their confessional divisions and provided a forum for organizing social life in a rapidly changing world."[12]

Personal parishes eschew traditional territorial lines to forge community out of shared purpose. This is "community without propinquity," to use the phrase of urban scholar Melvin Webber.[13] Pulling Catholics in from across a diocese, theirs is a wider, more asynchronous constitution of local religious organization. While some parishioners reside nearby, many do not. Nor do they need to—the personal parish derives its canonical decree not from shared territory, but shared purpose. Parish means place, but the personal parish prioritizes person. One personal parish pastor ascertains that while personal parishes are "not free of the rules," nonetheless, "it's a different feeling here than a territorial parish. It just feels different."

Structural changes decoupling parish and place are bred of broader social change. Predicting the transformation of modern cities, Webber also wrote in 1963 of how "the essential qualities of urbanness are *cultural* in character, not territorial."[14] Freed by the automobile and upward social mobility, urban dwellers (Catholics among them) reside ever further from urban cores. Modern cities are "neither concentrated nor concentric nor contained," where "space is distinguished from place."[15] Residents' relationships with each other grow independent of spatial propinquity. "Spatial separation or propinquity is no longer an accurate indicator of functional relations; and, hence, mere locational pattern is no longer an adequate symbol of order."[16]

Order in the Catholic Church is achieved through dioceses, managed by bishops, and organized in parishes. Personal parishes show that bishops approach the local Church increasingly through the lens of community without propinquity. "It really helps, to deal with certain things," says one pastor. Another states how personal parishes let bishops innovate around place to better meet lay need:

> It's creating a space for lay people to ask for, to demonstrate the need for, and to establish a place of worship. In some ways, I see it sort of as a replacement of what used to exist for centuries. It seems organic and revolutionary to me. I don't necessarily find it to be a conflict of any notion of the geographical parish. However, I'm sure I can hear the devil's advocate on the other side going, "What happens to our neighborhood ministry?" . . . I think there's a certain tension there that needs to be dealt with sensibly, at the administrative level. But I really see it as an advantage, because I think these places are only occurring where there is a core of need. It's being asked for and demonstrated.

In the Catholic Church and elsewhere, mobility generates innovative approaches to community and organization less reliant upon residential propinquity. "Fluidity and mobility are the keywords" in modern religion, writes sociologist Danièle Hervieu-Léger.[17] Mobility exacerbates personal choice in a religious marketplace, as "individuals travel increasingly long distances and start to think of their world (and possibly their religious and spiritual involvement) in terms of options that have a price, that may be consumed and that have to be chosen according to individual preferences."[18]

Today's personal parishes, more so than older national parishes that were coterminous with their ethnic neighborhoods, draw in Catholics on the move. Mobile Catholics are a byproduct of structural changes in the

US Catholic Church: more Catholics, fewer parishes, and new personal parishes. Catholics drive ever-further to reach an ever-smaller number of ever-larger parishes. Priests pastoring multiple parishes drive even more, serving a widely dispersed and increasingly diverse Catholic clientele. Catholics move farther across space to belong.

Personal parishes expose an emergent geography of belonging in the American Catholic Church. Whereas the narrative of neighborhood told the story of early American Catholicism—and especially that of more densely populated northeastern cities—narratives of mobility (and home) better capture today's story. Common purpose substitutes for common place. Institutionally, the Catholic Church responds to these emergent narratives of belonging by adapting its oldest organizational form—the parish—to a model less closely reliant upon neighborhood territoriality: the personal parish. Personal parishes build interconnected structures of community for people on the move. They organize an itinerant Catholic base.

If personal parishes pull together Catholics across space to coalesce in purpose, are they more akin to "imaginary communities"? This is the term Benedict Anderson used to describe nations whose symbolic expressions of community do not (and cannot) rely upon face-to-face contact.[19] "Community is shaped by cognitive and symbolic structures that are not underpinned by 'lived' spaces and immediate forms of social intimacy," summarizes Delanty of Anderson.[20] Anthropologist Fredrik Barth also writes of communities defined not by locality, but meaning and identity. "The boundaries to which we must give our attention are of course social boundaries, though they may have territorial counterparts."[21] Social boundaries make community; community is what people imagine it to be. Culture supplants place.

French sociologist of religion Danièle Hervieu-Léger captures some of this in describing religion as a "chain of memory." The chain links an individual believer to a broader community of past, present, and future believers. Tradition (collective memory) is core to religious communities' existence. Without this chain of memory, according to Hervieu-Léger, religion declines. Fragmentation and competing memories challenge continuity: if individual believers subjectively choose how they enact tradition and belief, this may shatter shared memories. By way of example, she describes "elective fraternities," or "a community of values and references which has developed through shared interests, experience, and hardships"—a concept applicable to personal parishes. Elective fraternities can either reconstruct memories through collective engagement, or clash with religion "each time it places the communion of the hearts and minds of its members above fidelity to the chain of belief."[22]

This would mean that personal parishes' emphasis on purpose rather than proximity can—but does not have to—compete with unity, tradition, and community. Pope Francis warns Catholics not to "withdraw into yourselves" in homogeneous parishes:

> This is a danger: we shut ourselves up in the parish, with our friends, within the movement, with the like-minded . . . but do you know what happens? When the Church becomes closed, she becomes an ailing Church, she falls ill!

To compensate, bishops rely upon the diocese and parish interdependence to sustain the chain of memory. "Ultimately, whoever's running the parish is subject to the dictates of the bishop, because it's his parish," says one pastor.

Another personal parish pastor explains management across aspatial boundaries as such:

> The idea of there being personal parishes that are overseen by bishops or archbishops falls in the context of a greater diocesan ministry. I think it's more regulated, for better or for worse. I think it demonstrates a certain freedom in a place where there really wasn't any before, at the diocesan level.

Bishops are still at the helm of parish boundaries: even social ones, absent propinquity. Hervieu-Léger says that, for Catholicism: "With its hierarchical structure directly threatened by the recognition that the growing number of new communities it is harbouring closely matches the tendency for belief to become individualized, it has reacted energetically by reaffirming the centrality of the doctrinal authority of Rome."[23]

Even to the extent that personal parishes bear the traits of imagined communities, they are nonetheless realized in place. Parishes still exist in fixed, stationary forms, in physical church buildings. Mobile people encounter immobile infrastructures. Parishes demonstrate one way in which "social life thus seems full of multiple and extended connections often across long distances" that is nonetheless "organized through certain nodes."[24] Churches are nodes of real, face-to-face community birthed in mobile environments. These spaces, write Sheller and Urry, "orchestrate new forms of social life around such nodes." Parishes command participants' physical proximity to engage in activities together—a collective performance in time. Seen in this way, mobility does not render the end of geography, but exists in relation to place.[25] Personal parishes are imagined through purpose and diffused residency, but real in particular, physical places. This is a logic of modern, local religious community that is neither wholly congregational nor wholly territorial. Parish and purpose congeal in place.

Returning to the question at hand, then: Do personal parishes reshape local religious community apart from propinquity? Should parishes be thought of as places with real boundaries, erected in space and lived out collectively, or places with only social boundaries, constructed through shared symbolic and cultural meaning? Bishops' use of personal parishes would argue that, to some degree, both are true. Community without propinquity describes modern American Catholicism to the extent that individual Catholics draw symbolic boundaries to generate belonging, apart from shared neighborhood space. But to suggest that community exists only without propinquity (or without official status as "parish") lacks a reference to the chain of memory and tradition that links voluntary groups to a broader, interconnected tradition and local leader. A bishop's authority defines a Catholic structure; lay Catholics come together face-to-face in weekly Masses and extra-Mass activities. Mobile Catholics necessarily live out their faith in immobile, institutionally defined, diocesan-embedded parish structures.

CHARTER CHURCHES

The Catholic Church is not alone in cutting creatively across spatial boundaries to build new communities of purpose. Public education presents a parallel institutional arena where questions of geography, purpose, community, and diversity arise: namely, in the phenomenon of public charter schools. Like personal parishes, charter schools find official designation through purposes aside from residential propinquity.

Charter schools sit among a growing set of schooling options that emphasize choice: magnet schools, voucher programs, and homeschooling also among them. They sit within bound school districts, but draw students from throughout the district. While public taxpayer dollars fund charter schools (like all public schools), the designation enables innovation through charters run by parents, educators, community groups, universities, or private organizations. Debuting in the early 1990s, charter schools have experienced exponential growth. As of the 2015–2016 school year, there were more than 6,800 charter schools serving nearly three million US children. Schools encompass a broad array of purposes: Afrocentrism, international studies, fine arts, classical education, and dedicated service to poor and urban students among them.[26]

Charter schools are the fastest-growing area of school choice. Research highlights how their emphasis on choice fosters innovation. A competitive marketplace promotes new forms and best practices, with the potential of better student outcomes. On the other hand, government bureaucracy and administrative oversight can make such innovations rare or short-lived. Research reveals mixed results regarding students' short-term academic gains, but positive long-term gains such as graduation rates and college enrollment.[27]

Back in personal parishes, a parallel to charter schools lends some predictions. Personal parishes, too, reflect a growing area of formally sanctioned choice. They are more common among some Catholics than others (e.g., disproportionately serving Asian Catholics). Choice and competition may breed innovation and better practice. This innovation may be less consequential due to the need to adhere to generic parish rules and oversight. Individual Catholic "outcomes" could be measured by retention in the faith, levels of parish involvement, or vocations. Pastors do note how personal parishes are "needed, because there are a whole bunch of Catholics who wouldn't be Catholic without that."

A "charter church" (or charter parish, or charter congregation) can offer a useful moniker to name the dynamic of sanctioned choice in local religion. Charter schools and charter churches (i.e., personal parishes) are both purpose-driven. They respond organizationally to transformations at the grassroots, but are formally embedded in hierarchical, bureaucratic structures. A charter church label—as opposed to a de facto congregational one—captures the influence of authority over organizational structures and outcomes. Loose ties are hardly the characteristic indicator of charter schools, or of personal parishes. Parishes are formally legislated entities; they are "mandated congregations" approved at the hands of external authorities.[28]

Charter schools, charter churches, and other choice-based reforms represent a slow evolution among institutions toward greater individual agency within the confines of institutional regulation. Charter schools are legal, legally regulated, and publicly funded. Proponents assert that they respond to a broken system of residential segregation, funding tiered by property value, and vested interest that undermines the geographically based school system. A choice-based system can also empower parents to control their children's education.[29] Districts advance school choice as social justice. Those opposed point to how charter and other semi-privatized schools take resources (and nonwhite students) away from other schools. Achievement outcomes also remain ambiguous.

The pace of a formal "parish choice" evolution in the institutional Catholic Church is slower than that of the public school system, but notable, nonetheless. Personal parishes are a (canonically) legal option; they are housed in and supported by their diocese. A "pro" personal parish argument centralizes comparable themes of social justice: the predominant territorial system of parishes replicates vested interests and keeps populations of Catholics apart from others in neighborhoods of their choosing. Personal parishes empower Catholics to live out their faith in ways that are most meaningful to them. Or, on the "con" side, personal parishes take Catholics away from territorial parishes . . . with ambiguous advantages.

In any case, it is worth noting that charter schools exist in tandem with neighborhood schools. Cities and school districts make localized decisions for how best to work out a balance between models. Both can and do thrive, simultaneously: having one system does not preclude the other. Such is the case, too, with personal parishes and territorial parishes. As one bishop put it, "I think every bishop has to find that balance." This is resource partitioning: using both specialist and generalist organizations, together.

Other interviewees agree that both territorial parishes and personal parishes can coexist. One pastor, for example, concludes:

> I think there is room for both. I always try not to be either/or. It's usually this *and* that. I think that territorial parishes have their role. There are many people who don't like driving too much. If you have school and church, it's good for neighborhoods. . . . Now, for personal parishes: military parishes, campus ministries, or hospital parishes—there are specific needs. And those needs cannot always can be best addressed in a territorial parish setting. So, territorial parishes? Yes. Personal parishes? Yes, as well.

In the US Catholic Church, bishops manage dioceses by utilizing both parish models. "I see the need for both," summarizes one pastor. "The territorial, and also to give the freedom to those that like to participate another place." Contemporary conditions in American Catholicism foster the vitality of both generalist and named specialist organizations. A charter system need not replace a neighborhood one. Both have their place and their purpose.

AS LONG AS THERE ARE PARISHES

This study of personal parishes cannot infer conclusively about the quality of community within any given personal parish. But sociologically, the structure and spatiality of community predicates experiences therein. Drawing on the parallel of the neighborhood, sociologist John Logan reminds us that "while segregation is all about neighborhoods, it is not much related to neighboring. Whether people even know their neighbors or not, they collectively experience the resources of the neighborhood, and neighborhoods reinforce inequality."[30] Whether and how Catholics commune inside the parish is predicated by (and dependent upon) whether and how the parish qua parish molds that experience in the first place.

In the American Catholic Church, there will always be parishes. Canonical regulations stipulate that all US territory be parsed into parish space such that even when the population moves and changes, the parish remains (albeit with redrawn boundaries). Contrasting the parish to the congregation, sociologist R. Stephen Warner paraphrases a metaphoric account of the parish as a city bus, driving through diverse and crowded streets to pick up all those who pay the fare. The chosen congregation, he writes, is more like a chartered bus, filled with like-minded people.[31]

While memorable, the parish-as-city-bus metaphor has its limitations. Most damning is the persistent reality of residential segregation in contemporary America, undermining the supposed randomness of the territorial parish. While the number of multiethnic neighborhoods is on the rise, black and whites still live mostly apart. Neighborhood integration between whites, Asians, and Latinos has changed little in recent years.[32] In this, the city bus metaphor breaks down: unless the bus journeys all the way from wealthier, predominantly white neighborhoods into lower-income, predominantly black neighborhoods ... over to enclaves dominated by first-generation Asians, and to heavily Latino neighborhoods ... it is hardly going to pick up a representative cross-section of American Catholics. Not to mention that it would be one long bus ride (and, someone has to sit in the back).

Congregationalism doesn't sufficiently explain it, either: divided parishes are not the mere progeny of parish choice. Segregated neighborhoods breed segregated territorial parishes. Kyle Crowder and Maria Krysan summarize three major explanations for neighborhood segregation, pertinent to their overlay with parishes: (1) people's in-group affinity and out-group avoidance; (2) inequality in resources to access "better" neighborhoods; and (3) discriminatory treatment in the market.[33] To the last point, if Catholic bishops are "realtors" playing to the resources and preferences of "homebuyers," then they exacerbate division in the US Catholic Church through the very structural arrangements of organizational Catholicism. If "residential segregation is the linchpin of racial stratification," per the title of a 2016 article by Douglas S. Massey, then residential segregation is the linchpin of parish segregation ... and, arguably, racial stratification by consequence. The territorial parish does not generate a utopia of representative Catholics congealed in community, together. Even to the extent that territorial parishes' geographic constitution facilitates diverse membership, segregation in other arenas of social life nonetheless undermines it.

Take, for example, the city of St. Louis, a city steeped in Catholic history as the "Rome of the West" and still among the most racially "hypersegregated" cities in the United States.[34] Leveling blame, urban historian Colin Gordon calls out "the historical choices made by public and private actors in St. Louis" as culpable for the city's urban crisis.[35] Hypersegregation is both an outgrowth of and precursor to segregated religious organizations. Personal (national) parishes dot St. Louis's early history. Bishop John Joseph Glennon (1903–1946) later oversaw a proliferation of neighborhood churches to meet nearby needs. Territorial ascription for those parishes was often quite small—in some instances, just a few blocks wide. Neighborhood, parish, and school were trifocal. In time, and through a mix of questionable urban policies, St. Louis neighborhood profiles changed dramatically. Racist zoning ordinances and white flight emptied many Catholic churches. The segregated city spawned segregated neighborhood parishes.

Describing congregations' typical encounter with significant ecological change, Ammerman predicts that "most will face a crisis," transform, and "either move or die."[36] In *Shades of White Flight*, Mark Mulder describes how white Christian Reform Church (CRC) congregations picked up and left in the wake of African American in-migration to Chicago.[37] Explaining their departure, Mulder cites three primary factors: (1) the denomination's historical precedence of schism and mobility; (2) a narrow conception of "place" centering on closed church networks rather than wider neighborhoods; and (3) a polity emphasizing de facto congregationalism and individual authority.

These explanations fail to explain the fate of Catholic parishes amid neighborhood change. Catholicism's organizational response to demographic change reiterates institutional authority. Catholic parishes exhibit (1) stability and staying power; (2) broad, territorial, and interconnected conceptions of place; and (3) a centralized polity that reduces congregationalism and individual authority. Returning to the example of St. Louis: the city's parishes couldn't leave. Many white Catholics, to be sure, did flock to the suburbs. But Catholic polity meant that diocesan leaders had to redraw parish boundaries where the population's carrying capacity was smaller. This meant suppressing some parishes, their territories absorbed by another parish. In the thirty years following the 1983 changes to canon law, the Archdiocese of St. Louis suppressed scores of parishes ... but left no block without an assigned parish.

Where redrawn boundaries emptied beautiful churches among populations too small to justify another territorial parish, the archdiocese established personal parishes. The city gained personal parishes for Hispanic Catholics, for Catholics attached to the Traditional Latin Mass, for Catholics committed to social justice, for Vietnamese and Korean Catholics, and more . . . even for the purpose of meeting tourist needs near the world-famous St. Louis Arch. The diocese capitalized on the opportunity of emptied churches to designate personal parishes with specialized purposes. Ironically, both territorial and personal parishes arrived at the same place: largely homogeneous, generally uniracial parishioners. But while St. Louis's territorial parishes arrived there as a consequence of segregated neighborhoods, St. Louis's personal parishes, as a consequence of formally named decree and specialization.[38]

Both territorial and personal parishes embody formal, organizational responses to diversity. For Catholics, the process is regulated. Historians credit the staying power of the Catholic Church in urban settings to the definitional character of parishes as geographically bound.[39] Parishes are comparatively more rooted. Amidst diocesan restructuring and grassroots transformation, personal parishes grant bishops another regulated, structural alternative to preserve Catholic presence and meet local need. As long as there are parishes, there will be a structural, organized process of sorting Catholics by place and purpose. Catholics' behavior necessarily acts within, around, and in sync with the structure of parishes—both personal and territorial.

LOCAL RELIGIOUS ORGANIZATION AND INTERDEPENDENCE

Robert Putnam famously bemoaned the loss of community in his 2000 book *Bowling Alone*, while nevertheless acknowledging that religion continues to act as "a central fount of American community life."[40] Perhaps, some posit, "the reason why commentators like Putnam have found a death of communities is that they have looked for them in the wrong places."[41] Or, perhaps, mobility and choice restructure community into a new form. A broader, interdependent lens sees community in structure and connections, rather than a "preoccupation with locating primary ties in local areas."[42] Grassroots transformations in Catholicism seed what one pastor calls "an opportunity for the church to struggle with its own relationship to the world, and to what its mission is."

Signaling increasing interdependence, trend data from the General Social Survey suggests that neighborhood social ties are in decline and non-neighborhood social ties are on the rise.[43] Sociologist Robert Sampson articulates an interdependent framework in his study of the city of Chicago, which he says exhibits a "spatial logic" wherein the neighbors of neighborhoods matter.[44]

In the American Catholic Church, bishops act on interdependence to forge community from the vantage point of the forest, rather than that of the trees. They treat single parishes not as self-contained units, but always and everywhere a part of a diocese. This structural reality suggests that a narrow, congregational focus misses how institutional leaders organize community, institutionally. While an ecological framing can appreciate proximate congregations' mutual influence, this interdependence is tied to polity. Catholic organizations, linked through dioceses led by bishops, illustrate "community as network." Leaders make interlocking parish decisions. In this, institutional responses to diversity imply compulsory connection and regulated structures.[45]

A similar logic guides Vatican II documents that talk about a single parish not as "Church" on its own, but as a "cell" of a diocesan or particular Church. "Church" denotes a diocese, not one parish. Vatican II advances a meso-level of understanding Catholicism, where a diocese sits meaningfully between (and thus embeds) the universal Church and the individual parish.[46] This is a "communion ecclesiology," to introduce a theological term with sociological consequences. Dioceses strategically subdivide into parishes to cultivate an interdependent notion of community. The parish as a diocesan cell serves as "an obvious example of the apostolate on the community level inasmuch as it brings together the many human differences within its boundaries and merges them into the universality of the Church."[47] Parishes unify Catholics together into a shared collective (whether decreed by place or person/purpose). More recent Vatican documents echo this description of the parish in its interdependent, community-building functions. People are linked to parishes; parishes are linked to dioceses; dioceses are linked to the Church. Community is interdependent.

What becomes apparent from bishops' applications of this is that, while a parish is "a certain community," it is, nonetheless, "*not* a church in the fullest theological sense of the term."[48] Bishops do not view single parishes as operating in isolation, but as always and necessarily a part of its diocese and ultimately a part of a unified (and hierarchical) global Roman Catholic Church.

The parish operates as one node in an interconnected institutional conception of community, shaping responses to diversity accordingly. Sociologically, this begs for an analysis of community that does presume its limits at a single, semiautonomous congregation. Parishes are interconnected. An interdependent approach to structuring (and understanding) local religion rationalizes fragmentation through interconnectivity. Bishops describe personal parishes as a constitutive part of a unified diocesan whole. Here, one describes his own interlocking approach to parishes:

> The "us" is the Catholic Church, and we are the Church—we are part of the Church. But other people are part of "us," and part of the Church. So it is very, very important that we pray as the Catholic Church prays, and not just at a particular moment someone in a particular congregation wants to organize an effort so we pray this way. All of this is part of living in a community; the Church has been doing it for years and will continue to do it.

Other leaders reason that specialized communities (personal parishes) are acceptable, "as long as they know that they're welcome in any parish, whether they're Korean, or African, or Hispanic, or whatever they might be."

The institutional structure of welcome—community—extends to the diocesan level rather than just to a single parish. Individual Catholics find a home somewhere in the diocese; all move to varying degrees across diocesan space to find and build meaningful community.

Applied to a more extreme degree, an interdependent approach could justify a parish structure with *only* personal parishes, and no territorial ones. The diocese already defines the wider territory. Could the diocese act as territory, the parish as "home"? I asked interviewees if the American Catholic Church should do this—erase parish boundaries (while preserving diocesan ones), instead privileging communities of purpose, identity, and choice. One pastor ruminates:

> That's basically what's happening already. So, I guess the question is: Should that be formalized? Should the Church in this country face facts? From a practical point of view, I can see that—because it's already happened. Just to say, "Well it's happened, so let's go along with it. Let's achieve their understanding of parish structure." On the other hand, would we be losing something by taking away the territorial parish idea? I don't know. I'm racking my brain here, trying to think what would we be missing. I don't know.

Given another moment, he speculates further:

> I think that one of the dangers if we went exclusively to personal parishes is that people would fall through the cracks. We would know about the people

that actually come to us, but there could be someone living out there that we have no idea, and they don't belong to any particular territory, so there is no one that would be looking for them. So we might lose that. I don't know.... Even though I've been Catholic for almost 30 years, much of my practical thinking when it comes to this sort of thing is still modeled on what I experienced growing up in the Protestant church. And it seemed to work perfectly well there.

Another leader deflects the question, saying that it opens up bigger questions:

I have no idea if eventually the notion of a personal parish may all but completely erode that notion of a geographical parish, or if both will continue to exist. But I think it really does invite the deeper question of, "In what way does the Church structure organizations and even its physical buildings a way in which the Church is meeting the needs, the deeply heartfelt needs of the people of this world? Who live with a lot of change, a lot of suffering and have a deep and rich need for God and for community?" It offers both opportunity and challenge, I think, for the already existing model. And I hope, if nothing, the personal parish model will provide an opportunity for the Church to more actively reflect upon its own way of leading people to God.

These institutional decisions matter to individual Catholics' experience of the Church.

By implication, this means that sociologists and other observers of religion in community (and Catholicism, in particular) must necessarily identify the characteristics of the *network*: the diocese, not just the parish. Catholicism is lived in and beyond the territorial parish (as territory) and personal parish (as person). Catholics traverse boundaries—geographic and social—to unify in a particular Church.

Sociologist of religion Omar McRoberts observed in *Streets of Glory* that churches in low-rent areas attract participants from elsewhere, limiting attachments to the neighborhood and its needs. Personal parishes suggest that the neighborhood is both everywhere and nowhere. Viewed in light of (a) the co-existence of territorial parishes (guaranteed to cover all territorial space in a diocese) and (b) the requisite connection of personal parishes to the diocese, this may predict different outcomes in linking local religious organizations to place, even amidst highly mobile populations. Catholic parishes are both rooted and interconnected. Their structural occurrence is purposeful and planned. This kind of thinking may foretell new conclusions about local religion and community.

Using personal parishes alongside territorial ones, the American Catholic Church structures community to balance both place and purpose. Local religious community bears both social and spatial roots. Catholics come together in parishes to be who they are: apart, but together. Whether bound by territory or purpose, religious structures designed from above comingle with lived practice from below. Community is thus both symbolic and structural. Parishes structure lay behaviors.

Far from an impetuous trend born of modern technology, community among Catholics has been evolving for some time. Catholics pass assigned territorial parishes to attend elsewhere. Territorial parishes boast far wider geographic catchment areas. Parishes within walking distance are now, by and large, a privilege of the few. The challenges of building community sans proximity is not new, but ever more acute. This is modern American Catholicism.[49]

Dwelling—in a mobile world—takes on new meaning for religious adherents. Even to the extent that Catholics still, by and large, experience their Catholicism at "home," this locality is undercut by new patterns of connection.[50] Like all Americans, the bonds (and fault lines) of social identities recast home beyond the neighborhood. Personal parishes sit between community-as-proximity and community-as-identity, or, put another way, real and symbolic forms of community. Akin to the "heterotopias" described by Michel Foucault, personal parishes operate on different spatial terms, atypical from the usual order.[51] Personal parishes engage a different logic than their territorial counterparts and non-Catholic counterparts. Heterotopias exist in real space, but subvert the regular arrangements of space. Personal parishes subvert the territorial structure of American Catholicism. They reconcile choice and agency among individual Catholics. They invite community in both real and symbolic forms, contained in place. At the nexus of top-down decision-making and bottom-up behavior, personal parishes assert a new kind of spatial logic. Accordingly, bishops adjudicate modern Catholic communities as both real and imagined communities. Both territorial and social boundaries envelop local religion.

Viewing community from a broader, interdependent place offers Church leaders a more satisfactory—albeit imperfect—solution to catholicity, to heterogeneity and homogeneity in Catholic community. If the territorial parish has failed to cultivate community and home for many Catholics—most prominently, those whose worship practices and preferences are othered within dominant American Catholic practice—then personal parishes are hardly to blame for undermining community.

Sociologist Herbert Gans instructs that "the negative consequences of heterogeneity are not inevitable, but they occur with regularity, even among the most well-intentioned people."[52] It might very well be that a "balanced community" can be structured only through a multi-parish, multi-locale, interrelated institutional whole.

Conclusion

We bless God for giving us the personal parishes that we've needed. I just think it's very important that we realize that these are not a toy. These are not a little instrument that we set up for ourselves . . . just to make it convenient to have our acquaintances together. No! That's not the purpose! There's no "Black Church"! There's no "White Church"! There's no "American Church"! There's just the Catholic Church. We don't want to separate people; we want to bring people together. We don't all have to have the same viewpoint in regard to liturgy, or any other aspect of the church. We want to be Catholic. And that means, "Bring everybody in."

—Cardinal Archbishop, United States

***

I want to say to these people, in one sense, "Way to go! You got your own place!" But, it's not over yet.

—Diocesan Multicultural Director

***

This book has focused on a distinctive subset of American Catholic parishes: *personal parishes*—defined not by territory, but by purpose. Serving Catholic groups bound by ethnicity, liturgical preference, or other unique mission, personal parishes represent a form of officially designated, local religious organization that prioritizes purpose over place. The novelty of personal parishes in the United States today refutes common presumptions that such a model for organizing local religion is now disallowed, aged, or extinct. While introduced with different origins, purposes, and functions than their historical counterparts, personal parishes are very much alive in the contemporary American Catholic Church. They make room for diverse expressions of American Catholicism.

Personal parishes showcase an emergent (and reclaimed) organizational form: they are named, specialist organizations. They eschew assimilation for specialization. They reconcile Americans' heterogeneity and propensity for choice with the Church's enduring authoritative, hierarchical polity. Personal parishes, in other words, present a strategy for religious leaders to manage internal diversity. Allowing for both generalist (territorial) organizations and named, specialist (personal) organizations means that both purpose and place can coexist.

Making room for diversity is a central challenge in contemporary American Catholicism. At stake is the just inclusion of all American Catholics within a single, unified, American Catholic Church. One parish constitutes but one part of a broader whole. The structural change wrought by personal parishes in recent years reflects transformations already underway at the grassroots, where individual Catholics navigate their own inclusion. We can ignore the role of social boundaries no more than we can ignore imperfect integration within territorial boundaries. As noted in the words of the diocesan multicultural director quoted at the outset of this chapter: it's not over yet. The story of organizing diversity in contemporary American Catholicism remains unfinished.

Having here considered parishes, boundaries, decisions, difference, fragmentation, and community, this book concludes with a handful of lessons that personal parishes offer for understanding local religion and institutional responses to diversity. Namely, the forthcoming pages explore: (1) ascription and achievement in local religion; (2) generalism and specialism in organizing diversity; (3) the future of personal parishes; and (4) the place of purpose in a heterogeneous (Catholic) America.

ASCRIPTION AND ACHIEVEMENT IN
RELIGIOUS ORGANIZATION
Local Religious Organizations Are Shaped by
Both Agency and Structure

Sociologists typically describe religion in the United States as highly voluntary. People choose whether to be religious, how and how much, and with whom (if anyone) to be religious. This is religious freedom. Structurally, this plays out into congregational forms of religion: local, churchlike organizations that are voluntary, not-for-profit, and semiautonomous. Legal and social norms sift all religious traditions through isomorphic pressures to conform and gain legitimacy in the American context. The lack of state regulation, moreover, enables religious groups to change and adapt, sans government intervention. Historically, such voluntary assemblies—particularly through their connections to ethno-national identities—have promoted the growth and vitality of American religion. Religion is less ascribed (whether as state-sponsored, state-regulated, or territorially assigned) and more achieved (voluntary, semiautonomous, and preferential).[1]

But upon closer examination, this privileging of achievement over ascription is insufficient to explain how American Catholics organize. Catholicism in the United States exists in "the tension between the traditional church principle of prescribed membership and the voluntary denominational principle dominant in the American religious environment," writes Jose Casanova.[2] A centralized polity structure determines formal parish status. Establishment, vitality, change, and survival turn not on the efforts of lay parishioners alone, but on that of bishops at the helm of wider dioceses. This comes through plainly in the words of one canon lawyer when he says, "There's just really no, I was going to say 'no realistic chance,' but it's really no—not even an *unrealistic* chance of overturning a bishop's decision not to give a personal parish. You really *have* to get along with your bishop." Ascription matters.

Local religion is necessarily examined not only from below—through the meaningful activities of religious actors themselves—but also from above. Catholicism's official parish structure itself offsets the tendency toward achievement: Catholics automatically belong to the geographic parish in which they reside, irrespective of their behavior. Even to the extent that American Catholics' practice belies this structure, the structure itself remains: parish boundaries stipulate who is in the parish, and who is not. Every inch of space, every Catholic in America, belongs. Personal parishes do not make territorial parishes congregational any more than an allowance for married priest-converts makes celibacy optional.[3] The exception proves the rule. Understanding organizational change requires looking not just through the perspective of individuals therein but also through that of the institution, and of institutional elites.

Seeing religious organizations as a product of structure alongside agency unsettles common modes of analyzing local religion. Take, for example, the concluding epigraph of an argument outlining de facto congregationalism, in which R. Stephen Warner describes his visit to a voluntary gathering of gay Catholics (Dignity-Chicago). "We have chosen to be here," Warner quotes from an attendee, "We are a congregation." Agency clearly shapes their religious involvement, and their collective identity vis-à-vis a shared institution. But, there's a catch: Dignity-Chicago isn't a parish. While voluntary association makes them a "congregation" by the logic and rubric of de facto congregationalism, it does not make them a Catholic parish. Likewise, for the independent communities Julie Byrne describes in *The Other Catholics*: theirs is a claimed Catholic status, but not a sanctioned institutional one. Parish status hinges upon a bishop's canonical decree, not upon lay Catholics' voluntary association.[4] Structure circumvents agency.

Sociologically, agency-oriented theories of local religion do well in capturing a narrative of cultural production in modern (especially American) religion. But religious organizations—like all of social life—are a mix of agency and structure. Institutions, and those endowed with the power of decision-making, are instrumental to lived outcomes. Seeing local religious organizations as structurally determined as well as voluntarily determined balances the scale. Even in a highly individualistic American context, religious organizations are structures, too, at the mercy of institutional elites.

To take another example, consider Catholics who, for months or years, stand vigil in their churches to protest parish suppression (i.e., church closure). They voluntarily assemble. They are localized. They lend their time, money, and leadership. They share in worship and fellowship, and claim a congregational identity. But alone, they do not hold the power to halt parish closure. Theologian John Seitz's ethnographic depiction of the wounds of parish closure includes an account of lay Catholics for whom closure represented "a deepened sense of scandal" that "caused people to lose their faith," and "a violation down to [the] core."[5] Needless to say, the Catholics Seitz interviewed would not have closed "their" parish. "Parish" is an institutional decision as much as it is a cultural production.

Theories of voluntary association also hinge upon a lack of regulation: believers belong where they want. Catholicism, however, is not an unregulated domain. We see this in sharp relief through personal parishes: bishops reigned in their proliferation by denying them for the better part of a century, then re-established their presence post-1983. Individual leaders make different choices in different circumstances, of course, but even that variation affirms the fact that lay Catholics are not at the helm of organizational outcomes. A voluntary religious context, mixed with increasing diversity therein, does not spawn subsidiarity at the expense of authority. This is a formal, structural response by a hierarchical institution reacting to grassroots change. Politics matter in a high polity Church.

A structural recalculation of local religion need not dismiss all agency-oriented thinking. Michele Dillon, for example, writes: "Being Catholic is both dependent on the church hierarchy's interpretation of Catholicism and simultaneously independent of it. It means being both the consumer and the producer of doctrine."[6] Catholics are both consumers and producers of Catholic parishes. Parish choice and lackluster administrative oversight provide evidence of increased flexibility and individual Catholics' imprint on parish practice, parish boundaries, and parish constitution. A bishop's decision to start a personal parish may stem from an empathetic response to the petition of a local community. We hear evidence of such grassroots sources for institutional change throughout this book. But in a tradition structured by hierarchical authority, formal institutional action (and lack thereof) presents a strong counterforce. Local, organized religion only is not merely subjectivity and social construction: it is structure, too.

The American Catholic Church remains territorially organized, while simultaneously fostering religious preference through the formal designation of personal parishes. Both generalist and named specialist organizations accommodate a diverse Catholic population. Personal parishes do not mimic congregations in allowing for choice: their institutional designation means that even voluntary association is institutionally prescribed. Personal parishes recognize and embed choice in a way that goes beyond a tacit acceptance of individuals' autonomy. Territorial parish ascription, moreover, does not rest upon the complete rejection of achievement: regulation does not nullify agency. Individual Catholics may "achieve" their parish participation even as the parish itself is ascribed. Within the social and geographic parameters of a diocese, personal parishes simultaneously affirm individual religious preference and reassert institutional control. This is a strategic organizational innovation.

GENERALISM, SPECIALISM, AND INSTITUTIONAL RESPONSES TO DIVERSITY
Organizational Structures Embed Formal Responses to Difference

Whether in churches, schools, voting precincts, workplaces, neighborhoods, or otherwise, the structure of organizations reflects (and shapes) institutional responses to diversity. Personal parishes reveal how the Catholic Church defines, allocates, and controls faith communities canonically (i.e., structurally) in response to internal diversity. The specific strategy that the American Catholic Church has deployed is a dual parish structure: both territorial parishes and personal parishes. Territorial parishes act as generalist organizations, serving all. Personal parishes act as specialist organizations, serving some.

Often, generalist organizations integrated across race, taste, class, and other lines of difference are heralded as the organizational form best suited to combat social problems associated with difference. Observers bemoan (for good reason) the lack of diversity in countless social institutions. Residential segregation, for example, acts as a fundamental barrier to racial equality. Sociologist Jonathan Kozol's many books heartbreakingly recount the impacts of segregation by race and class in America's highly unequal public school system. Most American congregations contain attendees of almost entirely one racial group. Race is the "problem" and the multiracial organizations the "answer," the "promised land." Homogeneity and apartness, assessed from the landscape of much of the sociological literature, is a deplorable reality in reflecting and refracting enduring social fissures along racial lines.[7]

But another problem is that the opposite—generalist, heterogeneous spaces—offer an imperfect solution. Americans stumble toward acceptance and equality across myriad lines of difference. Accounts from Catholics whose negative experiences pushed them into personal parishes echo this reality. Sheer internal diversity does not ensure an equal distribution of voice and power (especially for minority groups), nor ownership and empowerment for those already marginalized. Color-blind rhetoric and diversity talk in a world of "racism without racists" can conveniently blind Americans to the realities of difference, but does not erase the realities of difference.[8]

Some sociologists affirm this caveat in their own observations of integrated organizational structures. Sociologist Korie Edwards, for example, after conducting an in-depth ethnography of one multiracial church, wrote that "my observations of interracial churches ultimately led me to the following proposition: interracial churches with a substantial white attendance will work (by this I mean sustain a racially or ethnically diverse attendance) to the extent that they are first comfortable places for whites to attend."[9] In other words, if the integrated organizational structure doesn't work for privileged parties, it may not work at all. Sociologist Richard Pitt likewise critiques an overemphasis on racial "transcendence" in multiracial congregations, where participants' shared religion is assumed to trump racial dissimilarity. This is what people of color have to do all the time as minorities in white spaces, Pitt points out; hardly "a monumental shift in our understanding of race relations."[10] Both Edwards and Pitt level important critiques of institutional responses to diversity that (organizationally) bend to white privilege. As such, institutional structures can perpetuate the very inequalities they desire to undo. Generalist organizations don't always appeal to everyone equally.

Similar problems arise in Catholic parishes. Theologian Brett Hoover writes that the shared, multicultural parish "may provide us with valuable tools for living together well in a complex, multicultural society." But Hoover's use of the future tense here, paired with his cautious conclusion, is telling. Right now, shared parishes are fraught with tension: a "kind of permanent crucible of grief where resentments and frustrations dominate the scene over time."[11] The conclusion is hardly foregone. As I can attest in observing my own children's behavior, "sharing" is hardly a neutral or just enterprise. It matters who is doing the dividing.

Are other institutional sectors achieving more positive outcomes as they bend to welcome diversity internally? Writing about everyday public spaces like malls and museums, sociologist and ethnographer Elijah Anderson describes the "cosmopolitan canopy" in which individuals can "take leave of their particularism" and "connect across ethnic and racial lines."[12] But—painfully—Anderson describes how the cosmopolitan canopy is not an assuredly safe space. In his words:

> The affront very often takes place in a trusted social space or public environment like the cosmopolitan-oriented canopy, where a certain level of decorum and good-will is ordinarily expected. Emotions flood over the victim as this middle-class, cosmopolitan-oriented black person is humiliated and shown that he or she is, before anything else, a racially circumscribed black person after all. No matter what she has achieved, or how decent and law-abiding she is, there is no protection, no sanctuary, no escaping from this fact.

The insult of such an encounter, however minor, "can have significant impact," Anderson writes.

Assessed in another institutional context, sociologists Amanda Lewis and John Diamond write about the challenge of structuring schools to meet the needs of diverse student populations. Their book's title hints strongly of its findings: *Despite the Best Intentions: How Racial Inequality Thrives in Good Schools.* The authors conducted interviews and observations over the course of a school year in a highly resourced public high school whose administrators were baffled by persistent racial achievement gaps. Their findings reveal how even well-meaning actions can reproduce inequality. Remedies, Lewis and Diamond conclude, must shift away from individual blame and essentialist interpretations of culture, and toward evidence-based patterns in organizations. Put another way, cultural awareness does not sufficiently remedy inequality in schools. Structural and institutional awareness are needed, too.[13]

In yet another parallel, sociologists Richard Zweigenhaft and William Domhoff write about institutional responses to diversity in government and corporate organizations. There, the ideological push for multiculturalism often translates minimally into day-to-day practice due to stagnant organizational structures. "For all the changes in rationale and the emphasis on bottom-line business objectives, the actual practices of the corporations (and universities and large nonprofit organizations) remained about the same, based on the procedures and programs initially established by social movements and government laws."[14] This is the irony of diversity, they say: the illusion of multiculturalism in a milieu of unequal power. Unless and until organizational structures change through institutional regulation, individual behaviors will perpetuate the status quo.

Back in the Catholic Church, this brings a critical spotlight on why an alternative to the generalist organizational ideal has emerged: the named, specialist organization. The personal parish. Integration remains the ideal; intercultural competency the oft-cited strategy to achieve it. But while leaders' own cultural awareness matters, attitude adjustments neither resolve nor undo the differential experiences of some Catholics. Integrated attempts at "transcendence" may be insufficient to "overthrow the profound ways in which behavior and life circumstances are affected by ethnoracial categories."[15] Or, worse still: misguided attempts at color blindness in a racially inscribed world, mere "artifacts of a stereotypical understanding."[16] The structural, organizational response to diversity matters, too.

All this is to say that diversity for the sake of diversity—structured institutionally into generalist organizations—cannot be exalted as the clear, default, or only answer to cultivating inclusion and respect. It can even do the opposite—especially for those already disadvantaged vis-à-vis broader power structures. Diverse spaces may actually carry the most benefit to those already reaping the benefits of a broader power structure. Heterogeneity shines a light on the privilege of the privileged. Hoover, for example, notes that "shared parishes better prepare Euro-American people for a culturally diverse world simply by more realistically representing the demographic facts on the ground." A diverse organization, in other words, can decenter power for those in power. But even then, "greater awareness of these facts does not necessarily guarantee a positive adjustment or attitude toward them."[17]

Parishes are more than the sum of the Catholics therein. Structural adaptations to diversity matter as much as attempts to develop intercultural competency. There is space for innovation when it comes to making room for diversity in organizations, in a world that has yet to eliminate privileged hegemonies. The Catholic Church as an institution has introduced personal parishes as a novel organizational form, re-centering otherwise de-centered people and purposes. Personal parishes create a structural alternative to conformity, a named specialist organization alongside the generalist organization. Shared spaces are not the only response to difference.

WHITHER PERSONAL PARISHES?

Diverse Social Contexts Predict Multiple Organizational Forms

Throughout the course of this project, I have been asked to weigh in personally on whether personal parishes are a good thing or a bad thing. Should the Catholic Church have personal parishes (at all), or not? Most sociological questions don't lend themselves to a straightforward yes or no. As is often the case in studying people and society . . . it's complicated. Effective sociology appreciates these complexities and contradictions.

My best response to the question about personal parishes' relative worth is that the question itself is incomplete. Are personal parishes a good or bad thing . . . for whom? In what context? Requested for what purpose? Instigated how? In the past, the present, or the future? Further specification predicts important caveats to my response as to whether, when, and for whom to establish (or request) a personal parish. This is not to hedge indefinitely, nor to privilege unbridled relativism. I do believe—informed by my conversations with so many Catholics throughout the country deeply invested in personal parish decisions—that there are right and wrong answers to this question. But more than anything, I would argue that there can be multiple answers to this question. Committing to a single response (whether "yes" or "no") to fit every situation does not make for effective or collaborative policy, or vibrant parishes, or retention of Catholics and Catholic culture.

This ambiguity is reflected in what organizational scholars call the "contingency theory argument," or the idea that "there is no one best organizational form but many, and their suitability is determined by the goodness of fit between organizational form and the diverse environments to which they relate."[18] Complex institutions—and grassroots transformation therein—require organizational options. Heterogeneity in the Catholic population is increasing: a reality that predicts a diversity of solutions for its accommodation, organizationally.

Looking back, the liberal posturing of some US bishops that eliminated national parishes carte blanche—some lauded for their righteousness in racial justice at the time—brought with it the latent consequence of denying many Catholics a place to feel at home. The celebrated integration of territorial parishes arrived when newer immigrant Catholics most needed protected places of sanctuary in new locales. While white European Catholics had by then undergone decades of upward social mobility, fueled by their parochial infrastructure, their later, largely nonwhite immigrant counterparts faced a Church whose leaders' structural stance toward personal parish building discouraged them along a similar path. The organizational structure of parishes had changed. Post-1983, it changed again. Shifting circumstances require nimble institutions.

Broad-based, one-size-fits-all policies toward personal parishes are troubling when the Catholic hierarchy itself does not yet reflect the rich diversity of today's Catholics. The racial demographic of American bishops is far whiter than the racial demographic of American Catholics. Decisions regarding personal parishes are being adjudicated by leaders who, by and large, lack a personal connection to the challenges expressed by those petitioning for them. To put this more explicitly: (mostly) white bishops are deciding when and whether personal parish status is warranted for non-white Catholic groups. These institutional disjunctures breed disjunctures of power. Even to the extent that eventual parish outcomes may be the same, decision-makers do not yet represent all voices. If and when leadership changes, the Church itself—its structures, its practices, its holistic inclusion—will also change.

The example of personal parishes demonstrates that there is not a one-size-fits-all model for addressing diversity in today's increasingly diverse America. Just as the Catholic notion of subsidiarity emphasizes local decision-making, so, too, do the needs of individuals differ across social and geographic space. A generic, overarching policy stance—whether "for" or "against" personal parishes—does not honor the specificity and outright petitions of Catholics who seek them. Moreover, some groups of Catholics want personal parishes; others do not. The *sensus fidalum* predominant among one community ought not stipulate the lived outcome for another. Nor should leaders' well-intentioned, integrationist ethos rule out the possibility of a desired parish sanctuary requested by the impacted community itself.

Personal parish decisions require structural competence, intentionality, and an eye toward interdependence. This is best achieved through a mix of ordained and lay—top-down and bottom-up—collaborative diocesan consultation. Contemporary developments in the global and American Catholic Church predict continued use of—and debate surrounding—personal parishes. Tradition predicts continued use of—and debate surrounding—territorial parishes. Both lay Catholics and ordained leaders deserve a voice in these debates.

A PARISH, A PLACE, AND A PURPOSE

America is an extraordinarily diverse nation. Its population includes a record number of immigrants and people of color, foretelling no single racial or ethnic majority by the year 2055. Wealth inequality is at an all-time high. Residential segregation persists. Discrimination persists. Political races lay bare bitter ideological divides. Cities reel from the wounds of injustice. In short, unity in diversity is a struggle.[19]

How do American institutions reshape their local organizations amidst this diverse and diversifying public? The Catholic Church, the largest religious group in the United States with some 82 million self-identified Catholics, presents one litmus test. Nearly one in four Americans is connected to Catholicism in some meaningful way.[20] The number of American Catholics will continue to grow, as new migrant flows offset disaffiliation. Ever-more-diverse and (arguably) ever-more-divided, American Catholicism depicts the struggles and successes of one institution's attempts to honor, bridge, and unify difference through its local organizations.

This is a familiar role, of course. "From the very beginning the fundamental problem of the Catholic church in America has been how to form a unified body out of disparate and scattered Catholic parts," Jose Casanova wrote in *Public Religions in the Modern World*. "In order to maintain institutional unity, however, the church hierarchy has had to ensure that the most diverse Catholic groups would become one single American Catholic Church."[21] While this challenge parallels that of other faith traditions, Casanova remarks on a noteworthy difference. Unlike other religious bodies that split as a way to cope with irreconcilable difference, the American Catholic Church remains one (highly diversified) American Catholic Church. Its organizational structures change, but its overarching institutional framework holds.

America's diverse Catholics commune—they dwell together—within the social and territorial boundaries of "parish." Feeling the acuteness of difference, Catholics—like most religious adherents in the United States—tend to flock together with others like themselves. While typically unnamed through patterns of proximity and preference, personal parishes name that similarity that binds Catholics together in shared identity or purpose. They showcase the interplay between the values of homogeneity and heterogeneity, between institutional ascription and individual achievement. Their modern use represents an organizational innovation that is local in place, translocal in purpose, and interconnected on a higher diocesan plane.

Personal parishes offer an organizational means to preserve, celebrate, and retain particular cultural iterations of Catholicism. A way to be Catholic, to stay Catholic. Fitting America's diverse Catholics into one generalist mold risks excising minority expressions of the faith. Absent personal parishes, some will never reach a numerical majority in territorial parishes, nor adequate representation among leadership. As such, some liturgical styles, languages, music, and cultural celebrations will forever be the asterisk offering, at the mercy of a dominant group willing (or not) to grant permission, time, and space. This is the ready cry of personal parishes—whether by way of ethnicity, Traditional Latin rite, social mission, Anglican Use, college-focused, or otherwise—to have a parish home. A purpose, and a place.

Contemporary personal parishes tell the story of an institution appropriating resources to meet diverse needs and delineate meaningful spaces to do religion. This is a story about place and purpose, sameness and difference. Do we sacrifice "home" for heterogeneity? Unity for specificity? Viewed interdependently, perhaps the two are not mutually exclusive, after all. Exploring how this happens within the United States Catholic Church shines a light on questions germane to all institutions' responses to diversity, and to all places shaped by identity, community, and the power to draw (or erase) boundaries in-between.

APPENDIX A

The Study

Now can we go off the record?
TCB: Yeah. I can pause it, if you'd like me to.
I'd kind of prefer that.
TCB: Yeah, that's fine. I'll show you: I'm going to hit—
[Break in recording]

I just don't know if . . .
TCB: I understand.
I was telling you, sort-of, the real reason. The official reason.
TCB: Right.

* * *

This book used a mixed methodological approach to study personal parishes throughout the United States. Data are both quantitative (from an original, national survey) and qualitative (from in-person field visits and in-depth interviews). Research design prioritized both broad description and narrow focus. The study was preapproved by the Institutional Review Board of Maryville College.

I first piloted this research in 2010–2011 with a case study of a single diocese, funded by an Engaged Scholars Studying Congregations fellowship. During this pilot phase, I visited each personal parish in the case study diocese and conducted interviews with pivotal actors behind parish establishment. Findings confirmed that I needed to assess personal parishes from a broader, national perspective to understand their contemporary (and largely unknown) occurrence.

With additional funding from the National Science Foundation and Louisville Institute, I used the lessons of my pilot study (and corollary literature) to create a National Survey of Personal Parishes (NSPP). As seen in Appendix B, the survey inquired about the presence of personal parishes, special populations served, and factors related to parish creation and suppression. The survey went to all 178 Latin Rite US arch/dioceses (as of Fall 2012), making it a census rather than a sample. As such, no margin of error accompanies statistics used here. A total of 143 arch/dioceses returned the survey, for an 80 percent overall response rate. As evidenced by the high rate of return, I spent quite a bit of time researching and deploying strategies to maximize response rate. While tailored to this project, I share a few tactics here in hopes that they may also benefit future researchers.

Two weeks before the survey went out, I emailed all recipients (using personalized names inserted via mail merge), telling them to anticipate the survey's arrival and explaining its purpose. The Center for Applied Research in the Apostolate of Georgetown University (where I was once employed) managed the actual mailing. My cover letter and survey went out under joint letterhead (CARA and Maryville College), to enhance legitimacy and buy-in. Dioceses are familiar with CARA and its survey requests. Envelopes were addressed by name to the director of pastoral planning or director of research, if there was one. If not (as was the case for a large number of dioceses), it was addressed to the chancellor.

The literature on incentives shows that (1) any incentive trumps no incentive; (2) pre-incentives trump post-incentives; (3) guaranteed incentives trump lottery incentives; and (4) cash incentives trump gift card or coupon incentives. I generally followed this advice. To incentivize the person who opened the envelope, I enclosed a single dollar bill. While $1 is hardly a boon, research shows that it still ups response rates. It also generates a feeling of reciprocity. I also included a cover letter and a handwritten note that read "Please enjoy a cup of coffee on me as you complete the survey!—Tricia." The bit of feedback I received on this was positive: a few thanked me for the coffee, one respondent said she used it to get an ice cream, another put it into the donation basket at his parish. One returned the dollar with a note that read, "Here's your dollar back—I think you'll need the coffee more than I will!"

Also wanting to incentivize the diocese as an organization (and guessing that the envelope-opener would need to solicit information from others), I promised an annual subscription to *The CARA Report* for the first 25 responding dioceses (as a guaranteed rather than lottery incentive) and a summary of findings for all dioceses. This was quite popular; several followed up asking if they were among the first 25 respondents (and expressed disappointment, if not!). The mailing included a pre-addressed, pre-paid return envelope.

Two weeks following the mailing, and at approximately two week intervals for the next several months, staff from CARA followed up with non-respondents by mail. I personally called non-responding dioceses. CARA received the return envelopes and inputted all data electronically. A small number of dioceses scanned and emailed their completed surveys. Data collection concluded in early December 2012. After this date, I retrieved all original surveys from CARA and cross-checked data files. In the case of the 35 non-responding dioceses, I conferred with the 2012 Official Catholic Directory (the "OCD," which notes some parishes' ethnic designations) and diocesan webpages to generate the most complete list of all US personal parishes.

My survey queried dioceses a decade after abuse scandals rocked the American Church. Public perceptions of bishops had improved markedly since then. Some 70 percent of American Catholics were "somewhat" or "very" satisfied with bishops' leadership at the time the survey went out.[1] But the scandal's after-effects included numerous diocesan bankruptcies and financial cuts, which in some cases meant letting go of entire pastoral planning or research offices. This meant that some dioceses no longer had the resources or expertise to identify the information I requested. While I asked for a substantial amount of information in the four-page survey, I intentionally did not ask directly whether or not the diocese supported personal parishes. My questions focused on policy and practice, rather than subjective assessments of personal parishes' merit, given that the person filling it out was not necessarily privy to his or her bishop's stance.

National-level survey data in hand, my next step was to return to in-depth, in-person qualitative explorations of personal parishes as they appeared in contemporary forms across the United States. I used the *diocese*—as opposed to the individual *parish*—as my unit of observation and analysis. A theoretical approach emphasizing an interconnected organizational field requires this shift in the unit of observation and analysis: from individual congregations to interconnected organizations (which, for Catholics, means the diocese). This meant targeting dioceses showing personal parish activity in and after 1983. In this way, I chose on the variable of interest. My strategy intentionally prioritized those dioceses with personal parishes; data here should be read as such. Using my comprehensive list of personal parishes, I sorted first by diocese, then by the four major census regions. I then prioritized dioceses containing a higher number of new (1983 or after) personal parishes, along with those containing multiple personal parish types (specifically, ethnic versus non-ethnic). My diocesan case selection strategically ensured geographic and personal parish representativeness.

Through this process, I selected twelve (arch)dioceses across eleven states: three in the Midwest; two in the West; five in the South; and two in the Northeast. Dioceses in the South exhibit a higher likelihood to establish new (1983 or later) personal parishes. Dioceses generally include at least one mid-sized or larger city; such is the case with all dioceses selected for this study. Diocesan limits are not coterminous with city limits, though, meaning that this book's case studies incorporate urban, suburban, and rural dynamics—sometimes all within a single (arch)diocese.

Between April and October 2013, I traveled for ethnographic field visits (typically four days in length) to each of the selected dioceses. My visits always overlapped with a Sunday, to allow for Sunday Mass observations. Visits also overlapped weekdays (either Thursday/Friday or Monday/Tuesday) to accommodate interviewees' schedules, and to allow for additional observations of daily Mass. I visited and attended Masses at every personal parish in the diocese, requiring some tricky logistics! I observed the church building, the neighborhood, and the area of town. Often, my visits took me to the urban core of cities. One parish visit left me feeling too uncomfortable to get out of my car, knowing the crime statistics of that census region. I returned at another time of day, when I knew a crowd would be gathered near the church.

Parishioners were welcoming. Many greeted me upon observing my (occasionally quite apparent) visitor status. I sang along, participating in familiar rituals that cut across language difference. I covered my hair with a veil when appropriate. Twice, my Mass visit was unexpectedly announced by the pastor at the pulpit. One pastor handed me a beautiful rosary in the middle of his (non-English) homily. Even when language differences rendered my field notes less complete, every service provided ample material for observation. I ate many delicious post-Mass treats. I was twice asked out by other parishioners. I politely declined, sharing that I was married.

I requested interviews with every personal parish pastor. In a handful of instances, I interviewed a pastoral associate, associate pastor, or deacon rather than the pastor. I also contacted the diocesan chancery and requested interviews with the staff person responsible for pastoral planning, research, and/or multicultural ministry. Occasionally, this overlapped with the position of chancellor or vicar for clergy. A few case studies also included interviews with canon lawyers not employed by the diocese. I interviewed one additional pastoral planner not associated with a case study diocese.

It took time to establish trust and rapport with each interviewee. The nerves of some priests were apparent: one refused to be recorded, another closed his eyes throughout the interview, another kept looking around to make sure no one was listening, and another verified that my research would be published only after he was reassigned elsewhere. One priest asked if I had a "priest protector" (I did not). Another engaged in an extended, fruitful email exchange post-interview to clarify the role of sociology (from which he came away writing, "It strikes me as being something like aliens coming down from space to study this strange creature called human beings. There is no right or wrong to it; rather, just a study of behaviors and attitudes, etc., described in their own words"). I replied that that was pretty close.

Most priest interviewees displayed surprising candor. Many expressed gratitude (amazement, even) at my interest in personal parishes given their relatively unknown presence. One priest ran out to the parking lot after an interview I conducted alongside two undergraduate research assistants. He wanted to share a chocolate Easter bunny with my student. He then recommended a great diner down the street (we learned from our waiter there that he was a frequent customer). Another interviewee generously gifted rosaries for each of my children, blessed by the Pope. Several led me on tours of their churches. For all those honest and confidential conversations with priests (for which I am so grateful), this book is that much more true.

I also requested interviews with the (arch)bishop of each case study diocese. This was typically more formal and involved. Oftentimes, the answer to my request was no. Sometimes I simply got no response. Rationale varied for those who declined: the bishop was too busy, had nothing to say about personal parishes, wasn't interested, and so forth. Occasionally, the answer was "yes." I conducted in-depth, recorded interviews with five bishops and another five unrecorded interviews. Quoted material comes only from recorded interviews. My sample includes bishops, archbishops, and one cardinal. At the time of our interview, one bishop was retired. Half of bishop respondents held current or prior appointments in one of the twelve case-study dioceses. Bishops typically serve a few dioceses over their careers, so their responses typically pull from multiple contexts.

Altogether, I conducted 62 in-depth interviews with a total of 67 individuals. Each lasted approximately one hour and, unless refused, was recorded. I conducted every interview myself, except for one conducted by a trained research assistant while I conducted another simultaneously. Undergraduate students accompanied me to eight interviews. In some cases, a translator was present. Other times, two or three parish representatives joined for a collaborative conversation. A small number of interviews were conducted by phone, when a live interview proved unfeasible. Every recorded interview was later transcribed by a professional transcription company, and subsequently checked for accuracy (particularly when it came to Catholic terminology). In the case of interviews where a translator was present, both the English and non-English parts of the recording were transcribed in order to assess accuracy of the live translation. I subsequently coded all interviews personally using Atlas Ti—a time-consuming but highly valuable process of computer-assisted qualitative data analysis. This generated 95 codes, which I subsequently grouped into broader, thematic categories.

In addition to the national survey (which generated both quantitative and qualitative responses) and ethnographic field visits (which generated both observation and interview data), I also gathered relevant materials for content analysis: personal parish establishment decrees, restructuring documentation, parish websites and histories, and other available material related to personal parish decisions. In one diocese, I requested the proceedings of the presbyteral council and other consultative conversations during restructuring, but was told that such proceedings are subject to a 70-year rule of confidentiality. Some documents considered highly confidential, and/or including information about living bishops, stays confidential indefinitely. The extent to which dioceses were forthcoming in survey, interview, and archival data varied substantially. I was surprised in both directions (degree of openness, and degree of nondisclosure).

The elite-lean of my data means that I can provide intimate and rare access to a slice of American Catholicism rarely observed by sociologists, by lay Catholics, or even by the ranks of the Church elite. Interviews capture the voices of those involved in America's earliest Anglican Use personal parishes, Latin Mass personal parishes, and social justice personal parishes, among others. This is an insider look at decision-making in the American Catholic Church. Forty percent of my interviewees are people of color. This contextualizes scholarship on American Catholicism that disproportionately captures the voices of white Catholics. While white Catholics contribute heavily to this story (given their higher representation among elite leadership), so, too, do Catholics of color less often given voice. The majority of interviews (87 percent) are men, a statistic that overlaps with another: 64 percent are ordained as priests (another 5 percent are deacons or religious sisters).

Throughout data collection, I presented myself as a neutral sociologist observer, albeit one with deep familiarity and connection with Catholicism. While my own Catholicism lent a degree of insider access, I still felt acutely my positionality as an outsider—particularly when it came to my race, gender, and non-ordained status. Visiting personal parishes, I was frequently the only white person in attendance.

My outsider status was put in sharpest relief during priest interviews. All priests I interviewed, of course, were male. Unlike my last book project, which centered on a lay movement, this one consisted of predominantly non-lay interviews. This produced an overwhelmingly ordained, celibate male sample. I cannot recall a time prior to this research when I sat alone in a room with a priest, apart from confession. This is a point of access not commonly granted to a 30-something lay woman, especially apart from her male spouse. This may explain, in part, why much of the extant research on parishes has been conducted by men—often, by ordained priests.[2] I felt like—in an ever-so small way—I had been granted access to the inner circle, to the boys' club. I know of few sociologists of Catholicism who have been privy to these sorts of conversations, on this scale. My findings will undoubtedly differ from my predominantly male (and often ordained) sociologist counterparts.

Of course, any story—particularly one that examines elite institutional leaders—will assuredly leave things out. A sociologist cannot know what she cannot know via empirical data.

National Survey of Personal Parishes

The following questions (preceded by a cover letter and introduction) were included in the National Survey of Personal Parishes, sent in Fall 2012 to all (arch)dioceses in the United States. Formatting has been changed.

1. How many total parishes are currently in operation in your arch/diocese?

2. In what year was the most recent parish (not necessarily a personal parish) erected in your diocese?

3. Does your arch/diocese have any parishes designated by Canon Law as "personal parishes" currently in operation (see definition above)?

   ☐ Yes   ☐ No *(skip to question 8)*   ☐ Unsure

4. What special populations or purposes do personal parishes in your arch/diocese serve? Please provide the *total number of personal parishes* that fall within each category (or "0," if none).

   ___ Nationality, ethnic, or language group(s)   ___ College group(s)
   ___ Traditional Latin Mass group(s)   ___ Charismatic worship group(s)
   ___ Anglican Use group(s)
   ___ Other group(s) or purpose(s)
        (Please specify)

5. Were any of these personal parishes established in or after the year 1983?

   ☐ Yes   ☐ No   ☐ Unsure

6. In what year was the most recent personal parish established in your diocese?

7. Briefly describe the process for establishing the most recent personal parish in your diocese, if known:

8. Does your arch/diocese have a formal policy for determining whether and when to erect personal parishes?

   ☐ Yes *(please describe below)*   ☐ No   ☐ Unsure

9. To your knowledge, have any persons or groups *requested* or *petitioned* for a personal parish in your arch/diocese since 1982 (whether or not this has or will result in a parish)?

   ☐ Yes   ☐ No *(skip to question 11)*   ☐ Unsure

10. If *yes*, from what special category did this request emerge (check all that apply, if more than one)?

    ☐ Nationality, ethnic, or language group(s)   ☐ College group(s)
    ☐ Traditional Latin Mass group(s)   ☐ Charismatic worship
    ☐ Anglican Use group(s)   group(s)
    ☐ Other group(s) or purpose(s)
      (Please specify)

11. Are there any special populations in the arch/diocese currently moving toward personal parish status?

    ☐ Yes   ☐ No *(skip to question 13)*   ☐ Unsure

12. If *yes*, from what category (check all that apply, if more than one)?

    ☐ Nationality, ethnic, or language group(s)   ☐ College group(s)
    ☐ Traditional Latin Mass group(s)   ☐ Charismatic worship group(s)
    ☐ Anglican Use group(s)   ☐ Other group(s) or purpose(s)
                                                       (Please specify)

13. Many factors may influence whether or not a parish is erected for a specific population or purpose. For the ten factors listed below, please indicate their likely influence for your arch/diocese.

    [Respondents could select "not influential, somewhat influential, or highly influential for the following factors:]

    Unmet need among a particular population of Catholics
    Growth of a particular demographic group in the arch/diocese
    Conversation with religious groups (e.g., priests from the FSSP)

Conversations with interested lay people in the arch/diocese

Formal petition from a group of people in the arch/diocese

Arch/bishop support and/or advocacy

Multicultural office support and/or advocacy

Papal statements allowing for or encouraging the use of personal parishes

Financial resources made available for ministry to specific populations or purposes

Other (Please specify)

14. Which of the following criteria would likely need to be met before establishing a new personal parish for a specific population or purpose? Check all that apply.

☐ The special population must constitute a certain number in the diocese
☐ Local Catholics must petition the Arch/bishop
☐ A certain amount of funds must be raised
☐ Physical space for the personal parish must be secured
☐ A feasibility study must be conducted
☐ The diocesan presbyteral council must be consulted
☐ A priest must be made available to pastor the personal parish
☐ The Holy See must encourage, promote, or require the personal parish
☐ The Arch/bishop must provide written approval
☐ Other (*Please specify*).

15. Has the arch/diocese closed, suppressed, or merged any parishes since 2002?

☐ Yes (*How many?*)   ☐ No (*skip to question 17*)

16. *If yes*, were any of these closed/suppressed/merged parishes originally erected to serve a specific population of Catholics (e.g. Polish Catholics)?

☐ Yes (*How many?*)   ☐ No   ☐ Unsure

17. Has the canonical status of any arch/diocesan parish been changed from personal to territorial since 2002?

☐ Yes (*For how many parishes?*)   ☐ No   ☐ Unsure

18. Is the Traditional Latin Mass (the extraordinary form of the Roman Rite) currently offered at any territorial arch/diocesan parish(es)?

☐ Yes   ☐ No   ☐ Unsure

19. Are Anglican Use liturgies currently offered at any territorial arch/diocesan parish(es)?

☐ Yes   ☐ No   ☐ Unsure

20. In what ways does the arch/diocese minister to the following language, ethnic, or national groups? Please check each available ministry type for the communities listed below, or leave blank if no such ministry option is available.

[*Communities listed*: African Americans/Blacks; Africans; Brazilians; Chinese; Cubans; Deaf/Hearing-impaired; Dominicans (Dominican Republic); Filipinos; French; Haitians; Hispanics/Latinos (combined); Italians; Koreans; Mexicans; Native Americans; Polish; Puerto Ricans; Salvadorans; Vietnamese; Other language/ethnic/national groups (please specify).]

[*Selection options*: personal parish(es); dedicated parish(es) without personal parish status; mission(s) or apostolate(s); or territorial parishes offering special Masses and ministries.]

Lastly, please list the personal parishes in your arch/diocese on the attached sheet [parish name, city, year designated as a personal parish, number of attendees, and specific population/purpose served.]

Your arch/diocese: _____

(Optional) Your name: _____ *Phone number:* _____

Title: _____ *Email:* _____

NOTES

INTRODUCTION

1. Peter Berger, Grace Davie, and Effie Fokas (2008: 31) suggest that the volunteerism and congregationalism that characterizes US religious history set an "entirely different trajectory from that found in Europe." See Roof and McKinney 1987.
2. Liptak 1989; Dolan 1975: 169; 1985: 162; Stump 1986: 78.
3. Baggett 2009; Konieczny 2013; Warner 1994.
4. Lay leaders then exhibited strong influence on church development, a dynamic Dolan (1985: 192) calls "Catholic congregationalism." See Burns, Skerrett, and White 2000; Garces-Foley 2009; Gerson 2002; Matovina 2012. More on this in subsequent chapters.
5. CARA 2016; Pew Research Center 2014a; cf. CARA 2014; Coco 2014; D'Antonio, Dillon, and Gautier 2013; Hendershott and White 2013; Hoover 2014; Johnson, Wittberg, and Gautier 2014; Konieczny 2013; Konieczny, Camosy, and Bruce 2016.
6. CARA 2011. Parishes numbered more than 19,000 in the year 2000; down to 17,483 as of 2014. Total parishes decreased by 7 percent in the last decade alone. Only about one in ten US Catholic parishes were established after 1975. Facing shifting demographics, poor building conditions, priest shortages, and declining diocesan budgets, scores of dioceses have turned to parish consolidation and suppression (i.e., closure). See also CARA 2014; Edwards, Christerson, and Emerson 2013; Seitz 2011.
7. Aldrich and Ruef 2006; CARA 2011; National Congregations Study 2007 (Chaves and Anderson 2008); Hoover 2014. Offering a more critical assessment of this arrangement, Allen Deck (1989) calls them "divided" or "parallel" parishes, in which cultural groups exist basically in isolation.
8. CARA 2014; Pew Research Center 2007, 2014b. Two-thirds of Latinos attend predominantly Latino parishes; eight in ten Latinos whose dominant language is Spanish do so. Davis and Pope-Davis 2011; Pew Research Center 2013.
9. George 2011: 37.
10. For discussion of "niche," see Hannan, Carroll, and Pólos 2003.
11. On organizational change and Vatican II, see Wilde 2007. Personal parishes contrast "de facto congregations," "magnet" parishes, or the like. Cf. Baggett 2009; Brophy 2001; Hater 2004; Murnion 2004; Warner 1994.
12. Bruce 2011.

13. The most comprehensive look at America's national parishes was written as a doctoral dissertation in canon law from the Catholic University of America by Joseph E. Ciesluk, J.C.L., in 1944. Clearly, much has changed. This work was subsequently published by Catholic University of American Press in 1947, hence the 1947 date in all Ciesluk references cited herein.

CHAPTER 1

1. Adler, Bruce, and Starks 2018 explore this intersection of authority, community, and territory sociologically.
2. Coriden 1997; Vandenakker 1994.
3. Blöchlinger 1965: 34.
4. Berger et al. 2008: 25.
5. Duffy 2006: 61.
6. Koudelka 1921.
7. Vandenakker 1994: 58; Fox 2011.
8. Koudelka 1921.
9. Ciesluk 1947: 13.
10. Ciesluk 1947: 14–15.
11. Koudelka 1921: 13.
12. Koudelka 1921: 13.
13. Ciesluk 1947: 15.
14. MacDonald 1951: 48–49.
15. Ciesluk 1947: 29.
16. Ciesluk 1947: 38.
17. Ciesluk 1947: 32.
18. Fogarty 1985.
19. Leblebici et al. 1991. Until a 1908 apostolic constitution by Pope Pius X, Catholic assemblies in the United States were technically missions (Macdonald 1951). Catholic leaders and canon lawyers raised the parish status question again after the promulgation of the 1917 Code. Ciesluk 1947: 44.
20. Ciesluk 1947: 50.
21. Ciesluk 1947: 50.
22. 1917 Code #216.4, emphasis added.
23. Dolan 1985.
24. Morris 1997: 127.
25. Scholars including Timothy Matovina (2012) question whether the "immigrant-to-Americanization" paradigm is even sufficient to examine the history of Catholicism in the United States, recognizing the simultaneous role of other dynamics including, for example, a loosening attachment to the institutional church.
26. Stump 1986.
27. Matovina 1999: 47.
28. Ospino 2014: 6.
29. Harte (1951: 162) notes that the Catholic Directory was "the only source of information on the number and distribution of national parishes in the United States." Then—and now—personal parishes are not formally marked as such in the Official Catholic Directory. The closest measure comes through the foreign-language designation, which is indicated.
30. Vandenakker 1994: 45. See Wilde 2007 to understand the origins of Vatican II's progressive outcomes, or O'Malley 2010 for a general overall view of Vatican II changes.
31. Vandenakker 1994: 51.

32. Vatican Council II, *"Apostolicam Actuositatem."*
33. Vandenakker 1994.
34. Stravinskas and Shaw 1998.
35. Sacrosanctum Concilium.
36. Vandenakker 1994: 57.
37. Vandenakker 1994: 58.
38. Code of Canon Law 1983.
39. While Vatican II opened up new space for lay governance in parishes, tensions about this power shift bubbled between the end of the Council and the release of the new Code of Canon Law. This may have inhibited how lay autonomy was codified: for example, suggesting but not mandating pastoral councils.
40. Code of Canon Law 1983.
41. Vandenakker 1994: 59.
42. Vandenakker 1994: 59.
43. Renken 2000: 689.
44. Canon 518 and its commentary should not be confused with references to the territoriality of a "particular church" as discussed in canon 372. This is because a "particular church" in Catholicism means the diocese, not the parish. Warner (1994) uses commentary on Canon 372 in his discussion of congregationalism in a Catholic context, but this is misleading due to Canon 372's diocesan focus. While that commentary footnotes a parallel to personal parishes, the commentary on Canon 518 is the proper reference for territoriality when it comes to individual parishes.
45. Davis 2007: 346–347.
46. Coriden 1997.
47. Ammerman 2009: 259.
48. Parish rights are somewhat ambiguous given canon law's incomplete articulation of them. "It is a piece of unfinished business that remained after the canon law revisions following the Second Vatican Council were completed," says canon lawyer Coriden (1997: 71). Coriden's own list of twelve rights and obligations (1997: 72–79) from which I distill here is a combination of expressed and implied tenets from canon law.
49. Coriden 1997: 72.
50. See Gamm 2009. By way of example, one chancellor shared in our interview that a group without parish status was engaging in practices that he and the bishop disapproved of. They warned the group's leaders that, unless things changed, the diocese would revoke their approval to meet on church property or hold Mass. A couple months later, this is exactly what happened.
51. A parish (as a juridic person) includes the community and the pastor (Coriden 1997).
52. Stump (1986) notes that the longevity of older national parishes depends on their institutional environment: namely, the parish's ethnic affiliation, size of the ethnic community, the existence of national parishes elsewhere in the diocese, and parish consolidation processes.
53. 1983 Code of Canon Law: 515.
54. USCCB 2012.
55. Identifying an available priest, let alone one whose skills match that of the personal parish, can prevent personal parish status attainment in the first place. Even for some ethnic parishes who source their pastors from elsewhere, RI visas do not make the standard US six-year appointment possible.
56. Absent (or preceding) a physical church home, a parish may be called a "quasi-parish" with all the rights of a parish, but missing a key element—in this case, a building.

57. Canon 515.
58. This includes only those personal parishes still open as of 2012; it would exclude any personal parishes that may have been established after 1982 but suppressed prior to 2012.
59. Any decline is offset also by the fact that new parishes have started since Harte's assessment. Notre Dame Study of Catholic Parish Life 1981–1989. These prior studies counted only national parishes, excluding those serving African Americans (in the case of Harte 1951) and other personal parish types (for the Notre Dame study).
60. Bruce and Hoegeman 2013; CARA 2011. This fits urban sociologist Claude Fischer's (1975, 1995) assessment that the critical numbers of urban settings help to sustain subcultures, ethnic institutions, and religious involvement. Density, moreover, supports emergent organizational forms.
61. Alba 1981: 97.
62. Waters 1990.
63. NSPP data is limited to the personal parishes that were open at the time of the survey. If a parish was founded after 1983 but closed before 2012, it would not appear in these numbers.
64. CARA Hispanic Catholic Fact Sheet.
65. See Bruce 2018.
66. With the exception of Filipinos, as the Philippines is an overwhelmingly Catholic country. Some 19 percent of new Asian migrants are Catholic, though that varies substantially by ethnic group (Park, Bruce, and Cherry 2015).
67. Access to traditional forms of the Mass was promoted and protected by Vatican documents described in chapter 3.
68. Fichter 1951: 34; Badillo 2006: xvi.
69. See Padgett and Powell 2012.
70. http://dioknox.org/30924/divine-mercy-becomes-diocese-knoxvilles-49th-parish/.

CHAPTER 2

1. http://stjosephscamdennj.org/. The neighborhood today is called "Whitman Park."
2. George 2011: 36.
3. However, writing of parishes in medieval Ireland, historian Henry A. Jefferies (2006) argues that "the degree to which pastoral care was ever strictly circumscribed by parochial boundaries must be open to question" (216). Difficulties in travel meant that much of the rural population infrequently went to the church, and urban Catholics chose among several parish options based upon preference.
4. George 2011: 35–36.
5. McGreevy (1998) writes about how priests in earlier periods looked to precinct voting records and parish censuses to find the unchurched; community-level censuses today provide Catholic population estimates.
6. Maines and McCallion 2004: 93.
7. Canon 859 in the 1917 Code reads, "The faithful are to be persuaded to satisfy this precept in their own parishes; those who satisfy it in another parish should take care to let their own pastor know about their fulfilling the precept."
8. The Federal-Aid Road Act of 1916 was the first federal legislation to fund highway construction. See Kaszynski 2000.
9. McGreevy 1998.
10. Barker and Muse 1986; Dolan 2002.

11. A history that Gamm (2009) illustrates well in *Urban Exodus*.
12. http://www.smov.info/index.php/church-history/8-history.
13. See, e.g., Dillon (1999) for a discussion of Vatican II changes introducing the concept of Catholic laity as the "people of God." Before Vatican II, homilies were in the local language, but all else was in Latin.
14. Writing of de facto congregationalism's relevance to Catholicism, Maines and McCallion (2004) argue that both "de facto" and "de jure" aspects—notably, those institutionalized by the Second Vatican Council—need to be considered to understand increased elective affinity in American Catholicism. Baggett (2009) offers ample evidence of territorial parish diversification within a single diocese.
15. Notre Dame Study of Catholic Parish Life 1981–1989.
16. CARA 2012. Although this survey question asks Catholics if they drive by a closer parish to attend another, Mark Gray notes that "to be fair, in some cases, the closest parish may not be their territorial parish given the structure of boundaries."
17. Wade Clark Roof and William McKinney observed in 1987 that increasing religious individualism was among the most significant recent religious changes. The "new volunteerism," they called it, meant that Americans respected religion, while also viewing it through the frame of personal choice or preference.
18. CARA 2012. Maines and McCallion reported in 2004 that 43 percent of Catholic families in the Diocese of Detroit attended somewhere outside their home parish boundaries.
19. 62 percent reported in NSPP; overall parish numbers from CARA.
20. The Vatican's Congregation for the Clergy wrote the US bishops in 2006 to clarify that parishes should not be called "suppressed" or closed when, in fact, the parish has merged or amalgamated with one or more other parishes (Rasaian 2014). This speaks to the distinction between a territorial parish and the colloquial use of "parish" as a particular building or church community.
21. Ammerman 1997: 107
22. Catholic Canon Law no. 515:2 (1983).
23. McGreevy 1998.
24. Weldon 2004: 2. See also Seitz 2011.
25. The concept of "merging" does not even exist explicitly in canon law, but utilizes the allowances of Canon Law 121 stipulating the union between aggregates of "public juridic persons" (i.e., parishes). Canon Law 121 states: "If aggregates of persons (universitates personarum) or of things (universitates rerum), which are public juridic persons, are so joined that from them one aggregate (universitas) is constituted which also possesses juridic personality, this new juridic person obtains the goods and patrimonial rights proper to the prior ones and assumes the obligations with which they were burdened. With regard to the allocation of goods in particular and to the fulfillment of obligations, however, the intention of the founders and donors as well as acquired rights must be respected."
26. http://www.Oxforddictionaries.com
27. Kantowicz 1993.
28. CARA 2011.
29. Rasaian 2014; Renken 2010: 131.
30. Brinig and Garnett 2014; CARA "Frequently Requested Church Statistics."
31. Rapport and Dawson 1998: 68–69.
32. McRoberts 2003.
33. Aldrich 2008: 5.

34. CARA 2012. Gray also notes that "at the same time the survey data seem to indicate that this mobility may also make for happy parishioners."
35. George 2011: 36.

CHAPTER 3

1. Ciesluk 1947: 77.
2. Coriden 1997: 65.
3. A local bishop's approval for a new personal parish is canonically required, of course. The fact that some dioceses evaluate his support/advocacy as less influential may hint at the willingness of some bishops to act in ways that support lay need, even apart from their own position on personal parishes.
4. John Paul II, 2004: *Apostolorum Successores*, no. 206b.
5. Benedict XVI, 2007, emphasis added.
6. Art. 5, §1.
7. Personal parishes for Anglican Use in the United States, however, date back to 1983.
8. Vatican 2009, emphasis added.
9. Pontifical Council for the Pastoral Care of Migrants and Itinerant People 2004, emphasis added.
10. John Paul II, 2004: 622, emphasis added.
11. Matovina 1999: 55.
12. Ruef 2000.
13. A decade later, the same parish was turned over to the Priestly Fraternity of Saint Peter for leadership, again with little to no consultation of the extant pastor ("That shocked us all. I wasn't a part of it. I didn't know anything about it. And so I said 'Any reason?' and he said 'No, we just felt that we'd like to have it within the fraternity here.'")
14. Korean American Catholics are also less likely to feel as though pastors and staff understand their culture, which can further drive their desire for a personal parish. See Bruce, Park, and Cherry 2015.
15. For an expanded exploration of this phenomenon, see Bruce 2016b.
16. For more on this, see Thien-Huong T. Ninh 2014.
17. See Bruce and Packard 2016.
18. Arguably, changes to canon law in 1983 were tantamount to an institutional opportunity priming the Church for change from within. Much like political opportunities engender social movement activity targeted at the state, institutional opportunities create spaces whereby insiders—here, lay Catholics—can access authorities and promote change under receptive circumstances. For more on institutional opportunities, see Raeburn 2004. Intra-institutional social movements are defined in depth in my 2011 book, *Faithful Revolution*.
19. http://www.unavoceww.com/fssp-announcement-20081001.html.
20. Hart and Denison 1987. Byrne (2016) observes this even among independent Catholic collectives.
21. Aldrich and Ruef 2006: 182.
22. Meyer and Whittier 1994.
23. Ruef 2000. DiMaggio and Powell (1983) discuss organization fields.

CHAPTER 4

1. Pew Research Center 2015a, b. PEW counts adults only; accounting for children would further diversify this imaginary parish due to Latinos Catholics' younger average age.

2. Catholic Church 2011: Catechism of the Catholic Church, no. 1200.
3. Dulles 1987: 24.
4. DeYoung et al. 2003. Sociologists of religion vary in their use of language here—whether "multiracial," "multiethnic," or "multicultural." I interchange all three terms.
5. This evokes an earlier Catholic era whose leaders sought an answer to the "immigration problem." The post-1920 decline of the national parish and the successful "Americanization" of immigrant Catholics (the 1960 election of John F. Kennedy its pinnacle), meant that immigrants' differences could be transcended; their faith and national identity victorious. The integrated territorial parish emerged as the standard organizational structure for an increasingly diverse Church. See Dolan 1985; Fisher 2002; Hennesey 1981; Liptak 1985; Morris 1997.
6. Carroll (1985) discusses generalist organizations using the example of newspapers.
7. The most recent CARA/USCCB survey of new priests (2016) shows that 66 percent are white.
8. CARA 2014; Edwards, Christerson, and Emerson 2013; Emerson and Kim 2003; Emerson and Woo 2006.
9. E.g., Marti 2009b.
10. Hoover 2014: 2.
11. Some parishes do integrate parishioners in single Masses and embrace interracial contact across Mass times—as described by Kathleen Garces-Foley (2008), for example. But focusing on these proportionally few exceptions skews the reality that Catholics parishes remain highly segregated spaces.
12. Deck 1989; Garces-Foley 2008; John Paul II, 1999: 3.
13. My interviews are with individuals who have "opted out" of the territorial parish, in a sense, and are now in a personal parish—with the exception of diocesan interviewees. Thus, they are not a random sampling of Catholics in multiracial or territorial parishes and should not be read as such.
14. Hoover 2014: 222; Ospino 2014.
15. Ospino 2014.
16. Lee and Bean 2010.
17. Edwards 2008a, b.
18. Nelson 2009.
19. Bonilla-Silva 2003.
20. Aldrich and Ruef 2006.
21. Cimino 2011; DiMaggio 1998; Scheitle 2007.
22. Emerson and Woo 2006: 60.
23. This contrasts the specialization that Scheitle (2010) describes happening via "parachurch" organizations.
24. Carroll 1985; Carroll and Hannan 1995. Carroll and Swaminathan (2000) apply this to explain the emergence of microbreweries.
25. Carroll and Swaminathan 2000: 720.
26. Marti (2009) is among those who argue that "transcending" race is the key to effective multiracial congregations—an option which is not always readily available (nor even preferred) by Catholics of color.
27. See Ebaugh and Chafetz 2000, among others.
28. See O'Malley 2010.
29. Fears of culture loss can be justified given the way that the United States can operate as a figurative language graveyard. While many first-generation immigrants arrive with limited English proficiency, by the third generation

immigrants not only learn English but tend to speak English only (Portes and Rumbaut 2014).

30. See Ogbu and Simons 1998, Lee and Kye 2016; and Portes and Rumbaut 2014, among others.
31. Ethnicity is less of an option for nonwhites in the United States, notes racial theorist Mary Waters (1990).
32. As W. E. B. DuBois ([1903] 2014) put it more than a century ago in viewing "the color line" as the most central marker of division in the United States, "One ever feels his two-ness,—an American, a Negro; two souls, two thoughts, two unreconciled strivings; two warring ideals in one dark body, whose dogged strength alone keeps it from being torn asunder" (7).
33. Matovina 1999: 51.
34. McNally 1986. See also McGreevy 1998.
35. Matovina 1999: 52.
36. Brown 1998.
37. Fogarty 1985: 257.
38. Emerson, Mirola, and Monahan 2011: 165; Emerson and Smith 2000; Emerson, Smith, and Sikkink 1999.
39. Portes and Rumbaut 2014: 166.
40. Dulles 1987: 24.

CHAPTER 5
1. See Baggett 2009; D'Antonio, Dillon, and Gautier 2013; Dillon 1999.
2. Fischer and Mattson 2009: 436.
3. Hunter 1992; Park 1915.
4. McPherson, Smith-Lovin, and Cook 2001; Pew Research Center 2016.
5. Bishop 2008: 6.
6. Marcuse and van Kempton 2002.
7. Finke and Stark 2002: 33.
8. See Warner 1993, 2002.
9. Bellah et al. 1985: 72–73.
10. Pew Research Center 2012b.
11. Ammerman 1997; Baggett 2009; Brophy 2001; Cimino 2011; Cimino, Mian, and Huang 2013; Hater 2004; Livezey 2000; Murnion 2004; Scheitele 2007; Stark and Finke 2000; Warner 1993; Witham 2010.
12. Bender, Cadge, Levitt, and Smilde 2013; Marti and Ganiel 2014.
13. This research began prior to the formal creation of the Anglican Ordinariate in the United States, at which time all Anglican Use personal parishes were subsumed under the leadership of the Ordinariate rather than under individual, local dioceses.
14. Phillips 2011: 39.
15. http://cdlex.org/index.cfm?load=page&page=586.
16. Or, practice their Catholicism independent of Rome. See Byrne 2016.
17. Baggett 2009: 135.
18. See, for example, Becker 1999; Eiesland 2000; Lawson 1999; Reimer 2011.
19. Marcuse 1997.
20. Marcuse and van Kempen 2002: 8.
21. Baggett 2009; Clark 2005; Konieczny 2013.
22. Simmel 1997: 143.
23. Simmel 1997: 172.

CHAPTER 6

1. Code of Canon Law 1983, no. 515; George 2011.
2. Baggett 2009: 135–136. Although none of the parishes Baggett describes are canonical personal parishes, his latter two categories resonate with the outsider or countercultural dynamics of the communal narratives heard in personal parishes. Hometown parishes more closely approximate the ideal-typical territorial parish.
3. Cherry 2014: 4.
4. Delanty 2010: 71.
5. Ammerman 1997: 360.
6. See Fischel 2006; Putnam 2001.
7. Putnam 2001.
8. Swartz 2013: 43.
9. Chaves 2004.
10. Deck 1989; Dolan and Hinojosa 1994; Vidal 1990.
11. Garces-Foley 2018; Irby 2018.
12. Gillespie 2006.
13. Webber 1963.
14. Webber 1963: 30, emphasis added.
15. Webber 1963: 25.
16. Webber 1963: 49.
17. Hervieu-Léger 2000: 163.
18. Stolz and Usunier 2013: 5. The "new mobilities" paradigm (Sheller and Urry 2006) cuts across disciplinary boundaries to take seriously the extent and implications of America's now highly mobile population.
19. Anderson 2006.
20. Delanty 2010: xii.
21. Barth [1969] 1998: 15.
22. Hervieu-Léger 2000: 150, 152.
23. Hervieu-Léger 2000: 172.
24. Sheller and Urry 2006: 213.
25. Cresswell 2015: 84.
26. Berends 2015; National Alliance for Public Charter Schools 2016. Many charter schools are housed in closed Catholic schools. See Brinig and Garnett (2014) for a discussion of this phenomenon.
27. Berends 2015.
28. Emerson 2008.
29. Brinig and Garnett 2014.
30. Logan 2016: 23. This section's title is intentionally adapted from Logan's article title: "As Long as There Are Neighborhoods."
31. Warner 1994: 67.
32. Glaeser and Vigdor 2012; Massey 2015; Massey and Tannen 2015.
33. Crowder and Krysan 2016.
34. Massey and Tannen 2015. The criteria for this designation originated with Massey and Denton (1989). Urban historian Colin Gordon unpacks this in his book *Mapping Decline: St. Louis and the Fate of the American City*, writing that "political fragmentation enabled local and parochial interests to tear the city apart and reassemble it as a crazy quilt of fiercely segregated industrial, commercial, residential, and racial enclaves" (2008: 10).
35. Gordon 2008: 228.
36. Ammerman 1997: 106.

37. Mulder 2015.
38. See Bruce 2016b for a fuller description of personal parish establishment in St. Louis.
39. McGreevy 1998 and Gamm 2009.
40. Putnam 2001: 79.
41. Larsen, Urry, and Axhausen 2006: 23.
42. Wellman 1979: 1202.
43. Guest and Wierzbicki 1999.
44. Sampson 2012.
45. Eiesland 2000; Wellman 1979.
46. George 2011: 20, 22. This same change, of course, gives bishops a high level of power in the church—both local and universal.
47. Pope Paul VI 1965.
48. Christian 2011: 131, emphasis added.
49. Skerrett (1993) writes that "unlike the 'walking' parishes familiar to generations of Chicagoans, however, newer suburban parishes often cover eight square miles of territory." "The challenge of creating community in the city is as difficult today as it was in the 19th century. Without sacred spaces, it may well be impossible" (168); Fogarty 1985.
50. See Morley 2002.
51. Tonkiss 2005: 131.
52. Gans 1961: 178.

CONCLUSION
1. See Ammerman 2005; Berger, Davie, and Focas 2008; Warner 1994.
2. Casanova 1994: 175–176.
3. For an extended look at this, see Sullins 2016.
4. Warner 1994: 88; Byrne 2016.
5. Seitz 2011: 2.
6. Dillon 1999: 254.
7. DeYoung, Emerson, Yancey, and Kim 2003; Edwards, Christerson, and Emerson 2013; Garces-Foley 2007; Kozol 2012; Marti 2009b:180; Massey and Denton 1993.
8. Bonilla-Silva 2006.
9. Edwards 2008a, b.
10. Pitt 2010.
11. Hoover 2014: 222–223.
12. Anderson 2011: 43.
13. Lewis and Diamond 2015: 253.
14. Zweigenhaft and Domhoff 2006: 245.
15. Marti 2009a: 65.
16. Pitt 2010.
17. Hoover 2014: 181.
18. Scott and Davis 2007: 108.
19. Pew Research Center 2016.
20. Pew Research Center (2015c) measures this through personal affiliation, past affiliation, or the affiliation of a close family member to Catholicism.
21. Casanova 1994: 176.

APPENDIX A
1. Pew Research Center 2012a.
2. See Bruce 2018.

BIBLIOGRAPHY

Adler, Gary, Tricia C. Bruce, and Brian Starks. 2018. "Introduction." In *American Parishes: Remaking Local Catholicism*, edited by Gary J. Adler, Tricia C. Bruce, and Brian Starks. New York: Fordham University Press.

Alba, Richard D. 1981. "The Twilight of Ethnicity among American Catholics of European Ancestry." In *The Annals of the American Academy of Political and Social Science*. Vol. 454, *America as a Multicultural Society*, 86–97.

Aldrich, Howard E. 2008. *Organizations and Environments*. Stanford, CA: Stanford University Press.

Aldrich, Howard E., and Martin Ruef. 2006. *Organizations Evolving*. 2d ed. London: Sage Publications.

Ammerman, Nancy. 1997. *Congregation and Community*. New Brunswick, NJ: Rutgers University Press.

Ammerman, Nancy. 2005. *Pillars of Faith: American Congregations and their Partners*. Berkeley: University of California Press.

Ammerman, Nancy. 2009. "Congregations: Local, Social, and Religious." In *Oxford Handbook of the Sociology of Religion*, edited by P. B. Clarke, 562–580. New York: Oxford University Press.

Anderson, Benedict. 2006. *Imagined Communities: Reflections on the Origin and Spread of Nationalism*. London: Verso Books.

Anderson, Elijah. 2011. *The Cosmopolitan Canopy: Race and Civility in Everyday Life*. New York: WW Norton.

Badillo, David A. 2006. *Latinos and the New Immigrant Church*. Baltimore: Johns Hopkins University Press.

Baggett, Jerome P. 2009. *Sense of the Faithful: How American Catholics Live Their Faith*. New York: Oxford University Press.

Barker, Bruce, and Ivan Muse. 1986. "One-Room Schools of Nebraska, Montana, South Dakota, California, and Wyoming." *Research in Rural Education* 3 (3): 127–130.

Barth, Fredrick, ed. (1969) 1998. *Ethnic Groups and Boundaries: The Social Organization of Culture Difference*. Long Grove, IL: Waveland Press.

Becker, Penny Edgell. 1999. *Congregations in Conflict: Cultural Models of Local Religious Life*. New York: Cambridge University Press.

Bellah, Robert N., Richard Madsen, William M. Sullivan, Ann Swidler, and Stephen M. Tipton. 1985. *Habits of the Heart: Individualism and Commitment in American Life*. Berkeley and Los Angeles: University of California Press.

Bender, Courtney, Wendy Cadge, Peggy Levitt, and David Smilde, eds. 2013. *Religion on the Edge: De-centering and Re-centering the Sociology of Religion*. New York: Oxford University Press.

Benedict XVI. 2007. *Summorum Pontificum*. http://w2.vatican.va/content/benedict-xvi/en/motu_proprio/documents/hf_ben-xvi_motu-proprio_20070707_summorum-pontificum.html.

Berends, Mark. 2015. "Sociology and School Choice: What We Know After Two Decades of Charter Schools." *Annual Review of Sociology* 41:159–180.

Berger, Peter. 1969. *The Sacred Canopy*. New York: Anchor Books.

Berger Peter, Grace Davie, and Effie Fokas. 2008. *Religious America, Secular Europe? A Theme and Variations*. Aldershot, UK: Ashgate.

Bishop, Bill. 2008. *The Big Sort: Why the Clustering of Like-Minded America is Tearing Us Apart*. New York: Houghton Mifflin.

Blau, Peter M. 1977. *Inequality and Heterogeneity*. New York: Free Press.

Blöchlinger, Alex. 1965. *The Modern Parish Community*. New York: P. J. Kenedy & Sons.

Bonilla-Silva, Eduardo. 2006. *Racism without Racists: Color-Blind Racism and the Persistence of Racial Inequality in the United States*. 2d ed. Lanham, MD: Rowman & Littlefield.

Brinig, Margaret F., and Nicolle Stelle Garnett. 2014. *Lost Classroom, Lost Community: Catholic Schools' Importance in Urban America*. Chicago: University of Chicago Press.

Brophy, Don. 2001. "The Parish of Choice." *America* 185 (16): 12–14.

Brown, Joseph A., S.J. 1998. *To Stand on the Rock: Meditations on Black Catholic Identity*. Eugene, OR: Wipf & Stock.

Bruce, Tricia C. 2011. *Faithful Revolution: How Voice of the Faithful Is Changing the Church*. New York: Oxford University Press.

Bruce, Tricia C. 2016a. "Polarized Preferences, Polarized Pews." In *Polarization in the US Catholic Church: Naming the Wounds, Beginning to Heal*, edited by Mary Ellen Konieczny, Charles C. Camosy, and Tricia C. Bruce, 33–45. Collegeville, MN: Liturgical Press.

Bruce, Tricia C. 2016b. "Preserving Catholic Space and Place in 'The Rome of the West.'" In *Spiritualizing the City: Agency and Resilience of the Urban and Urbanesque Habitat*, edited by Victoria Hegner and Peter Jan Margry, 46–62. London: Routledge.

Bruce, Tricia C. 2018. "Hogar Parroquial: Hispanic 'Personal Parishes' in the Contemporary U.S. Catholic Church." *Journal of Prevention & Intervention in the Community* 46(4).

Bruce, Tricia C. 2018. "A Brief History of Sociology and Parishes in the United States." In *American Parishes: Remaking Local Catholicism*, edited by Gary J. Adler, Tricia C. Bruce, and Brian Starks. New York: Fordham University Press.

Bruce, Tricia C., and Catherine Hoegeman. 2013. "Leadership Characteristics and Responses to Diversity: Catholic Bishops' Use of 'Personal Parishes'." Society for the Scientific Study of Religion Annual Meeting, Boston, MA.

Bruce, Tricia C., and Josh Packard. 2016. "Organizational Innovation." In *Handbook of Religion and Society*, edited by David Yamane, 155–175. Switzerland: Springer.

Bruce, Tricia C., Jerry Park, and Stephen Cherry. 2015. "Asian and Pacific Island Catholics in the United States." Washington, DC: United States Conference of Catholic Bishops. http://www.usccb.org/issues-and-action/cultural-diversity/asian-pacific-islander/demographics/upload/API-Catholics-in-the-US-Report-October-2015.pdf.

Burns, Jeffery M., Ellen Skerrett, and Joseph Michael White, eds. 2000. *Keeping Faith: European and Asian Catholic Immigrants*. Maryknoll, NY: Orbis.

Byrne, Julie. 2016. *The Other Catholics: Remaking America's Largest Religion*. New York: Columbia University Press.

CARA. 2011. "The Changing Face of U.S. Catholic Parishes." *Emerging Models of Pastoral Leadership*. Washington, DC: Center for Applied Research in the Apostolate.

CARA. 2012. "Parish Drive By." *Nineteen Sixty-four* blog (June 11, 2012). http://nineteensixty-four.blogspot.com/2012/06/parish-drive-by.html.

CARA. 2014 "Cultural Diversity in the Catholic Church in the United States." Washington, DC: Center for Applied Research in the Apostolate.

CARA. 2016. "Ordination Class of 2016." http://www.usccb.org/beliefs-and-teachings/vocations/ordination-class/upload/2016-Ordination-Class-News-Release.pdf.

CARA. n.d. "Fact Sheet: Hispanic Catholics in the U.S." http://cara.georgetown.edu/staff/webpages/Hispanic%20Catholic%20Fact%20Sheet.pdf.

CARA. n.d. "Frequently Requested Church Statistics." http://cara.georgetown.edu/frequently-requested-church-statistics/.

Carroll, Glenn R. 1985. "Concentration and Specialization: Dynamics of Niche Width in Populations of Organizations." *American Journal of Sociology* 90 (6): 1262–1283.

Carroll, Glenn R., Stanislav D. Dobrev, and Anand Swaminathan. 2002. "Organizational Processes of Resource Partitioning." In *Research in Organizational Behavior* Volume 24, edited by Barry Staw and Roderick M. Kramer, 1–40. Amsterdam: Elsevier.

Carroll, Glenn R., and Michael T. Hannan. 1995. "Resource Partitioning." In *Organizations in Industry: Strategy, Structure and Selection*, edited by Glenn R. Carroll and Michael T. Hannan, 215–221. New York: Oxford University Press.

Carroll, Glenn R., and Anand Swaminathan. 2000. "Why the Microbrewery Movement? Organizational Dynamics of Resource Partitioning in the U.S. Brewing Industry." *American Journal of Sociology* 106 (3): 715–762.

Casanova, Jose. 1994. *Public Religions in the Modern World*. Chicago: University of Chicago Press.

Catholic Church. 2001. *The 1917 Or Pio-Benedictine Code of Canon Law*, curated by Edward N. Peters. San Francisco: Ignatius Press.

Catholic Church. 2011. *Catechism of the Catholic Church*. 2d ed. Washington, DC: United States Conference of Catholic Bishops.

Chaves, Mark. 2004. *Congregations in America*. Boston: Harvard University Press.

Chaves, Mark, and Shawna L. Anderson. 2008. "Continuity and Change in American Congregations: Introducing the Second Wave of the National Congregations Study." *Sociology of Religion* 69 (4): 415–440.

Cherry, Stephen M. 2014. *Faith, Family, and Filipino American Community Life*. New Brunswick, NJ: Rutgers University Press.

Christian, Robert, OP. 2011 "Bonds of Communion among Parishes and among Pastors." In *What is a Parish? Canonical, Pastoral, and Theological Perspectives*, edited by Thomas A. Baima, 130–144. Chicago: Hillenbrand Books.

Ciesluk Joseph E., J.C.L. 1947. *National Parishes in the United States*. Washington, DC: Catholic University of America Press.

Cimino, Richard. 2011. "Neighborhoods, Niches, and Networks: The Religious Ecology of Gentrification." *City & Community* 10 (2):157–181.

Cimino, Richard P., Nadia A. Mian, and Weishan Huang, eds. 2013. *Ecologies of Faith in New York City: The Evolution of Religious Institutions*. Bloomington: Indiana University Press.

Clark, William A. 2005. *A Voice of Their Own: The Authority of the Local Parish*. Collegeville, MN: Liturgical Press.

Coco, Angela. 2014. *Catholics, Conflicts, and Choices: An Exploration of Power Relations in the Catholic Church*. London: Routledge.

Code of Canon Law. 1983. http://www.vatican.va/archive/ENG1104/_INDEX.HTM.

Coriden, James A. 1997. *The Parish in Catholic Tradition: History, Theology and Canon Law*. New York: Paulist Press.

Cresswell, Tim. 2015. *Place: An Introduction*. 2d ed. Malden, MA: Wiley Blackwell.

Crowder, Kyle, and Maria Krysan. 2016. "Moving beyond the Big Three: A Call for New Approaches to Studying Racial Residential Segregation." *City and Community* 15 (1): 18–22.

D'Antonio, William V., Michele Dillon, and Mary L. Gautier. 2013. *American Catholics in Transition*. Lanham, MD: Rowman & Littlefield.

Davis, Darren W., and Donald B. Pope-Davis. 2011. "National Black Catholic Survey." Washington, DC: United States Conference of Catholic Bishops. http://www.usccb.org/issues-and-action/cultural-diversity/african-american/news/upload/exec-summary-key-findings.pdf.

Davis, Kenneth G. 2007. "Built from Living Stones: Hispanic Catholic Parishes Without Boundaries or Buildings." *New Blackfriars* 88 (1015): 335–352.

Deck, Allen Figueroa. 1989. *The Second Wave: Hispanic Ministry and the Evangelization of Cultures*. New York: Paulist Press.

Delanty, Gerard. 2010. *Community*. 2d ed. London: Routledge.

DeYoung, Curtiss Paul, Michael O. Emerson, George Yancey, and Karen Chai Kim. 2003. *United by Faith: The Multiracial Congregation as an Answer to the Problem of Race*. New York: Oxford University Press.

Dillon, Michele. 1999. *Catholic Identity: Balancing Reason, Faith and Power*. Boston: Cambridge University Press.

DiMaggio, Paul. 1998. "The Relevance of Organization Theory to the Study of Religion." In *Sacred Companies: Organizational Aspects of Religion and Religious Aspects of Organizations*, edited by N. J. DemerathIII, Peter Dobkin Hall, Terry Schmitt, and Rhys H. Williams, 7–23. New York: Oxford University Press.

DiMaggio, Paul J., and Walter W. Powell. 1983. "The Iron Cage Revisited: Institutional Isomorphism and Collective Rationality in Organizational Fields." *American Sociological Review* 48 (2): 147–160.

Dolan, Jay P. 1975. *The Immigrant Church: New York's Irish and German Catholics 1815–1865*. Baltimore: Johns Hopkins University Press.

Dolan, Jay P. 1985. *The American Catholic Experience: A History from Colonial Times to the Present*. Garden City, NJ: Doubleday & Company.

Dolan, Jay P. 2002. *In Search of an American Catholicism*. New York: Oxford University Press.

Dolan, Jay P., and Gilberto M. Hinojosa, eds. 1994. *Mexican Americans and the Catholic Church, 1900–1965*. Notre Dame, IN: University of Notre Dame Press.

DuBois, W. E. B. (1903) 2014. *The Souls of Black Folk*. New York: Pocket Books.

Duffy, Patrick J. 2006. "The Shape of the Parish." In *The Parish in Medieval and Early Modern Ireland: Community, Territory, and Building*, edited by Elizabeth FitzPatrick and Raymond Gillespie, 33–61. Dublin: Four Courts Press.

Dulles, Avery. 1987. *The Catholicity of the Church*. Oxford: Clarendon Press.

Ebaugh, Helen Rose. 2003. "Religion and the New Immigrants." In *Handbook of the Sociology of Religion*, edited by Michele Dillon, 225–239. Boston: Cambridge University Press.

Ebaugh, Helen Rose, Jennifer O'Brien, and Janet Saltzman Chafetz. 2000. "The Social Ecology of Residential Patterns and Membership in Immigrant Churches." *Journal for the Scientific Study of Religion* 39:1–11.

Ebaugh, Helen Rose, and Janet Saltzman Chafetz. 2000. *Religion and the New Immigrants: Continuities and Adaptations in Immigrant Congregations*. Walnut Creek, CA: Altamira Press.

Edwards, Korie. 2008a. *The Elusive Dream: The Power of Race in Interracial Churches*. New York: Oxford University Press.

Edwards, Korie. 2008b. "Bringing Race to the Center: The Importance of Race in Interracial Churches." *Journal for the Scientific Study of Religion* 47:30–52.

Edwards, Korie, Brad Christerson, and Michael O. Emerson. 2013. "Race, Religious Organizations, and Integration. *Annual Review of Sociology* 39: 211–228.

Eiesland, Nancy L. 2000. *A Particular Place: Urban Restructuring and Religious Ecology in a Southern Exurb*. New Brunswick, NJ: Rutgers University Press.

Emerson, Michael O., and Karen Chai Kim. 2003. "Multiracial Congregations: An Analysis of Their Development and a Typology." *Journal for the Scientific Study of Religion* 42 (2): 217–227.

Emerson, Michael, William Mirola, and Susanne C. Monahan. 2011. *Religion Matters: What Sociology Teaches Us about Religion in Our World*. London: Routledge.

Emerson, Michael O., and Christian Smith. 2000. *Divided by Faith: Evangelical Religion and the Problem of Race in America*. New York: Oxford University Press.

Emerson, Michael O., Christian Smith, and David Sikkink. 1999. "Equal in Christ, But Not in the World: White Conservative Protestants and Explanations of Black–White Inequality." *Social Problems* 46 (3): 398–417.

Emerson, Michael O., and Rodney M. Woo. 2006. *People of the Dream: Multiracial Congregations in the United States*. Princeton, NJ: Princeton University Press.

Fichter, Joseph Henry. 1951. *Southern Parish*. Vol. 1. Chicago: University of Chicago Press.

Finke, Roger, and Rodney Stark. 2002. "Beyond Church and Sect: Dynamics and Stability in Religious Economies." In *Sacred Markets, Sacred Canopies: Essays on Religious Markets and Religious Pluralism*, edited by Ted G. Jelen, 31–62. Lanham, MD: Rowman & Littlefield.

Fischel, William A. 2006. "Why Voters Veto Vouchers: Public Schools and Community-specific Social Capital." *Economics of Governance* 7:109–132.

Fischer, Claude. 1975. "Toward a Subcultural Theory of Urbanism and the Subcultural Theory of Urbanism." *American Journal of Sociology* 80 (6): 1319–1341.

Fischer, Claude. 1995. "The Subcultural Theory of Urbanism: A Twentieth-Year Assessment." *America Journal of Sociology* 101 (3): 543–577.

Fischer, Claude S., and Greggor Mattson. 2009. "Is American Fragmenting?" *Annual Review of Sociology* 35:435–455.

Fisher, James Terence. 2002. *Communion of Immigrants: A History of Catholics in America*. New York: Oxford University Press.

Fogarty, Gerald. 1985. "The Parish and Community at the Third Plenary Council of Baltimore." *U.S. Catholic Historian* 4:233–257.

Fox, Joseph, OP. 2011. "The Status of the Parish in the 1983 *Code of Canon Law*." In *What is a Parish? Canonical, Pastoral, and Theological Perspectives*, edited by Thomas A. Baima, 39–66. Chicago: Hillenbrand Books.

Gamm, Gerald. 2009. *Urban Exodus: Why the Jews Left Boston and the Catholics Stayed*. Boston: Harvard University Press.

Gans, Herbert J. 1961. "The Balanced Community: Homogeneity or Heterogeneity in Residential Areas?" *Journal of the American Institute of Planners* 27 (3): 176–184.

Garces-Foley, Kathleen. 2007. *Crossing the Ethnic Divide: The Multiethnic Church on a Mission*. New York: Oxford University Press.

Garces-Foley, Kathleen. 2008. "Comparing Catholic and Evangelical Integration Efforts." *Journal for the Scientific Study of Religion* 47 (1): 17–22.

Garces-Foley, Kathleen. 2009. "From the Melting Pot to the Multicultural Table: Filipino Catholics in Los Angeles." *American Catholic Studies* 120 (1): 27–53.

Garces-Foley, Kathleen. 2018. "Parishes as Homes and Hubs." In *American Parishes: Remaking Local Catholicism*, edited by Gary J. Adler, Tricia C. Bruce, and Brian Starks. New York: Fordham University Press.

George, Francis Cardinal, OMI. 2011. "The Parish in the Mission of the Church." In *What Is a Parish? Canonical, Pastoral, and Theological Perspectives*, edited by Thomas A. Baima, 18–38. Chicago: Hillenbrand Books

Gerson, Jeffrey N. 2002. "Latino Migration, the Catholic Church, and Political Division: Lowell." In *Latino Politics in Massachusetts: Struggles, Strategies, and Prospects*, edited by Carol Hardy-Fanta and Jeffrey N. Gerson, 127–152. London: Routledge.

Gillespie, Raymond. 2006. "Urban Parishes in Early Seventeenth Century Ireland: The Case of Dublin." In *The Parish in Medieval and Early Modern Ireland: Community, Territory, and Building*, edited by Elizabeth FitzPatrick and Raymond Gillespie, 228–241. Dublin: Four Courts Press.

Glaeser, Edward, and Jacob Vigdor. 2012. "The End of the Segregated Century: Racial Separation in American Neighborhoods 1890–2010." New York: Manhattan Institute for Policy Research.

Gordon, Colin. 2008. *Mapping Decline: St. Louis and the Fate of the American City*. Philadelphia: University of Pennsylvania Press.

Guest, Avery M., and Susan K. Wierzbicki. 1999. "Social Ties at the Neighborhood Level: Two Decades of GSS Evidence." *Urban Affairs Review* 35 (1): 92–111.

Hannan, Michael T., Glenn R. Carroll, and László Pólos. 2003. "The Organizational Niche." *Sociological Theory* 21 (4): 309–340.

Hart, Stuart, and Daniel R. Denison. 1987. "Creating New Technology-Based Organizations: A System Dynamics Model." *Policy Studies Review* 6 (3): 512–528.

Harte, Thomas J., C.Ss.R. 1951. "Racial and National Parishes in the United States." In *The Sociology of the Parish*, edited by C.J. Nuesse and Thomas J. Harte, C.Ss.R., 154–177 Milwaukee, WI: Bruce Publishing Company.

Hater, Robert J. 2004. *The Catholic Parish: Hope for a Changing World*. New York: Paulist Press.

Hendershott, Anne, and Christopher White. 2013. *Renewal: How a New Generation of Faithful Priests and Bishops Is Revitalizing the Catholic Church*. New York: Encounter Books.

Hennesey, James, S.J. 1981. *American Catholics: A History of the Roman Catholic Community in the United States*. New York: Oxford University Press.

Hervieu-Léger, Danièle. 2000. *Religion as a Chain of Memory*. New Brunswick, NJ: Rutgers University Press.

Hoover, Brett C. 2014. *The Shared Parish: Latinos, Anglos, and the Future of U.S. Catholicism*. New York: New York University Press.

Hunter, James Davison. 1992. *Culture Wars: The Struggle to Control the Family, Art, Education, Law, and Politics in America*. New York: Basic Books.

Irby, Courtney. 2018. "Preparing to Say 'I Do.'" In *American Parishes: Remaking Local Catholicism*, edited by Gary J. Adler, Tricia C. Bruce, and Brian Starks. New York: Fordham University Press.

Jefferies, Henry A. 2006. "Parishes and Pastoral Care in the Early Tudor Era." In *The Parish in Medieval and Early Modern Ireland: Community, Territory, and Building*, edited by Elizabeth FitzPatrick and Raymond Gillespie, 211–227. Dublin: Four Courts Press.

John Paul II. 1999. *Ecclesia in America*. http://w2.vatican.va/content/john-paul-ii/en/apost_exhortations/documents/hf_jp-ii_exh_22011999_ecclesia-in-america.html.

John Paul II. 2004. "*Apostolorum Successores* [Directory for the Pastoral Ministry of Bishops]." http://www.vatican.va/roman_curia/congregations/cbishops/documents/rc_con_cbishops_doc_20040222_apostolorum-successores_en.html.

Johnson, Mary, S.N.D. de N., Patricia Wittberg, S.C., and Mary L. Gautier. 2014. *New Generations of Catholic Sisters: The Challenge of Diversity*. New York: Oxford University Press.

Kantowicz, Edward R. 1993. "The Ethnic Church." In *Catholicism, Chicago Style*, edited by Ellen Skerrett, Edward R. Kantowicz, and Steven M. Avella, 574–603. New Orleans: Loyola University Press.

Kantowicz, Edward R. 1995. "Polish Chicago: Survival through Solidarity." In *Ethnic Chicago: A Multicultural Portrait*, edited by Melvin Holli and Peter d'Alroy Jones, 173–198. Grand Rapids, MI: Eerdmans.

Kaszynski, William. 2000. *The American Highway: The History and Culture of Roads in the United States*. Jefferson, NC: McFarland.

Konieczny, Mary Ellen. 2013. *The Spirit's Tether: Family, Work, and Religion among American Catholics*. New York: Oxford University Press.

Konieczny, Mary Ellen, Charles C. Camosy, and Tricia C. Bruce. 2016. *Polarization in the US Catholic Church: Naming the Wounds, Beginning to Heal*. Collegeville, MN: Liturgical Press.

Koudelka, Charles J., J.C.L. 1921. "Pastors, Their Rights and Duties According to the New Code of Canon Law." PhD dissertation. Washington, DC: Catholic University of America.

Kozol, Jonathan. (1992) 2012. *Savage Inequalities: Children in America's Schools*. New York: Broadway Books.

Larsen, Jonas, John Urry, and Kay Axhausen. 2006. "Social Networks and Future Mobilities." Report to the UK Department for Transport. http://www.forschungsnetzwerk.at/downloadpub/mobility_transport_future.pdf.

Lawson, Ronald. 1999. "Internal Political Fallout from the Emergence of an Immigrant Majority: The Impact of the Transformation of Seventh-Day Adventism in Metropolitan New York." *Review of Religious Research* 41 (1): 20–46.

Leblebici, Hussein, Gerald Salancik, Anne Copay, and Tom King. 1991. "Institutional Change and the Transformation of Interorganizational Fields: An Organizational History of the U.S. Radio Broadcasting Industry." *Administrative Science Quarterly* 36 (3): 333–363.

Lee, Jennifer, and Frank D. Bean. 2010. *The Diversity Paradox: Immigration and the Color Line in Twenty-first Century America*. New York, NY: Russell Sage Foundation.

Lee, Jennifer, and Samuel Kye. 2016. "Racialized Assimilation of Asian Americans." *Annual Review of Sociology* 42:253–273.

Lewis, Amanda E., and John B. Diamond. 2015. *Despite the Best Intentions: How Racial Inequality Thrives in Good Schools*. New York: Oxford University Press.

Liptak, Dolores Ann, R.S.M. 1985. "The National Parish: Concept and Consequences for the Diocese of Hartford, 1890–1930." *Catholic Historical Review* 71 (1): 52–64.

Liptak, Dolores Ann, R.S.M. 1989. *Immigrants and Their Church*. New York: Macmillan.

Livezey, Lowell (ed.). 2000. *Public Religion and Urban Transformation*. New York: New York University Press.

Logan, John R. 2016. "As Long as There Are Neighborhoods." *City and Community* 15 (1): 23–28.

MacDonald, Fergus, C.P. 1951. "The Development of Parishes in the United States." In *The Sociology of the Parish*, edited by C. J. Nuesse and Thomas J. Harte, C.Ss.R., 45–71. Milwaukee, WI: Bruce Publishing Company.

Maines, David R., and Michael J. McCallion. 2004. "Evidence of and Speculations on Catholic De Facto Congregationalism." *Review of Religious Research* 46:92–101.

Marcuse, Peter. 1997. "The Enclave, the Citadel, and the Ghetto: What Has Changed in the Post-Fordist U.S. City." *Urban Affairs Review* 33 (2): 228–264.

Marcuse, Peter, and Ronald van Kempen. 2002. "States, Cities, and the Partitioning of Urban Space." In *Of States and Cities: The Partitioning of Urban Space*, edited by Peter Marcuse and Ronald van Kempen, 3–10. New York: Oxford University Press.

Marti, Gerardo. 2009a. "Affinity, Identity, and Transcendence: The Experience of Religious Racial Integration in Diverse Congregations." *Journal for the Scientific Study of Religion* 48 (1): 53–68.

Marti, Gerardo. 2009b. *A Mosaic of Believers: Diversity and Innovation in a Multiethnic Church*. Bloomington: Indiana University Press.

Marti, Gerardo. 2012. *Worship across the Racial Divide: Religious Music and the Multiracial Congregation*. New York: Oxford University Press.

Marti, Gerardo, and Gladys Ganiel. 2014. *The Deconstructed Church: Understanding Emerging Christianity*. New York: Oxford University Press.

Massey, Douglas S. 2015. "The Legacy of the 1968 Fair Housing Act." *Sociological Forum* 30 (1): 571–588.

Massey, Douglas S., and Nancy A. Denton. 1989. "Hypersegregation in US Metropolitan Areas: Black and Hispanic Segregation along Five Dimensions." *Demography* 26 (3): 373–391.

Massey, Douglas S., and Nancy A. Denton. 1993. *American Apartheid: Segregation and the Making of the Underclass*. Boston: Harvard University Press.

Massey, Douglas S., and Jonathan Tannen. 2015. "A Research Note on Trends in Black Hypersegregation." *Demography* 52 (3): 1025–1034.

Matovina, Timothy M. 1999. "The National Parish and Americanization." *U.S. Catholic Historian* 17 (1): 45–58.

Matovina, Timothy M. 2012. *Latino Catholicism*. Princeton, NJ: Princeton University Press.

McGreevy, John T. 1998. *Parish Boundaries : The Catholic Encounter with Race in the Twentieth-Century Urban North*. Chicago: University of Chicago Press.

McNally, Michael J. 1986. "A Peculiar Institution: Catholic Parish Life and the Pastoral Mission to the Blacks in the Southeast, 1850–1980." *U.S. Catholic Historian* 5 (1): 67–80.

McPherson, Miller, Lynn Smith-Lovin, and James M. Cook. 2001. "Birds of a Feather: Homophily in Social Networks." *Annual Review of Sociology* 27:415–444.

McRoberts, Omar M. 2003. *Streets of Glory: Church and Community in a Black Urban Neighborhood*. Chicago: University of Chicago Press.

Merton, Robert K. 1968. *Social Theory and Social Structure*. New York: Free Press.

Meyer, David S., and Nancy Whittier. 1994. "Social Movement Spillover." *Social Problems* 41 (2): 277–298.

Morley, David. 2002. *Home Territories: Media, Mobility and Identity*. London: Routledge.

Morris, Charles. 1997. *American Catholic: The Saints and Sinners Who Built America's Most Powerful Church*. New York: Vintage.

Mulder, Mark T. 2015. *Shades of White Flight: Evangelical Congregations and Urban Departure*. New Brunswick: Rutgers University Press.

Murnion, Philip J. 2004. "The Catholic Parish in the Public Square." In *American Catholics and Civic Engagement: A Distinctive Voice*, edited by Margaret O'Brien Steinfels, 71–91. Lanham, MD: Rowman & Littlefield.

National Alliance for Public Charter Schools. 2016. "A Closer Look at the Charter School Movement." http://www.publiccharters.org/wp-content/uploads/2016/02/New-Closed-2016.pdf.

NCCB. 2000. "Welcoming the Stranger among Us: Unity in Diversity: Issued by the United States Catholic Conference, Inc.

Nelson, Timothy J. 2009. "At Ease with Our Own Kind: Worship Practices and Class Segregation in American Religion." In *Religion and Class in America: Culture, History, and Politics*, edited by Sean McCloud and William Andrew Mirola, 45–68. Leiden: Brill.

Ninh, Thien-Huong, Keith Camacho, Sylvia Chan-Malik, and Khyati Joshi. 2014. "Colored Faith: Vietnamese American Catholics Struggle for Equality within Their Multicultural Church." *Amerasia Journal* 40 (1): 80–96.

Notre Dame Study of Catholic Parish Life. 1981–1989. http://icl.nd.edu/initiatives-projects/church-life-research/.

O'Malley, John W. 2010. *What Happened at Vatican II*. Boston: Harvard University Press.

Ogbu, John U., and Herbert D. Simons. 1998. "Voluntary and Involuntary Minorities: A Cultural-Ecological Theory of School Performance with Some Implications for Education." *Anthropology & Education Quarterly* 29 (2): 155–188.

Ospino, Hosffman. 2014. "Hispanic Ministry in Catholic Parishes." http://www.bc.edu/content/dam/files/schools/stm/pdf/2014/HispanicMinistryinCatholicParishes_2.pdf.

Padgett, John Frederick. 2012. "The Problem of Emergence." In *The Emergence of Organizations and Markets*, edited by John Frederick Padgett and Walter W. Powell, 1–30. Princeton, NJ: Princeton University Press.

Park, Jerry, Tricia C. Bruce, and Stephen Cherry. 2015. "White Paper: Asian Pacific Islander Catholics in the United States." Washington, DC: United States Conference of Catholic Bishops. http://www.usccb.org/issues-and-action/cultural-diversity/asian-pacific-islander/resources/upload/Asian-Pacific-Islander-Catholics-in-the-United-States-A-Preliminary-Report.pdf.

Park, Robert Ezra. 1915. "The City: Suggestions for the Investigation of Human Behavior in the City Environment." *American Journal of Sociology* 20:577–612.

Pew Research Center. 2007. Changing Faiths: Latinos and the Transformation of American Religion. http://www.pewforum.org/2007/04/25/changing-faiths-latinos-and-the-transformation-of-american-religion-2/.

Pew Research Center. 2012a. "Catholics' Views of U.S. Bishops." http://www.pewforum.org/Christian/Catholic/Catholics-Views-of-U-S--Bishops.aspx.

Pew Research Center. 2012b. "The Rise of Residential Segregation by Income." http://www.pewsocialtrends.org/2012/08/01/the-rise-of-residential-segregation-by-income/.

Pew Research Center. 2013. "The Rise of Asian Americans." http://www.pewsocialtrends.org/asianamericans/.

Pew Research Center. 2014a. "Religious Landscape Survey." http://www.pewforum.org/religious-landscape-study/.

Pew Research Center. 2014b. "The Shifting Religious Identity of Latinos in the United States." http://www.pewforum.org/2014/05/07/the-shifting-religious-identity-of-latinos-in-the-united-states/.

Pew Research Center. 2014c. "The Number of U.S. Catholics Has Grown, So Why Are There Fewer Parishes?" http://www.pewresearch.org/fact-tank/2014/11/06/the-number-of-u-s-catholics-has-grown-so-why-are-there-fewer-parishes/.

Pew Research Center. 2015a. "A Closer Look at Catholic America." http://www.pewresearch.org/fact-tank/2015/09/14/a-closer-look-at-catholic-america/.

Pew Research Center. 2015b. "The Most and Least Racially Diverse U.S. Religious Groups." http://www.pewresearch.org/fact-tank/2015/07/27/the-most-and-least-racially-diverse-u-s-religious-groups/.

Pew Research Center. 2015c. "U.S. Catholics Open to Non-Traditional Families." http://www.pewforum.org/2015/09/02/u-s-catholics-open-to-non-traditional-families/.

Pew Research Center. 2016. "The Demographic Trends Shaping American Politics in 2016 and Beyond." http://www.pewresearch.org/fact-tank/2016/01/27/the-demographic-trends-shaping-american-politics-in-2016-and-beyond/.

Phillips, Christopher G. 2011. "An Example of What It's Like to Come Home to Rome." *Anglicans and the Roman Catholic Church: Reflections on Recent Developments*, edited by Stephen E. Cavanaugh. San Francisco: Ignatius Press.

Pitt, Richard N. 2010. "Fear of a Black Pulpit? Real Racial Transcendence versus Cultural Assimilation in Multiracial Churches." *Journal for the Scientific Study of Religion* 49 (2): 218–223.

Pontifical Council for the Pastoral Care of Migrants and Itinerant People. 2004. "Erga migrantes caritas Christi." [The love of Christ towards migrants] http://www.vatican.va/roman_curia/pontifical_councils/migrants/documents/rc_pc_migrants_doc_20040514_erga-migrantes-caritas-christi_en.html#.

Pope Francis. 2013a. "General Audience, Saint Peter's Square." https://w2.vatican.va/content/francesco/en/audiences/2013/documents/papa-francesco_20130925_udienza-generale.html.

Pope Francis. 2013b. Evangelii Gaudium. http://w2.vatican.va/content/francesco/en/apost_exhortations/documents/papa-francesco_esortazione-ap_20131124_evangelii-gaudium.html.

Portes, Alejandro, and Rubén G. Rumbaut. 2014. *Immigrant America: A Portrait.* Berkeley: University of California Press.

Putnam, Robert D. 2001. *Bowling Alone: The Collapse and Revival of American Community*. New York: Simon and Schuster.

Raeburn, Nicole Christine. 2004. *Changing Corporate America from Inside Out: Lesbian and Gay Workplace Rights*. Minneapolis: University of Minnesota Press.

Rapport, Nigel, and Andres Dawson. 1998. "Home and Movement: A Polemic." In *Migrants of Identity: Perceptions of Home in a World of Movement*, edited by Nigel Rapport and Andres Dawson, 19–35. New York: Oxford University Press.

Rasaian, Lawrence. 2014. "Collaboration between the Parochus and the Parish Finance Council in the Protection of Parish Property." PhD dissertation, Saint Paul University, Ottawa, Canada.

Reimer, Sam. 2011. "Orthodoxy Niches: Diversity in Congregational Orthodoxy among Three Protestant Denominations in the United States." *Journal for the Scientific Study of Religion* 50 (4): 763–779.

Renken, John A. 2000. "Parishes, Pastors, and Parochial Vicars [cc:515–552]." In *New Commentary on the Code of Canon Law*, edited by John P. Beal, James A. Coriden, and Thomas J. Green, 673–724. New York: Paulist Press.

Renken, John A. 2010. "The Stable Patrimony of Public Juridic Persons." *The Jurist* 70:131–162.

Roof, Wade Clark, and William McKinney. 1987. *American Mainline Religion: Its Changing Shape and Future*. New Brunswick, NJ: Rutgers University Press.

Ruef, Martin. 2000. "The Emergence of Organizational Forms: A Community Ecology Approach." *American Journal of Sociology* 106 (3): 658–714.

Sampson, Robert J. 2012. *Great American City: Chicago and the Enduring Neighborhood Effect*. Chicago: University of Chicago Press.

Scheitle, Christopher P. 2007. "Organizational Niches and Religious Markets: Uniting Two Literatures," *Interdisciplinary Journal of Research on Religion* 3 (2): 1–29.

Scheitle, Christopher P. 2010. *Beyond the Congregation: The World of Christian Nonprofits*. New York: Oxford University Press.

Scott, W. Richard, and Gerald F. Davis. 2007. *Organizations and Organizing: Rational, Natural and Open Systems Perspectives*. London: Routledge.

Seitz, John C. 2011. *No Closure: Catholic Practice and Boston's Parish Shutdowns*. Boston: Harvard University Press.

Sheller, Mimi, and John Urry. 2006. "The New Mobilities Paradigm." *Environment and Planning A* 38 (2): 207–226.

Simmel, Georg. 1997. *Simmel on Culture: Selected Writings*. Edited by David Frisby and Mike Featherstone. London: Sage Publications.

Skerrett, Ellen. 1993. "Sacred Space: Parish and Neighborhood in Chicago." In *Catholicism, Chicago Style*, edited by Ellen Skerrett, Edward R. Kantowicz, and Steven M. Avella, 137–169. New Orleans: Loyola University Press.

Smith, Christian, and Michael Emerson. 1998. *American Evangelicalism: Embattled and Thriving*. Chicago: University of Chicago Press.

Stark, Rodney, and Roger Finke. 2000. *Acts of Faith: Explaining the Human Side of Religion*. Berkeley: University of California Press.

Stolz, Jörg, and Jean-Claude Usunier. 2013. *Religions as Brands: New Perspectives on the Marketization of Religion and Spirituality*. London: Routledge.

Stravinskas, Peter, M.J., and Russell B. Shaw. 1998. *Our Sunday Visitor's Catholic Encyclopedia*. Huntington, IN: Our Sunday Visitor.

Stump, Roger W. 1986. "Patterns in the Survival of Catholic National Parishes, 1940–1980." *Journal of Cultural Geography* 7 (1): 77–97.

Sullins, D. Paul. 2016. *Keeping the Vow: The Untold Story of Married Catholic Priests.* New York: Oxford University Press.

Swartz, David L. 2013. *Symbolic Power, Politics, and Intellectuals: The Political Sociology of Pierre Bourdieu.* Chicago: University of Chicago Press.

Tonkiss, Fran. 2005. *Space, the City and Social Theory: Social Relations and Urban Forms.* Malden, MA: Polity.

USCCB. 2012. "Canon 522—Stability of Office of Pastor." Available http://www.usccb.org/beliefs-and-teachings/what-we-believe/canon-law/complementary-norms/canon-522-stability-of-office-of-pastor.cfm.

Vandenakker, John Paul. 1994. *Small Christian Communities and the Parish: An Ecclesiological Analysis of the North American Experience.* Lanham, MD: Rowman & Littlefield.

Vatican Council II. 1963. "*Sacrosanctum Concilium* [Constitution on the Sacred Liturgy]." http://www.vatican.va/archive/hist_councils/ii_vatican_council/documents/vat-ii_const_19631204_sacrosanctum-concilium_en.html.

Vatican Council II. 1965. "*Apostolicam Actuositatem* [Decree on the apostolate of lay people]." http://www.vatican.va/archive/hist_councils/ii_vatican_council/documents/vat-ii_decree_19651118_apostolicam-actuositatem_en.html.

Vatican. 2009. *Apostolic Constitution Anglicanorum Coetibus Providing for Personal Ordinariates for Anglicans Entering into Full Communion with the Catholic Church. 2009.* http://press.vatican.va/content/salastampa/it/bollettino/pubblico/2009/11/09/0696/01642.html.

Vidal, Jamie R. 1990. "The American Church and the Puerto Rican People." *U.S. Catholic Historian* 9:119–135.

Warner, R. Stephen. 1993. "Work in Progress Toward a New Paradigm for the Sociological Study of Religion in the United States." *American Journal of Sociology* 98 (5): 1044–1093.

Warner, R. Stephen. 1994. "The Place of the Congregation in the American Religious Configuration." In *American Congregations*, Vol. 2: *New Perspectives in the Study of Congregations*, edited by James P. Wind and James W. Lewis, 54–99. Chicago: University of Chicago Press.

Warner, R. Stephen. 2000. "Epilogue." In *Public Religion and Urban Transformation: Faith in the City*, edited by Lowell W. Livezey, 295–308. New York: New York University Press.

Warner, R. Stephen. 2002. "More Progress on the New Paradigm." In *Sacred Markets, Sacred Canopies: Essays on Religious Markets and Religious Pluralism*, edited by Ted G. Jelen, 1–29. Lanham, MD: Rowman & Littlefield.

Warner, R. Stephen, and Judith G. Wittner, eds. 1998. *Gatherings in Diaspora: Religious Communities and the New Immigration.* Philadelphia, PA: Temple University Press.

Waters, Mary. 1990. *Ethnic Options: Choosing Identities in America.* Berkeley: University of California Press.

Waters, Mary C., and Tomás R. Jiménez. 2005. "Assessing Immigrant Assimilation: New Empirical and Theoretical Challenges." *Annual Review of Sociology* 31:105–125.

Webber, Melvin. M. 1963. "Order in Diversity: Community without Propinquity." In *Cities and Space: The Future Use of Urban Land*, edited by Lowdon Wingo Jr., 23–54. Baltimore: Johns Hopkins University Press.

Weldon, Michael. 2004. *A Struggle for Holy Ground: Reconciliation and the Rites of Parish Closure*. Collegeville, MN: Liturgical Press.

Wellman, Barry. 1979. "The Community Question: The Intimate Networks of East Yorkers." *American Journal of Sociology* 84 (5): 1201–1231.

Wilde, Melissa. 2007. *Vatican II: A Sociological Analysis of Religious Change*. Princeton, NJ: Princeton University Press.

Witham, Larry. 2010. *Marketplace of the Gods: How Economics Explains Religion*. New York: Oxford University Press.

Zweigenhaft, Richard L., and G. William Domhoff. 2006. *Diversity in the Power Elite: How It Happened, Why It Matters*. Lanham, MD: Rowman & Littlefield.

INDEX

Note: Page numbers followed by *t* or *f* indicate tables or figures, respectively. Numbers followed by n indicate notes.

Adler, Gary, viii, 220n1, 229
advocacy, 94–95, 96*t*
affinity, 166, 186–187, 223n14
Africans and African Americans, 108–109
  approaches to ministry for, 41*t*
  personal parishes for, 7, 39, 40*t*, 41*t*, 98, 108, 119, 125, 131–133, 187
  services for, 117–118
age differences, 116
Alba, Richard D., 222n61, 229
Aldrich, Howard E., 219n7, 223n33, 224n21, 225n20, 229
American Catholic Church, 134, 203–205
  Anglican Use parishes, 4, 39, 67, 78, 97, 140, 152–153, 224n7, 226n13
  community in, 170–193
  demographics, 6, 37–39, 38*f*, 96, 96*t*, 108–109, 117, 187, 203–205, 219n6
  fragmentation in, 137–169
  future directions, 202–205
  historic development of, 5–6, 20
  organizational strategy, 19
  parish(es), 12–44, 178
  parish boundaries, 14–15, 45–69
  parish decisions, 70–107
  research study, 207–213
  structure of, 4–8, 187, 192–193
American Catholicism, 42, 134, 220n25
Americanization, 19, 127, 129, 225n5
The American Parish Project, viii

Ammerman, Nancy, 25, 56, 175, 221n47, 223n21, 226n11, 227n5, 227n36, 228n1, 229
Anderson, Benedict, 227n19, 228n12, 229
Anderson, Elijah, 200, 229
Anderson, Shawna L., 219n7, 231
Anglican Ordinariate, 78, 226n13
"Anglicanorum Coetibus," 78
Anglican Use Mass, 152
Anglican Use parishes, 4, 39, 67, 78, 97, 140, 152–153, 224n7, 226n13
antagonism, out-group, 155–160
Apostolorum Successores, 77, 79, 224n4
archdioceses. *See also dioceses and specific dioceses*
  approaches to ethnic or language ministry, 41, 41*t*
  policy regarding personal parishes, 74–75
Asians and Asian Americans, 108–109
  migrants, 222n66
  parishes for, 6–7, 35, 37, 39, 40*t*, 42, 184
  services for, 117–118
assimilation, cultural, 109, 127–130
Axhausen, Kay, 229n41, 235

Badillo, David A., 222n68, 229
Baggett, Jerome P., 137, 139, 161, 173, 219n3, 219n11, 223n14, 226n1, 226n11, 226n17, 226n21, 227n2, 229

baptism, infant, 47
Barker, Bruce, 222n10, 229
Barth, Fredrick, 181, 227n21, 229
Basilica of St. Louis, King (The Old
    Cathedral), 89, 90f, 91f
Bean, Frank D., 225n16, 236
Becker, Penny Edgell, 226n18, 229
Belgian Catholics, 20, 21t
Bellah, Robert N., 139, 226n9, 229
Bender, Courtney, 226n12, 230
Benedict XVI, 77–78, 145, 224n5, 230
Berends, Mark, 227nn26–27, 230
Berger, Peter, 219n1, 220n4,
    228n1, 230
Bishop, Bill, 139, 226n5, 230
bishops
    authority of, 95, 104–105, 107, 183
    management of parishes by, 80–85,
        94–95, 96t, 104–107, 179, 224n3
    racial demographics, 203
    reasons for establishing parishes,
        85–87, 96t, 224n3
    reasons for not establishing parishes,
        82–85, 96t
    satisfaction with, 209
blacks, 125, 130–133. See also Africans
    and African Americans
Blau, Peter M., 230
Blöchlinger, Alex, 220n3, 230
Bohemian Catholics, 20, 21t
Bonilla-Silva, Eduardo, 117, 225n19,
    228n8, 230
boundaries, 45–69, 168
    enforcement of, 49, 53–55,
        155–160
    out-group antagonism, 155–160
    redrawing, 56–59, 188
Bourdieu, Pierre, 176
Brazilians, 41t
breastfeeding, 146
Brinig, Margaret F., 223n30, 227n26,
    227n29, 230
Brophy, Don, 219n11, 226n11, 230
Brown, Joseph A., 226n36, 230
Bruce, Tricia C., 219n5, 219n12,
    220n1, 222n60, 222nn65–66,
    224nn14–15, 224n17, 228n2,
    228n38, 229–230, 235, 237
Brunett, Alexander, 98, 100–104
Brunett, Joseph, 71

Burns, Jeffery M., 219n4, 231
Byrne, Julie, 197, 224n20, 226n16,
    228n4, 231

Cadge, Wendy, 226n12, 230
cafeteria Catholics, 137
Camacho, Keith, 224n16, 237
Camden, New Jersey, 45–46, 49
Camosy, Charles C., 219n5, 235
Campbell Soup, 45
Canon Law, 6, 15–16, 18–19, 23–24,
    43, 222n7
    no. 121, 223n25
    no. 515, 22, 75
    no. 518, 3
Cape Verdian Catholics, 20, 21t
capital, social, 176
CARA. See Center for Applied Research
    in the Apostolate
Carroll, Glenn R., 219n10, 225n6,
    225nn24–25, 231, 234
Carroll, John, 17
Casanova, Jose, 196, 204, 228n2,
    228n21, 231
cathedraticum, 34
Catholic Church, 223n22, 223n25,
    225n2, 231. See also American
    Catholic Church
    future directions, 202–203
    parish boundaries, 45–69
    racial diversity, 108
    territoriality, 45–69
Catholic Housing Services, 99
Catholicism, 189, 192–193
    American or US, 42, 134, 220n25
    charismatic, 4
    as community, 126
    cultural, 120, 135
    niche, 113–114, 140
    as pluralist, 137
    territorial model, 67–68
Catholicity, 109
Catholic organizations, 189
Catholic schools, 62–64
Center for Applied Research in the
    Apostolate (CARA), 208–209,
    219nn5–8, 222n60, 222n64,
    223n16, 223nn18–19,
    223n28, 223n30, 224n34,
    225nn7–8, 231

Chafetz, Janet Saltzman, 225n27, 233
Chan-Malik, Sylvia, 224n16, 237
charismatic Catholics, 4, 154
charter churches, 183–185
charter schools, 183–184, 227n26
Chaves, Mark, 177, 219n7, 227n9, 231
Cherry, Stephen M., 174, 222n66,
    224n14, 227n3, 230–231, 237
Chicago, Illinois, 187
children, 224n1
Chinese, 20, 21t, 41t
choice
    parish selection, 4–5, 51–55, 67–68,
    184–185
    religious preference, 138–141
Christerson, Brad, 219n6, 225n8,
    228n7, 233
Christian, Robert, 228n48, 231
Christian Reform Church (CRC), 187
Christ Our Hope (Seattle, Washington),
    70–71, 72f, 73f, 74f, 90–91,
    102–103
church(es), 47, 89–92, 90f, 91f, 189
The Church of Divine Mercy (Knoxville,
    Tennessee), 43–44
Ciesluk, Joseph E., 15–16, 18–19,
    220nn9–10, 220n13,
    220nn15–17, 220nn19–21,
    224n1, 231
Cimino, Richard, 225n21, 226n11,
    231–232
cities, 180, 228n49
citizenship, 25–26
city bus metaphor, 186
civic engagement, 174
Clark, William A., 226n21, 232
class differences, 116
clustering, 60–61
Coco, Angela, 219n5, 232
Code of Canon Law, 6, 15–16, 18–19,
    22–24, 43, 75, 220n22, 221n38,
    221n40, 221n53, 222n7,
    227n1, 232
code switching, 113–114
collaboration, 60–61
collective conscience, 126
collectivity, 126
college-based parishes, 153–154
college ministry, 39
color-blindness, 199

Commission for the Authentic
    Interpretation of the Code of
    Canon Law, 18
community, 2, 170–193
    building, 125–126, 180, 228n49
    of communities, 111, 173–174
    faith communities, 98–99, 103
    ghettos, 141, 165–166
    lifestyle enclaves, 139, 165–166
Congregation for the Clergy, 223n20
congregations and congregationalism, 4,
    17, 186–187, 219n4
    charter congregations, 183–185
    de facto congregations, 5, 196–197,
    219n11, 223n14
    definition of, 25, 61
    de jure congregations, 223n14
    mandated congregations, 184
    multiracial congregations, 225n26
conservative Catholics, 155
Cook, James M., 226n4, 237
Copay, Anne, 220n19, 235
Coriden, James A., 26, 76, 220n2,
    221n46, 221nn48–49, 221n51,
    224n2, 232
cosmopolitanism, 200
Council of Trent, 14–15
countercultures, 27
Cresswell, Tim, 227n25, 232
Crowder, Kyle, 186, 227n33, 232
Cubans, 41t
cultural activities, 126–127
cultural assimilation, 109, 127–130
cultural Catholicism, 120, 135
cultural competency, 110
cultural differences, 117, 120, 127–130
cultural preservation, 124–128, 225n29
culture wars, 138

D'Antonio, William V., 219n5,
    226n1, 232
Davie, Grace, 219n1, 220n4, 228n1, 230
Davis, Darren W., 219n8, 232
Davis, Gerald F., 228n18, 239
Davis, Kenneth G., 24, 221n45, 232
Dawson, Andres, 223n31, 239
deaf/hearing-impaired, 41t, 154
decisions, 70–107
Deck, Allen Figueroa, 219n7, 225n12,
    227n10, 232

Delanty, Gerard, 175, 181, 227n4, 227n20, 232
demographic changes, 6, 37–39, 38f, 96, 96t, 108–109, 117, 187, 203–205, 219n6, 220n25
Denison, Daniel R., 224n20, 234
Denton, Nancy A., 227n34, 228n7, 236
Detroit, Michigan, 223n18
DeYoung, Curtiss Paul, 225n4, 228n7, 232
Diamond, John B., 200, 228n13, 236
difference, 108–136
Dignity-Chicago, 196–197
Dillon, Michele, 197, 219n5, 223n13, 226n1, 228n6, 232
DiMaggio, Paul, 224n23, 225n21, 232
dioceses, 14, 189. *See also archdioceses and specific dioceses*
    approaches to ethnic or language ministry, 41–42, 41t
    bridging, 176–179
    management of, 185
    with personal parishes, 85
    policy regarding personal parishes, 74–75
    restructuring, 89, 90f, 91f
discrimination, 111–119, 226n32
diversity, 51, 164
    parish, 111–118, 133, 134–136
    responses to, 167–169, 195, 198–201, 225n5
divided parishes, 219n7
Dobrev, Stanislav D., 231
Dolan, Jay P., 5, 19, 219n2, 219n4, 220n23, 222n10, 225n5, 227n10, 232
Domhoff, G. William, 200, 228n14, 241
Dominicans, 41t, 131
DuBois, W. E. B., 226n32, 232
Duffy, Patrick J., 14, 220n5, 232
Dulles, Avery, 109, 136, 225n3, 226n40, 232
Durkheim, Émile, 126, 175

Easter obligations, 49
Ebaugh, Helen Rose, 225n27, 233
Ecclesia Dei, 77
Ecclesia Dei of Western Washington, 99–100
ecclesiology, 189

economic changes, 37–39, 38f, 50
Edwards, Korie, 199, 219n6, 225n8, 225n17, 228n7, 228n9, 233
Eiesland, Nancy L., 226n18, 228n45, 233
80 percent rule, 110
elderly, 39
elementary schools, 63–64
elites, 106–107
Emerson, Michael O., 133, 219n6, 225n4, 225n8, 225n22, 226n38, 227n28, 228n7, 232–233, 239
enclaves, 139, 165–166
enculturation, 109
engagement, civic, 174
"Erga migrantes caritas Christi" (The love of Christ toward migrants), 78
ethnic Catholics, 4, 36–39, 38f, 111–118, 135
    ministry for, 41–42, 41t, 79, 164
    parishes for, 39–42, 40t, 41t, 120–124, 121f, 122f, 123f, 126–127
ethnicity, 124–125, 159, 226n31
European parishes, 36–40, 40t
exclusion, 155–160

faith communities, 98–99, 103
faith retention, 126
family, 125–127, 159
Federal-Aid Highway Act, 50, 222n8
fellowship, 173
Fichter, Joseph Henry, 222n68, 233
Filipinos, 20, 21t, 41t, 174, 222n66
financial resources
    disparities, 116
    funding for personal parishes, 92–94, 96t
Finke, Roger, 226n7, 226n11, 233, 239
Fischel, William A., 227n6, 233
Fischer, Claude, 138, 222n60, 226n2, 233
Fisher, James Terence, 225n5, 233
Flores, Patrick, 152
fluidity, 180
Fogarty, Gerald, 131, 220n18, 226n37, 228n49, 233
Fokas, Effie, 219n1, 220n4, 228n1, 230
food, 126
Ford, Henry, 50

foreign-born Catholics, 108–109
Foucault, Michel, 192
Fox, Joseph, 220n7, 233
fragmentation, 137–169
    political, 227n34
    rationale for, 85–86, 95, 124, 140, 161, 163–164
Francis, 173–174, 182, 238
fraternity, 173
French, 18, 20, 21t, 41t
FSSP. See Priestly Fraternity of Saint Peter
funding, 92–94, 96t, 116
future directions, 202–205

Gamm, Gerald, 221n50, 223n11, 228n39, 234
Ganiel, Gladys, 226n12, 236
Gans, Herbert J., 193, 228n52, 234
Garces-Foley, Kathleen, 111, 219n4, 225nn11–12, 227n11, 228n7, 234
Garnett, Nicolle Stelle, 223n30, 227n26, 227n29, 230
Gautier, Mary L., 219n5, 226n1, 232, 235
gay Catholics, 151, 155
generalism, 198–201
generalist organizations, 136, 198–199
generational differences, 116
geographic information system (GIS) software, 57
geographic parishes, 65, 118. See also territorial parishes
geography, 51
George, Francis Cardinal, 7, 46–47, 69, 219n9, 222n2, 222n4, 224n35, 227n1, 228n46, 234
Georgetown University, 208
Germans and German Americans, 17–18, 20, 21t, 50, 170
Gerson, Jeffrey N., 219n4, 234
ghettos, 141, 165–166
Gillespie, Raymond, 179, 227n12, 234
Glaeser, Edward, 227n32, 234
Glennon, John Joseph, 187
globalization, 109
Gordon, Colin, 187, 227nn34–35, 234
grassroots transformations, 188
Gray, Mark, 68, 223n16, 224n34
Guest, Avery M., 228n43, 234

Haitians, 41t, 131
Hannan, Michael T., 219n10, 225n24, 231, 234
Hart, Stuart, 224n20, 234
Harte, Thomas J., 220n29, 222n59, 234
Hater, Robert J., 219n11, 226n11, 234
hearing impairment. See deaf/ hearing-impaired
Hendershott, Anne, 219n5, 234
Hennesey, James, 225n5, 234
Hervieu-Léger, Danièle, 180–182, 227n17, 227nn22–23, 234
Hinojosa, Gilberto M., 227n10, 232
Hispanics/Latinos, 108–109, 219n8
    average age, 224n1
    ministry for, 41–42, 41t
    parishes for, 2–3, 6–7, 20, 37, 39–42, 40t, 41t, 93–94, 127, 131, 161, 188
    services for, 117–118
Hoegeman, Catherine, 222n60, 230
Hollandish Catholics, 20, 21t
Holy Trinity (Philadelphia, Pennsylvania), 17, 36, 170, 171f, 172f
homelessness, 149
home parishes, 64–68, 123–124
hometown parishes, 227n2
homilies, 223n13
homophily, 138–141
Hoover, Brett C., 7, 110, 199–200, 219n5, 219n7, 225n10, 225n14, 228n11, 228n17, 235
Huang, Weishan, 226n11, 232
Hungarians, 20, 21t, 36, 50
Hunter, James Davison, 138, 226n3, 235
Hunthausen, Raymond, 98
hypersegregation, 187

identity, 124–125, 135, 155–160
ideology, 159
imagery, 173
imaginary community, 180
immigrants, 134–135, 220n25, 225n5, 225n29
    personal parishes for, 121, 124, 127–128
incentives, 208
individualism, 51–52
infant baptism, 47
innovation, 106–107

institutional containment, 160–164
institutional elites, 106–107, 165
integration, 111–118
international priests, 87
interracial interactions, 111, 225n11
Irby, Courtney, 235
Ireland, 179, 222n3
Irish Americans, 18
isolationism, 127, 155–160
Italians, 20, 21t, 37, 41t

Jefferies, Henry A., 222n3, 235
Jesuits, 100
Jiménez, Tomás R., 240
John Paul II, 22, 111, 142, 224n4,
    224n10, 225n12, 235
Johnson, Mary, 219n5, 235
Josephinium, 99, 102
Joshi, Khyati, 224n16, 237

Kantowicz, Edward R., 223n27, 235
Kaszynski, William, 222n8, 235
Kim, Karen Chai, 225n4, 225n8, 228n7,
    232–233
King, Tom, 220n19, 235
Knoxville, Tennessee, 12–13, 43–44
Konieczny, Mary Ellen, 219n3, 219n5,
    226n21, 235
Koreans and Korean Americans, 224n14
    ministry for, 41t
    parishes for, 35, 41t, 83, 87–89,
        98–99, 103–104, 124, 126,
        159–160, 188
Koudelka, Charles J., 220n6, 220n8,
    220nn11–12, 235
Kozol, Jonathan, 199, 228n7, 235
Krysan, Maria, 186, 227n33, 232
Kye, Samuel, 226n30, 236

laity, 96, 96t, 97, 105, 223n13
language differences, 7, 42, 113, 116–117,
    123f, 124–125, 220n29
language lessons, 126
language preservation, 124
Larsen, Jonas, 228n41, 235
Latin, 7
Latin Mass. See Traditional Latin
    Mass (TLM)
Latino Catholics. See Hispanics/Latinos
Lawson, Ronald, 226n18, 235

leadership, shared, 116–117
Leblebici, Hussein, 220n19, 235
Lee, Jennifer, 225n16, 226n30, 236
Levitt, Peggy, 226n12, 230
Lewis, Amanda E., 200, 228n13, 236
lifestyle enclaves, 139, 165–166
linguistic ministry, 41, 41t, 42, 79
Liptak, Dolores Ann, 225n5, 236
Lithuanians, 20, 21t
Livezey, Lowell, 226n11, 236
local religion, 5–8, 52–53, 139, 168, 188–
    191, 195–198
Logan, John R., 185–186, 227n30, 236
Los Angeles, California, 97
Louisville Institute, 207

MacDonald, Fergus, 17, 220n14,
    220n19, 236
Madsen, Richard, 139, 226n9, 229
Magnano, Paul, 71
magnet parishes, 140, 219n11
Maines, David R., 222n6, 223n14,
    223n18, 236
Maltese, 20, 21t
mapping, 56–57
Marcuse, Peter, 165, 226n6,
    226nn19–20, 236
marketplace, 50–56
Mark Twain Expressway, 50
Marti, Gerardo, 225n9, 225n26, 226n12,
    228n7, 228n15, 236
Massey, Douglas S., 186, 227n32,
    227n34, 228n7, 236
Mass times, 7
Matovina, Timothy M., 19–20, 80,
    130–131, 219n4, 220n25, 220n27,
    224n11, 226n33, 226n35, 236
Mattson, Greggor, 138, 226n2, 233
McCallion, Michael J., 222n6, 223n14,
    223n18, 236
McGreevy, John T., 58, 222n5, 222n9,
    223n23, 226n34, 228n39, 236
McKinney, William, 223n17, 239
McNally, Michael J., 226n34, 237
McPherson, Miller, 226n4, 237
McRoberts, Omar M., 67, 191,
    223n32, 237
membership, 48–49
memory, 180
mergers and merging, 60–61, 223n25

Merton, Robert K., 237
Mexicans, 20, 21t, 41t, 93, 126
Meyer, David S., 224n22, 237
Mian, Nadia A., 226n11, 232
microaggressions, 120
minorities and minority groups, 88–89,
    114, 125, 177
Mirola, William, 226n38, 233
missions, 220n19
mission statements, 120
mixed/other racial backgrounds,
    108–109
mobility, 50, 52–53, 65, 68–69,
    180–181, 227n18
modernity, 109
Monahan, Susanne C., 226n38, 233
Morley, David, 228n50, 237
Morris, Charles, 19, 220n24, 225n5, 237
Most Holy Redeemer Parish, 151
Mulder, Mark T., 187, 228n37, 237
multiculturalism, 83, 96t, 108–110, 173,
    199–201, 225n4
  ideal territorial parishes, 111–118
multiracial congregations, 6, 109–111,
    199, 225n4, 225n26
multiracial organizations, 199, 225n4
multiracial parishes, 110, 225n4
Mundelein, George, 19
Murnion, Philip J., 219n11, 226n11, 237
Murphy, Thomas Joseph, 98
Muse, Ivan, 222n10, 229
music, 126
mutual affinity, 166

named spaces, 120
named specialist organizations, 136
narcissism, 139
National Alliance for Public Charter
    Schools, 227n26, 237
National Congregations Study, 219n7
national parishes, 4–5, 16–20, 24,
    123–124
  bishops and, 80–81
  development of, 20
  ethnic composition of, 20, 21t
  first, 170, 171f, 172f
  old, 36–39, 38f
  pastors for, 16
  policy on, 80–81
  schools, 63

National Science Foundation
    (NSF), 207
National Survey of Personal Parishes
    (NSPP), 10, 35, 74, 76, 79–80, 82–
    83, 86, 155, 207–208, 215–218,
    222n63, 223n19
  questions, 215–218
Native Americans, 39, 40t, 41t
NCCB, 237
neighborhood churches, 187
neighborhood parishes, 50, 67–68, 187
neighborhood schools, 187
Nelson, Timothy J., 225n18, 237
niche Catholicism, 113–114, 140
Niebuhr, H. Reinhold, 138
Ninh, Thien-Huong, 224n16, 237
non-assimilation, 127–130
noncompliance, 53–54
non-English language services, 110,
    116–117
North American Martyrs (Seattle,
    Washington), 99–101
Notre Dame Study of Catholic Parish
    Life, 51, 222n59, 223n15, 237
Novus Ordo Mass, 146, 157
NSPP. See National Survey of Personal
    Parishes

O'Brien, Jennifer, 233
Official Catholic Directory (OCD),
    209, 220n29
Ogbu, John U., 226n30, 237
Omaha, Nebraska, 7–8
O'Malley, John W., 220n30, 225n28, 237
orthodoxy, 161
Ospino, Hosffman, 20, 116, 220n28,
    225nn14–15, 237
othering, 115, 155–160

Packard, Josh, 224n17, 230
Padgett, John Frederick, 222n69, 237
pan-Hispanic personal parishes, 42
papal statements, 96t
parachurch organizations, 225n23
parallel parishes, 111, 219n7
parish(es), 12–44, 178, 223n20. See also
    specific churches
  approaches to, 41, 41t, 164
  bonding, 176–179
  boundaries of, 14–15, 45–69

parish(es) (*Cont.*)
    as cells, 189
    characteristics of, 33
    charter, 183–185
    as city buses, 186
    as communal spaces, 51, 189
    constitutive characteristics of, 15–16
    contemporary, 35–42
    decisions, 70–107
    definition of, 4, 14–16, 22, 29, 173
    diversification of, 51, 133, 134–136
    divided, 219n7
    durability of, 28
    establishment of, 73, 224n3
    ethnic composition of, 20, 21*t*
    future directions, 202–203
    as home, 64–68
    hometown, 227n2
    interdependence of, 188–191
    as juridic persons, 26, 31, 221n51
    jurisdiction over, 14–15
    legal components of, 15
    limits, 33–34
    marketplace, 50–56
    membership, 48–49
    mergers, 60–61, 223n25
    multiracial, 110–111
    national (*see* national parishes)
    organization of, 62, 72, 179, 188–191,
        202–203
    overlapping, 57–58
    oversight of, 19, 34
    parallel, 111, 219n7
    personal (*see* personal parishes)
    physical home, 31–33, 32*f*
    planning, 57, 60, 78
    quasi-parishes, 221n56
    reallocations, 56
    renewal, 88–89
    requirements for, 74–75
    rights of, 221n48
    segregated, 130–133
    selection of, 4–5, 51–55, 67–68,
        184–185
    shared, 7, 110–111
    stability of, 26–29
    status of, 24–34, 42–43
    suburban, 228n49
    supersizing, 110
    territorial (*see* territorial parishes)
    walking, 228n49
    Whitman Sampler approach to, 164
parish-as-place principle, 4
parish family, 125–127
parish home, 64–68
parish maps, 54
parish or parochial schools, 62–64
Park, Jerry, 222n66, 224n14, 230, 237
Park, Robert Ezra, 138, 226n3, 238
parking lots, 111, 115
partitioning, 119, 139–140, 168
    self-sorting, 155–160
pastoral councils, 116, 221n39
"Pastoral Provision," 152
pastors and pastoral care, 14–17, 29–30
Paul VI, 228n47
personal parishes, 3–4, 7–8, 11–17, 165–
       167, 192–195, 199–201
    absenteeism, 80
    advantages for pastors, 161
    advocacy for, 94–95
    Anglican Use parishes, 4, 39, 67, 78,
       97, 140, 152–153, 224n7, 226n13
    approaches to, 41, 41*t*, 164
    bishops and, 81–83
    as bonding, 176–179
    boundaries, 55–56, 59–62
    categories or purposes of, 39, 40*t*
    charter parishes, 183–185
    coexistence with territorial
       parishes, 185
    college-based, 153–154
    as community of communities, 174
    as containment, 161–162
    contemporary, 35–42
    criteria for, 76–77, 86, 86*t*
    definition of, 23, 194
    dioceses that use, 41, 41*t*
    durability of, 28
    establishment of, 20, 73–82, 85–106,
       86*t*, 96*t*
    ethnic, 120, 121*f*
    factors influencing, 95–96, 96*t*
    first, 170, 171*f*, 172*f*
    as fragmentation, 137–169
    funding, 92–94
    future directions, 202–205
    as home away from home, 123–124
    as home church, 31–33, 32*f*,
      89–92, 90*f*

as institutional strategy, 67
management of, 94–95, 106
multisite, 62
national-level influence on, 80–81
negative outcomes of, 165
new, 35–39, 71
non-assimilative, 127–130
non-ethnic purposes for, 39, 40t
old, 36–39, 38f
older, 67
pan-ethnic, 42
parishioners, 87–89
pastors for, 16, 29–30
planning, 74–75
policy regarding, 74–75
positive outcomes of, 165
post-1983, 39–42, 40t
priests, 86–87, 163
pull factors, 119–125
push factors, 119–125
rationale for, 85–86, 95, 124, 140,
    161, 163–164, 184
reasons for denying requests
    for, 84–85
reasons for not starting, 82–84
renewal, 88
as response to diversification,
    167–169
as safe spaces, 119, 166
segregated, 130–133
self-sorting, 155–160
social mission, 148–152, 161–162
as specialist, 118–130, 165
stability of, 26–27
status, 25, 161
Traditional Latin Mass (TLM)
    parishes, 142–148, 143f, 144f (see
    also Traditional Latin Mass (TLM)
    parishes)
petitions, 96t, 97
Pew Research Center, 219n5, 219n8,
    224n1, 226n4, 226n10, 228n1,
    228n19–228n20, 238
Philadelphia, Pennsylvania, 17
Philippines, 222n66
Phillips, Christopher G., 152–153,
    226n14, 238
Pitt, Richard N., 199, 228n10,
    228n16, 238
planning, 57, 60, 74–75

Plenary Council of Baltimore (1866), 18
pluralism, 137–138
Polish, 20, 21t, 41t, 45–46, 49, 166
Polishtown (Camden, New Jersey), 45
political fragmentation, 227n34. See also
    fragmentation
Pólos, László, 219n10, 234
Pontifical Council for the Pastoral Care
    of Migrants and Itinerant People,
    78–79, 224n9, 238
Pope-Davis, Donald B., 219n8, 232
Portes, Alejandro, 135, 226n30,
    226n39, 238
Portuguese, 20, 21t
Powell, Walter W., 222n69, 224n21,
    224n23, 232
praise gatherings, 179
Priestly Fraternity of Saint Peter (FSSP),
    100–101, 142, 224n13
priests, 86–87, 96t, 105, 211, 225n6
    appointments, 163
    international, 87
    Jesuit, 100
progressivism, 150, 155, 161
property, 17, 89–92, 90f, 91f
propinquity, 179–183
Puerto Ricans, 41t, 131
Putnam, Robert D., 176, 188, 227nn6–7,
    228n19, 228n40, 239

quasi-parishes, 221n56
"Quattuor Abhinc Annos" (John Paul
    II), 142

racial discrimination, 111–118,
    128–129, 226n32
racial diversity, 7, 108–109
racial grammar, 117–118
racial integration, 111–118, 128
racial transcendence, 199, 201, 225n26
racism, 135, 187, 199
Raeburn, Nicole Christine, 224n18, 239
Rapport, Nigel, 223n31, 239
Rasaian, Lawrence, 223n20, 223n29, 239
RCA Victor, 45
registration, 48–49
Reimer, Sam, 226n18, 239
religion, 180
religious community, 179–183. See also
    community

religious education, 126
religious groups and organizations, 96*t*, 195–198
    Catholic organizations, 189
    local, 195–198
    non-assimilative, 127–130
religious identity, 124–125, 135
religious preference, 138–141
Renken, John A., 221n43, 223n29, 239
research, 207–213
resource allocation, 74–75
    funding for personal
        parishes, 92–94
    partitioning, 119
Roman Catholic Church. *See*
    Catholic Church
Romanians, 20, 21*t*
Roman Rite parishes, 42
Roof, Wade Clark, 223n17, 239
Ruef, Martin, 107, 219n7, 224n12, 224n21, 224n23, 225n20, 229, 239
Rumbaut, Rubén G., 135, 226n30, 226n39, 238

sacramental church(es), 47
sacred spaces, 228n49
Sacrosanctum Concilium, 221n35
safe spaces, 119
Saint Joseph (Omaha, Nebraska), 37
Salancik, Gerald, 220n19, 235
Salvadorans, 41*t*
Sampson, Robert J., 189, 228n44, 239
San Antonio, Texas, 151–153
San Jose, California, 8
Scheitle, Christopher P., 225n21, 225n23, 226n11, 239
schools
    charter, 183–184, 227n26
    parochial, 62–64
Scott, W. Richard, 228n18, 239
Seattle, Washington, 98–104
    Christ Our Hope parish, 70–71, 72*f*, 73*f*, 74*f*, 90–91, 102–103
    North American Martyrs
        parish, 99–101
    Sisters of Saint Joseph of Peace, 99
    St. Andrew Kim parish, 99
    St. Paul Chong Hasang parish, 99
Second Vatican Council. *See* Vatican II

segregation, 165, 185–187
    hypersegregation, 187
    parish, 130–133, 225n11
Seitz, John C., 197, 219n6, 223n24, 228n5, 239
self-sorting, 155–160
separatism, 128
shared leadership, 116–117
shared parishes, 7, 110–118
Shaw, Russell B., 221n34, 239
Sheller, Mimi, 182, 227n18, 227n24, 239
signs, 120
Sikkink, David, 226n38, 233
Simbang Gabi Mass, 126
Simmel, Georg, 168–169, 226nn22–23, 239
Simons, Herbert D., 226n30, 237
Sisters of Saint Joseph of Peace (Seattle, Washington), 99
Skerrett, Ellen, 219n4, 228n49, 231, 239
Slovaks, 20, 21*t*
Smilde, David, 226n12, 230
Smith, Christian, 133, 226n38, 233, 239
Smith-Lovin, Lynn, 226n4, 237
social boundaries, 61
social capital, 176
social justice, 4, 39
social justice parishes, 148–152, 161–162, 188
social media, vii
social ministry, 162. *See also* social justice parishes
social services, 126
Society of St. Pius X (SSPX), 154–155
solidarity, 175
Spanish Masses, 124
Spanish speakers. *See also* Hispanics/Latinos; *specific ethnic groups*
    disenfranchisement of, 116–117
    parishes for, 7, 20, 21*t*, 42, 120, 123*f*, 124
specialism, 136, 198–201
specialization, 78, 118–130, 190
    approaches to ethnic or language
        ministry, 41–42, 41*t*
    fragmentation, 137–169
    named, 136
Spellman, Francis, 19
SSPX. *See* Society of St. Pius X

St. Andrew Kim parish (Seattle, Washington), 99
St. Joseph's Church (Camden, New Jersey), 45–46, 49
St. Louis, Missouri, 8
  Archdiocese of St. Louis, 187
  Basilica of St. Louis, King (The Old Cathedral), 89, 90f, 91f
  personal parishes, 188
  St. Mary of Victories, 50
St. Mary of Victories (St. Louis, Missouri), 50
St. Paul Chong Hasang parish (Seattle, Washington), 99
staffing, 116
Stark, Rodney, 226n7, 226n11, 233, 239
Starks, Brian, viii, 220n1, 229
statues, 120, 121f, 122f, 123f
Stika, Richard F., 44
Stolz, Jörg, 227n18, 239
Stravinskas, Peter, M. J., 221n34, 239
students, 79
Stump, Roger W., 219n2, 220n26, 221n52, 239
subcultures, 222n60
subsidiarity, 81–85
suburbs, 50, 228n49
Sullins, D. Paul, 228n3, 240
Sullivan, William M., 139, 226n9, 229
Summorum Pontificum (Benedict XVI), 77–78, 100, 145
supersizing, 110
Swaminathan, Anand, 225nn24–25, 231
Swartz, David L., 227n8, 240
Swidler, Ann, 139, 226n9, 229
symbolic boundaries, 62
symbolic capital, 177
symbols, 120, 121f, 122f, 123f

Tannen, Jonathan, 227n32, 227n34, 236
territorial parishes, vii, 13–15, 18–20, 51, 135–136, 139–140, 223n20
  black parishes, 131–132
  boundaries, 45–69
  coexistence with personal parishes, 185
  contemporary, 36
  definition of, 23
  emergence of, 225n5
  as generalist, 6–7, 109–111, 118

ideal, 111–118
Mass offerings, 7
missions in, 82
reallocations, 56
schools, 63–64
selection of, 4–5, 51–53
Texas, 152–153
theology on tap, 179
Tipton, Stephen M., 139, 226n9, 229
TLM. *See* Traditional Latin Mass
Tonkiss, Fran, 228n51, 240
tourists and tourism, 4, 39, 154
Traditional Latin Mass (TLM), 142, 146, 157
Traditional Latin Mass (TLM) parishes, 1–4, 39, 40t, 42, 66, 142–148, 143f, 144f, 155–158, 188
  advantages for pastors, 161–162
  bishops and, 82
  establishment of, 77–78, 97
  funding for, 92–93
  North American Martyrs (Seattle, Washington), 99–101
  reasons for attendance and joining, 99–102, 146–147
transcendence, racial, 199, 201, 225n26
tribalism, 139
Tridentine Rite, 77, 142
trustees, 17
Tyrolese, 20, 21t

Una Voce, 97, 99–100, 102
uncertainty, 106
unfairness, 106
United States, 108–136
  Midwest, 35
  Northeast, 35, 39
  population, 6, 203–205
  South, 35, 39, 63
  West, 63
United States Anglican Use Ordinariate, 78, 226n13
United States Catholic Church. *See* American Catholic Church
United States Conference of Catholic Bishops (USCCB), 221n54, 225n7, 240
  Committee on Cultural Diversity, 80
  guides for intercultural competency, 110

United States Conference of Catholic
      Bishops (USCCB) (*Cont.*)
   influence on personal parish
      decisions, 80–81
university parishes, 39, 40*t*, 153–154
urbanization, 180, 222n60, 228n49
Urry, John, 182, 227n18, 227n24,
      229n41, 235, 239
USCCB. *See* United States Conference of
      Catholic Bishops
Usunier, Jean-Claude, 227n18, 239

Vandenakker, John Paul, 21, 23, 220n2,
      220n7, 220nn30–31, 221n33,
      221nn36–37, 221nn41–42, 240
van Kempen, Ronald, 165, 226n6,
      226n20, 236
Vatican, 19, 79–80, 223n20, 224n8, 240
   Congregation for the Clergy, 223n20
   influence on personal parish
      decisions, 77–80
   Pontifical Council for the Pastoral
      Care of Migrants and Itinerant
      People, 78–79
Vatican Council II, 6, 8, 21–24, 43,
      50–51, 142, 173, 221n32,
      221n39, 240
Vidal, Jamie R., 227n10, 240
Vietnamese, vii, 8
   ministry for, 41*t*
   North American Martyrs parish
      (Seattle, Washington), 99–101
   parishes for, 12–13, 35, 41*t*, 43–44,
      67, 87, 92, 95, 98–106, 114,
      124–128, 188
   Parish Pastoral Council, 125–126
Vigdor, Jacob, 227n32, 234
Virgin Mary, Our Lady of Guadalupe
      (Nuestra Señora de Guadalupe), 2–3

Voice of the Faithful, 8
voluntary association, 196–197
volunteerism, 223n17

walking parishes, 228n49
Warner, R. Stephen, 5, 186, 196,
      219n3, 219n11, 221n44, 226n8,
      226n11, 227n31, 228n1,
      228n4, 240
Waters, Mary, 222n62, 226n31, 240
Webber, Melvin. M., 179–180,
      227nn13–16, 240
welcome therapy, 122–123, 190
welcoming, 111–118, 120, 123*f*
Weldon, Michael, 60, 223n24, 241
Wellman, Barry, 228n42, 228n45, 241
White, Christopher, 219n5, 234
White, Joseph Michael, 219n4, 231
white flight, 187
whites, 6–7, 108–109, 111–118,
      178, 203
Whitman Park, 222n1
Whitman Sampler approach, 164
Whittier, Nancy, 224n22, 237
Wierzbicki, Susan K., 228n43, 234
Wigilia Mass, 126
Wilde, Melissa, 219n11, 220n30, 241
Witham, Larry, 226n11, 241
Wittberg, Patricia, 219n5, 235
Wittner, Judith G., 240
women's involvement, 151, 155
Woo, Rodney M., 225n8, 225n22, 233

Yancey, George, 225n4, 228n7, 232
young adults, 155, 179

zoning, 187
Zweigenhaft, Richard L., 200,
      228n14, 241